The History of the London Cab Trade

From 1600 to the Present Day

By
Philip Warren

Taxi Trade Promotions Ltd, London

To my late wife Joyce for the help and encouragement she gave to me during my research.

First published 1995
ISBN 0 9522052 1 1

Published by Taxi Trade Promotions Ltd.
431 Caledonian Road
London N7 9BG

Printed by Chandlers Printers Limited
Saxon Mews, Reginald Road,
Bexhill- on- Sea, East Sussex TN39 3PJ

Philip Warren was born in London in 1927. Most of his childhood was spent in the Elephant & Castle district of South London. As a result of being bombed out during the blitz in 1940 the family moved to Oxfordshire. After leaving school in 1941 he worked as an apprentice gardener on a nearby estate, Watlington Park, until he joined the army in 1944. On his demob in May 1948 he returned to London, working for the Gardens Department of the London County Council.

In April 1955 he decided to follow in his father's and grandfather's footsteps by becoming a licensed taxi driver; gaining his badge in 1956. From the start he took a keen interest in trade matters. In 1961, for example, he was an active member of the Cab Trade Crisis Committee, formed to combat the Welbeck Motors minicab venture. This was followed by a long involvement with the Cab Section of the T. & G.W.U., becoming Chairman of the Cab Trade Committee and editor of Cab Trade News.

Other roles in the trade have been the editorship of Steering Wheel in 1975 and co-writing with Malcolm Linskey, "Taxicabs - A Photographic History" published in 1976.

From 1980 to 1987 he worked for Mann & Overton Limited as Regional Sales Executive; simultaneously editing their house magazine Newslink. Throughout his career he had been conducting on-going research into the history of the taxi trade. His expertise was such that in 1984 he assisted in the publication of a book commemorating the 75th Anniversary of the London General Cab Company.

Unfortunately, his wife's ill health led to early retirement in 1987. However, this gave him the time to complete his many years of research, culminating in this book.

Other recent moments of pride in his career have included, in 1993 his son Timothy becoming a licensed taxi driver and in 1994 being Master of the Fellowship of Hackney Carriage Drivers when the trade celebrated 300 years of continuous licensing of hackney carriages.

Contents

ACKNOWLEDGMENTS

I cannot express my gratitude enough to Mr. J.R.L. King formerly of the Guildhall Library, to whom I am indebted for his assistance during my research. It was probably due more to him than anyone else that I was able to make any progress at all. To the staff of the Guildhall Record Office for their painstaking help with primary source material of the 17th century. I would also like to thank all of the staff of the Guildhall Library in the City of London.

My thanks are also due to the staff of the House of Lords Record Office, the Record Office, Chancery Lane; the British Museum staff at Bloomsbury and Colindale and Miss Williams of the Minet Library, Lambeth. I owe a special debt of gratitude to Mr. George Astley of the Society of Authors and the Phoenix Trust for the grant which allowed me to finish my research and for all the trouble he went to on my behalf during that period. My gratitude also to Stephen Watts of Chelsea for all his time he spent checking the manuscript and in particular to the late Alec Clifton-Taylor who finally steered me in the right direction.

My sincere thanks to Sue Smith of Bexhill-on-Sea, East Sussex, for all her assistance in the initial typing.

ILLUSTRATIONS

I would like to make grateful acknowledgment for the use of 12 illustrations from Malcolm Linskey's collection and the following individual items:- Page 147 - Brian West; Page 155 - London Transport Museum; Page 165 - Stanley Roth; Page 170 - The Editor, Taxi Magazine and Page 181 - The Fellowship of Hackney Carriage Drivers.

The remaining illustrations are from my private collection.

INTRODUCTION

There are many gaps in the transport and social history of London, apocryphal stories abound concerning the history of stage coaches, Sedan chairs and London's horse drawn cabs and motorised taxis. London's licensed taxi trade has more than three hundred years of Parliamentary control behind it, but how much of its history is known? Outwardly mundane, it has often been the centrepiece of royal patronage, of fierce Parliamentary debate and political intrigue.

This story traces the development of the horse drawn coach plying for hire with its roots firmly planted in the reign of Richard II. It describes the opposition from the Thames watermen and how the growth of London in the 17th and 18th centuries brought the watermen to the edge of disaster. It tells when these coaches were first licensed in 1654, by whom and why and what effect the religious and political bigotry had on the infant cab trade. It explains who, where, when and why the stage coach service was begun and the growth of the short stage coach and how they grew away from London's licensed hackney coach trade to become the present day London Transport bus service.

It relates the development of the Hansom cab in the 19th century, its decline and the advent of the motor cab. The industrial problems of the trade are examined and how the growth of the cab trade unions led to the formation of the Transport & General Workers Union. It deals with the end of Railway Privilege system in London and the strikes against government and employers. In short it fills a gap in the social and transport history of London.

AUTHOR'S NOTE

Throughout this story the term 'Bills of Mortality'* will appear. To give the reader a better understanding of the meaning of the term, these were the collection of records compiled by the Company of Parish Clerks in London, which recorded all deaths within the area of the city and beyond. In 1536, Thomas Cromwell, Chancellor of England ordered that, "the incumbent of every parish is to keep a true record and exact register of all christenings, weddings and funerals". In 1598 this was carried out in parchment books which have survived to this day.

The weekly 'Bills' proper began on December 21st 1592 and continued until the last burial recorded in the city on April 29th, 1856 and the last christening entered in the 'Bills' at St. Mildreds Poultry, on August 3rd 1858. Prior to 1639, the 'Bills' covered a total of 97 parishes of medieval London and 16 parishes without the walls, they gradually grew in size to include Middlesex and Southwark. The first addition after 1639 was St. Paul's Covent Garden, followed by the riverside parishes of St. Paul's Shadwell and Christchurch Southwark in 1671.

At the time the 'Bills' were discontinued there were a total of 159 parishes within the area of the Bills of Mortality; 97 city parishes; 16 without the walls; 38 out parishes and 8 district churches. Most of them were within three miles of the traditional centre of the city from which milestones were measured, at the point of the standard water supply at the junction of Cornhill and Gracechurch Street.

* The Parish Clerks of London, R.H. Adams. GRL (L.14.71) pp.48,62.

ABBREVIATIONS

GRL .... Guildhall Reference Library
GRO .... Guildhall Record Office
PRO .... Public Record Office
HOLRO .... House of Lords Record Office
BRIT. MUS. .... British Museum Library
SMA .... Science Museum Annexe
PARLY. PAPERS. .... Parliamentary Papers
HIST. MAN. COM. .... Historical Manuscripts Commission Reports
IBID .... As before

Chapter One

The Growth of London

The history of the London cab trade is synonymous with the growth of London itself; it is also inextricably entwined with the social and economic development of the capital. More apparent, as we shall see, is the part the cab trade played in laying down the pattern for the development of transportation especially in the 18th century, along lines that as far as public road transport is concerned have changed little to this day. But the story of all that is to come, we must go back to the year before the Norman Conquest.

From that moment when Edward the Confessor decided to build a monastery church at Westminster which was consecrated in 1065, the ascendance of London as the capital was assured. Before then it could just have easily been Kingston-on-Thames where eleven English kings were crowned between 856 AD and 978 AD, or Winchester, where Edward the Confessor himself had been crowned in 1043 AD and where six kings were buried, from Alfred the Great in AD 901 to William II in 1134.

From 1065 then, until Henry VIII took possession of Cardinal Wolsey's Palace, York House in Whitehall on November 2nd 1529,(1) the main place of residence for our monarchs had been the Palace of Westminster. The Confessor had built his palace opposite Westminster Abbey so that he could be near to the church that was rising from the marshy ground of the Isle of Thorney as the district was called.

In 1197 when it was thought expedient for the Archbishop of Canterbury to have his palace near to that of the monarch, it was accomplished by transferring the Manor of Lambeth from the See of Rochester, in exchange for the Manor of Dartford. (2) Sixty years later in 1257 the Great Council assembled in the Chapter House of Westminster Abbey on March 26th of that year. Thus had come together the three estates of Monarchy, Church and Government which in the main comprise the establishment, placed conveniently near to one another.

The dominating feature of London is it's rivers and it is not without good reason that the Thames has been called 'liquid history'. London probably owes it's existence to it's river and the Romans had chosen their site for a permanent city because of the river's strategic importance. The twin hills now dominated by St. Pauls in the west and Leadenhall Market in the east, formed a natural defensive position and the relatively hard ground which was surrounded by marshland added further to its defences. The River Fleet that emptied itself into the Thames at the city's western extremity, provided a natural harbour for the ships which were to carry on an extensive trade with the continent.

Orientated to the river as it was, London's early development naturally followed it's course. Prior to 1500 only the area within the old city walls was heavily populated. The strip development of Fleet Street and the Strand followed the course of the river, joined Whitehall and ran down to Westminster Abbey and the Palace. The larger houses were occupied by religious orders and members of the nobility, Carmelite Street perpetuates the memory of the Carmelite Priory that stood on this site until the dissolution of the monasteries in 1539. Somerset House, facing the river close to Waterloo Bridge is the direct successor to the Somerset House that stood here in the years between 1549 and 1776. The Savoy Hotel stands on the site of the former residence of the Dukes of Savoy and Burgundy.

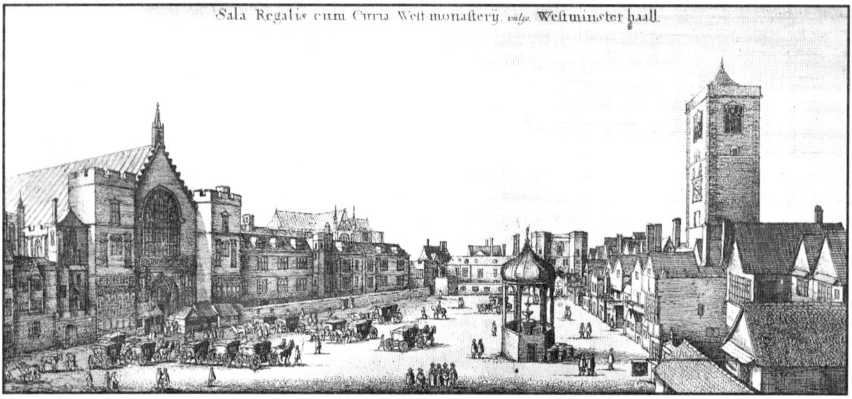

London's cab trade has a long association with Parliament as this line-up of horse cabs outside Westminster Hall demonstrates - c.1654.

All these buildings stood in their own grounds and very little was allowed by way of encroachment. Beyond this area was open country with small villages dotted about; Fulham, Chelsea, Lambeth, Islington, Hampstead and Stepney were but a few of the villages which then surrounded London. The only other built up area was Southwark which then extended south to where St. Georges Church now stands, west to Blackfriars Bridge and eastwards to Tower Bridge. This then was the extent of the built up area and as such was well served by the Watermen for both public travel along and across the river and for the transportation of goods.

Between the years 1500 and 1600 this area practically doubled in size and such was the rate of growth during this period that Elizabeth I issued a proclamation on July 7th 1580, forbidding any building within three miles of the city gates. (3) This sufficed for a short time but while it curbed the spread it increased the density, as builders added to existing buildings until it was almost possible to shake hands with people on the opposite side of the street.

The continuing growth of London was only momentarily checked by the plague in 1665 and the Great Fire of 1666. The provisions of the rebuilding act of 1667 laid down the standard and type of houses that were to be built. It forbade the erection of the kind of houses that had existed before the fire - the tenements and garrets that were a constant source of overcrowding. Once the regulations were complied with as to which type of house should be built, the architect was given a free hand as to how it should be constructed and to what extent he could use the materials available. Pictures and drawings of post fire London show that the city achieved a certain dignity in it's rows of well constructed houses of red brick; Wren's beautiful churches and by 1711 his masterpiece, St. Paul's Cathedral dominating the entire city.

During the next hundred years, London again doubled in size and by 1800 it covered an area which stretched roughly from Paddington to Bethnal Green, west to east and from King's Cross to the Elephant and Castle, north to south. As London grew, so too did the need for transport and between 1711 and 1800 twenty five Acts of Parliament were passed either wholly or partly concerned with London's licensed hackney carriage trade. During the 17th century as we shall see, when a few of London's hackney coachmen begun the long stage coach network, so too in the 18th century others were responsible for the development of the short stage network in and around London.

The growth of London affected not only the hackney coach it also threw up many social and economic problems. The general pattern of expansion was for the richer folk i.e., the nobility, merchants and the more prosperous tradesmen to move west and north-west. This move in one general direction was motivated by the prevailing wind which blew from west to east. As the use of coal increased so the effects of it's smoke and the noise and smells of industry became worse, the only way to escape was to move westward which only the wealthy could afford to do. Even today the terms West End and East End indicate a higher standard of living for the former and a depressed area for the latter.

As one class of people moved out so their former residences were taken over by the 'meaner people' amongst whom were a large proportion of the criminal class. The houses were adapted to provide for up to ten families and the alterations included adding several doors that led off into alleys and courts thus making escape easy if the need arose. The population being increased tenfold meant the rapid deterioration of the area into slums. This large influx of people often resulted in increased unemployment and more and more people were forced to go 'on the parish'.

Social Security is not a modern invention, it is merely the modern equivalent of the former Poor Laws. In 1795 for example a labourers' wage was eight shillings a week and his wife earned another sixpence, probably taking in washing. Their weekly living requirements were eleven shillings and twopence, a deficit of two shillings and eight pence which was made up by poor relief distributed by the parish. (4)

Despite the appalling conditions of the poor, London continued to expand and during the 18th century two new bridges were built across the Thames; Westminster Bridge opened in 1750 and Blackfriars Bridge in 1769. For hundreds of years the city had resisted the building of new bridges because the City Corporation, jealous of their position as the centre of trade and commerce, was afraid that new routes across the Thames would divert trade.

Their attitude is highlighted by a remarkable series of events in 1664 when various people were petitioning Charles II to be allowed to build a bridge across the river at Westminster. But they had reckoned without the City Corporation who had the measure of their king. On October 25th 1664, the Court of Common Council made an order, "on the King's pleasure", to grant the king a loan of £100,000 because he had prevented the building of the bridge. (5)

A few days later the Earl of Manchester said in a speech to the Common Council, "his majesty will never forget your demonstration of loyalty and affection and will not be wanting in care and kindness to the happiness and advantage of the city". (6) The eventual construction of Westminster Bridge was accomplished in 1750 by which time the inhabitants of Lambeth and Westminster had increased so as to overcome opposition to the bridge. The main fear of the Corporation appears to have been a loss of tolls from reduced traffic over London Bridge and a corresponding loss of profits from the city's markets both of which as it turned out were unfounded.

By 1760 the last of the old buildings on London Bridge had been pulled down and the roadway widened to allow for the easier access of traffic to and from the city. By this time even the City Corporation could not resist progress and between 1760 and 1780 most of the old Roman Wall and gates of the city were demolished, giving greater freedom of movement to the ever increasing road traffic.

One particular source of annoyance to traffic entering and leaving the city by way of Fleet Street was Temple Bar and the narrow streets in the vicinity. At one time it was even contemplated pulling down St. Clement Danes Church such was the need for better road communication. In 1787 the Common Council of the City of London rejected by one vote, a resolution to pull down Temple Bar and it continued to obstruct traffic until 1887, when it was at last taken down and re-erected in Theobald's Park in Hertfordshire. It was not until 1887 with the construction of the Royal Courts of Justice and the Kingsway, Aldwych and Strand widening scheme from 1900 to 1905 that traffic could at last flow with ease.

The 19th century saw more in the way of expansion than at any time before and London took on the shape it is today, except for the urban development of this century. The construction of the Thames Embankments and the layout of Trafalgar Square are two good examples, the Queen Victoria Street and Cannon Street clearances are two more.

Beyond any doubt the most important single social event of the 19th century was the coming of the railways. In 1836 the first passenger train to leave a London station left London Bridge for Greenwich. Euston, London's second main line station was opened in 1838; Paddington in 1841 and Waterloo in 1848. (7) Following the completion of London's main line stations by 1875 the Railway Commissioners had intended that all the stations should be connected by a circular railway. It was only partially carried out with the construction of the Inner Circle, part of London's Underground Railway system.

Cannon Street Station, a typical Victorian development that accommodated the growing demand for travel, 1866.

By the end of the 19th century London covered an area bounded by Highgate in the north, Dulwich in the south, in the east as far as Stratford and to Hammersmith in the west. The demand for travel was now so great that when the Metropolitan Railway from Paddington to Farringdon Street was opened in 1863, nine and a half million people used it in it's first year of operation. (8) At the end of the century, 12,000 Hansom cabs and 'growlers' were licensed yet by 1914 nearly all had gone as the London cab trade switched to mechanical power.

It is possible to observe now that from 1750 to 1900, London's true formative years, have given us a remarkable city. The pattern is now thoroughly established, the old city, formerly residential but now 98 per cent offices and the financial centre for half the world. The judicial centres both civil and criminal are in close proximity to the barristers and solicitors of the Temple and it's various associated Inns of Court. Both are relatively close to Whitehall the seat of government with it's supporting cast - the Civil Service. The main residences of the Monarch and the Archbishop of Canterbury are conveniently sited, as we have seen, to constitute the higher echelons of the establishment.

As in this chapter we have seen how London grew to a vast Metropolis so the succeeding chapters chart the growth of wheeled transport through the social and economic conditions of three centuries. How the long stage coach, short stage coach and the omnibus all stemmed from an obscure Act of Oliver Cromwell's Parliament. The growth of London and the growth of public travel go hand in hand and as the Industrial Revolution brought wealth to many of London's citizens, so their travel demands had to be met. The following chapters tell how this was done.

References used in Chapter One

1. Kings and Queens of England, Sir George Bellew K.C.V.O.
2. Lambeth Palace, a guide to home and history, D. Willis, p. 8.
3. Bibliotheca Lindesiana (GRL)
4. The Case of Labourers Husbandry, Rev. David Davies 1795, from the history of the Cost of Living. J. Burnett.
5. State Papers Domestic 1664. p. 145. (GRL)
6. Ibid.
7. The Face of London. H.P. Clunn.
8. Ibid.

Chapter Two

The Beginning

"Give the losers leave to speak"

"Sir, ye know well that except the hackney horses between Gravesend and Dovour there is no usual conveyance in post for men of this realme as in the accustomed places of France and other parts". So wrote Brian Tuke, Master of Posts, to Thomas Cromwell, Chancellor of England on August 11th 1553. (1) From this passage in Tuke's letter it would appear that the London to Dover road was the only road in England that had a system known as 'hackney stages'. That this service had been in use since at least 1396 is evident from a patent of Richard II in that year which read:-

"There shall be taken for the hire of a hakenie from Suthwuk to Rochester 12d; from Rochester to Canterbury 12d; and from Canterbury to Dovour 6d; and from town to town according to the rayte of 12d and the number of miles". (2)

These references to 'hackney' refer to the type of horse used for the conveyance of men who hired horses from the various Hackneymen's stables set at intervals along the route from London to Dover. These became known as 'hackney stages' and when centuries later the coach was used for travel along this and similar routes they became stage coaches.

Within a few years of Richard II's patent the Mayor and Aldermen of Rochester had drawn up a set of bye-laws known as 'The Custumale' for the better regulation of tradesmen in the city. The contents of the Custumale, although written in the 16th Century, date mostly from before that time. The local laws of the city are described, together with the form of oath, to be sworn to Edward IV (1461-1483) by municipal officers when taking up office. (3) A peculiarity of these bye-laws was the great stress they laid upon Hackneymen and Victuallers as to the conduct of their trade. Whatever their profits must have been, the pleasure of carrying on their business must have been small.

One bye-law in the interest of the Hackneymen stated, "no person shall go out of the citie to hyre no horse". Outside the city limits were speculators who, having no city rate or fee to pay could afford to hire out horses at a cheaper rate. "No Hackneyman shall breke another's hyre". This was enacted to prevent one Hackneyman from taking away the legitimate fare of another. In current cab trade legislation this appears as "if any driver or proprietor shall wrongfully, or in a forcible or clandestine manner take away the fare of another driver, he shall be liable to a fine of £1". Taxicabs are officially described as hackney carriages, the former reduced road tax for taxis was known as hackney road tax and a London cabdriver's licence refers to "Acts relating to hackney carriages".

It would appear then that there is a definite connection between the fares laid down by Richard II's patent of 1396, the Custumale of the following century and current legislation. The term 'hackney' has been passed down through the centuries, applicable at first to the horse, then the horse drawn vehicle and lastly the motor cab. The word 'hackney' is derived from the Flemish term 'haquenue' meaning ambling nag, a dappled grey horse which came originally from Flanders. It has nothing to do with the London borough of that name.

Following the introduction of the coach into England during the reign of Queen Elizabeth I, it was a natural progression for it to be used as a passenger carrying vehicle. Whether eventually hackney coaches were so named because they were drawn by hackney horses, or because they served the same functional purpose is not known, though their use as hackney coaches was not immediate. The first recorded use of a hackney coach carrying fare paying passengers seems to have been in 1588 on the occasion of a thanksgiving service at St. Paul's Cathedral, attended by Elizabeth I, following the defeat of the Spanish Armada. (4)

At this time any person owning a coach was required to pay to the Exchequer £50 per annum, a form of Road Fund tax which cost more than the coach itself. It was to recoup some of the high cost of owning a coach that their owners, mostly nobility, hired them out for others to drive. By 1601 this habit was the cause of some concern and an attempt was made to put an end to the practice. Consequently in November of that year a Bill was placed before the House of Lords which read, "an act to restrain the excess and superfluous use of coaches within this Realme of England". The noble lords spoke of "the Saddlers trade is like to be ruined, evil disposed persons securely convey themselves in coaches and cannot be discerned from persons of honour". The Bill provided for a penalty of £5 for every offence of wrongful use and "no p'son to let a coach or coach horses to any but those authorised to use them on pain of forfeiting same". (5)

As many of the lords who were to examine the Bill stood to lose their income from hiring out their coaches, the Bill did not get a second reading. Proof that some of the nobility were hiring out their coaches in this manner comes from Thomas Platter who recorded that the coachman he tried to hire to take him from Oxford to Cambridge, excused himself by saying "the coach is very expensive and belongs to a great lord from whom I have hired it, as I am newly set up house should the coach get stuck in the mud I shall be a ruined man for life". (6)

The practice of using coaches continued to grow and they were well established by the early 17th century. Travel by coach opened up hitherto closed avenues for a great number of people; family could visit family, whereas before it had been necessary to ride horseback or by the carriers long wagon which only travelled a prescribed route and was of no use to anyone wanting to make a spontaneous journey. Large numbers of people had difficulty riding horses, for some it was impossible; the sick the aged and the infirm. It was also possible to travel in reasonable comfort in inclement weather and a good deal more safely since the streets were infested with footpads.

COACH and SEDAN,

Pleaſantly Diſputing for Place and Precedence;

The *Brewers-Cart* being Moderator.

Spectatum admiſſi, riſum teneatis amici?

LONDON:

Printed by *Robert Raworth*, for *Iohn Crowch;* and are to be ſold by *Edmund Paxton*, dwelling at *Pauls* chayne, neere Doctors-Commons. 1636.

This illustration shows the primitive design of early hackney coaches and sedan chairs - 1636.

In 1614 another attempt was made to stop coaches from being hired and a Bill entitled "a Bill against the outrageous hackney coaches" was rejected by the House of Commons on May 7th of that year. (7) Perhaps the most surprising fact to emerge from this early period is not that various attempts were made to stop the growth of hackney coaches but that the authorities seemed reluctant to control them. An example of this occurred in 1633 when the Churchwardens and Parish Constables of Blackfriars in the City of London, petitioned the Privy Council concerning the problems caused by the presence of the Playhouse theatre and particularly of the number of hackney coaches bringing playgoers there.

The Privy Council upheld the petition and issued an order of the Star Chamber requiring all hackney coachmen to leave the Playhouse as soon as they set down and not to return until the play was over. Any coachman disobeying the order was to be committed to Newgate prison. (8) Although the Privy Council thought it necessary to commit offenders to prison, no steps were taken to suppress them, as there would have been had they been considered to be a public nuisance. No form of control was envisaged at this stage which is somewhat strange when at that time all other trades in the city were firmly controlled.

An early Hackney Coach in Fleet Street, close to the Maypole in the Strand. The Temple Bar is featured in the background - c.1656.

The method of plying for hire at this time was not on ranks, openly, but to tuck themselves away in the yards of the numerous inns dotted about the city; here they would wait until approached by a prospective customer. There was no official tariff and fares went up or down according to public demand. In 1634 an attempt was made to stand coaches in Fleet Street but the coachmen were prevented from doing so by an order of Common Council in the City of London.

However in 1636 the modus operandi that had previously existed ceased almost overnight and the pattern of plying for hire was laid down that has existed up to the present day. A certain Captain Bailey, a retired mariner, was responsible for the experiment. He had four hackney coaches constructed, attired his drivers in livery and instructed them what fares to charge, but most important he brought his coaches out into the open and stood them one behind the other close to the Maypole in the Strand.

Captain Bailey's choice of the Maypole was wise for it was the focal point of the parish, where proclamations and newsheets were posted and where therefore people would congregate. The rank thus set up by Captain Bailey soon attracted the attention of other hackney coachmen who flocked there seeking work. It became so crowded that the practice of driving slowly along the street was begun, waiting for a vacancy on the rank. The Reverend Mr. Garrod commenting on these events in a letter to Lord Strafford said, "everybody is much pleased with it, for, whereas coaches could be had at great rates now a man can hail one much cheaper". (9)

This latest innovation on the part of the coachmen infuriated the Thames watermen and brought to a climax the hostility which had been festering for some years. It was from London's watermen that the fiercest opposition to the hackney coach came for the growth of the coaches was largely at the expense of the men who worked on the river.

As early as 1612 the watermen had expressed their concern at the growth of the hackney coach. Previously they had benefited considerably from the trade provided by actors and their patrons crossing the river to the theatres on Bankside in Southwark. But about this time the theatres in the city - the Playhouse for example already referred to - came into fashion and boats were no longer required in such numbers as formerly. The hackney coaches were soon catering for the passengers who had formerly used the river.

The watermen went to a great deal of trouble in an effort to stem this new trend with its resulting loss of revenue, even to the extent of petitioning James I. The king set up a commission of inquiry to study the charges made but when it's chairman, Sir Walter Cope died, the commission was dissolved. (10) Every crisis, so it is said, produces a leader and the watermen were no exception. They were fortunate to have among them John Taylor, a staunch crusader on their behalf. Apart from his profession as a waterman he was also a poet and an author, he often composed water pageants for Lord Mayor's processions on the river. In an effort to rouse the watermen he wrote the following verse.

"Coaches, Garroaches, Jades and Flanders Mares, do rob us of our fares, our wares and our tares, while we stand and click our heels all our profit runs away on wheels".

By 1623 John Taylor was firmly established as the watermen's champion. He redoubled his efforts to obtain some form of restriction against the hackney coach, bombarding influential people with tracts and pamphlets he had written. To some extent the ground had been prepared for him because public opposition to the coach had arisen even before the end of the 16th century. People using coaches were often described as wantons. There seemed no objection to coaches being used by officers of state or those suffering some kind of infirmity for "to ride in coaches they need not shame". There was an element of resentment against the wealthy who used coaches, succinctly put in one tract published "as poorer trules must ride in carts so coaches are for prouder hearts". (11)

John Taylor blamed hackney coaches for reasons that the citizens could easily recognise. "Whence cometh leather so dear", he wrote in 1623, "by reason of the hackney coach that doth consume all the best hides in the kingdom wherebye many poor shoemakers are undone and many poor christians go barefoot at Christmas". He was particularly resentful of the fact that hackney coaches plied for hire near the Temple Gate and carried members of the legal profession to Westminster Hall and back, with three or four passengers sharing a coach at fourpence each", which was cheaper than the fare by boat. "If the coaches would carry people north or south", he said, "there would be no grievance but their carrying east and west will ruin the watermen". (12)

Even the Sedan chair came under attack from the watermen for they claimed that Sedan chairs were taking almost as much work away from them as were the hackney coaches. The hackney coachmen looked upon Sedan chairs as having an unfair advantage, though the watermen eyed them both with suspicion. "They deserve to bee both thrown in the Theames", said a waterman in 1636, "and but for stopping the channel I would they were; for I am sure that where I was woont to have eight or tenne fares in a morning, I scarce now get two in a whole day". (13)

Although the profession of watermen on the river was centuries old and at least two ferries, at Putney and London Bridge were mentioned in the Domesday Book, the passenger boats were only successful while the Thames was London's high street and the majority of journeys followed the east-west axis of the river. As London grew north and south the hackney coach began to predominate. Apart from John Taylors reference to members of the legal profession sharing coaches to Westminster Hall, there is evidence to suggest that the sharing of coaches was quite common, especially to official functions.

Meanwhile, John Taylor pressed on, trying to obtain some form of restriction against hackney coaches. He was helped to some extent because Charles I did not view hackney coaches in a very favourable light either. In 1630 the monarch had granted 'letters patent' to a Sir Saunders Duncombe to let out Sedan chairs for hire in London (See Chapter 6). The king may have thought that if hackney coaches became very popular they would adversely affect Sedan chairs thereby reducing the income he received from Duncomb's concession.

Whatever the reasons were, John Taylor's efforts were successful and Charles I issued a proclamation on January 19th 1636, restricting the number of hackney coaches to fifty throughout London, Westminster and the suburbs. Moreover, they were only allowed to pick up passengers who were travelling more than three miles. (14) This effectively gave the Sedan chairs a monopoly of the short distance journeys, confirming earlier suspicions that Charles I was acting more in his own interests than those of the watermen.

Detail from a print showing watermen plying their trade across the Thames at the Pool of London - c.1660.

When issuing a proclamation the monarch's actions were restricted as to what he could or could not do. What was really required was an Act of Parliament, but here Charles' hands were tied. Parliament did not sit between 1629 and 1640 and from 1642 to 1648 the country was embroiled in a civil war and legislation was out of the question. Within two years of the proclamation, it was if it had never been made for hackney coaches were working very much as before; because the people wanted them.

John Taylor seemed to sense that his profession was doomed, yet he still kept up his attacks. "I do not inveigh against any coaches that belong to a person of quality", he wrote, "the hackney coaches have undone my poor trade of which I am a member; and though I look for no reformation yet I expect the benefit of the old proverb "give the losers leave to speak".

From about this time he seems to have given up his unequal struggle chiefly because he was disillusioned by his fellow watermen, for though his costs had amounted to £34.0.0 and a fund had been raised to assist him, it only amounted to £19.4.0. even so some of them accused him of swindling them. In 1649 after an eventful life at sea and on the river he took an inn at Pheonix Alley off Long Acre. At first he intended to call it 'the Mourning Crown' for he was staunchly royalist but he was persuaded to change it to 'The Poet's Head', upon which there hung a sign.

"There's many a kings head hung up for a sign why not mine".

References used in Chapter Two

1. Packhorse, Wagon and Post, Croftie. (GRL)
2. Ibid.
3 The original Custumale can be seen in the Town Clerk's office in Rochester.
4. History, Origin and Progress of the Watermen's Company. H. Humerous. (GRL)
5. Hist. Man. Com. 4th Report. (GRL)
6. Packhorse, Wagon and Post, Croftie. (GRL)
7. Hist. Man. Comm. 4th Report. (GRL)
8. Bibliotheca Lindesiana. (GRL)
9. London in the time of the Stuarts. Sir Walter Besant. (GRL)
10. History, Origin and Progress of the Watermen's Company. H. Humerous. (GRL)
11. The Development of Transportation in Modern England. W.T. Jackman. (Brit. Mus. 08235 p.22)
12. The Writings and Tracts of John Taylor, in particular 'Thief'. (GRL)
13. Coach and Sedan presently disputing, Henry Peachum, 1636. (GRL)
14. Bibliotheca Lindesiana. (GRL)

Chapter Three

"Leave to labour for our living"

In June 1636 five months after Charles I proclamation against hackney coaches, the coachmen petitioned Charles protesting at the general use of coaches by Chandlers, Innkeepers, Brokers and others who were intruding into the profession of coachman. They asked for a charter of incorporation with powers to make rules for the future governing of hackney coaches under the auspices of the Lord Chief Justice. (1)

By examining what facts there are it would seem that two groups of coachmen existed. First were those who relied solely upon driving a coach for a living. These were the men who had stood their coaches in the yards of inns and who had later followed Captain Bailey's example and worked from the Maypole in the Strand. This group were known as the 'ancient coachmen' and have come down through the centuries as the licensed taxi trade.

The second group were comprised of coaches owned by merchants, shopkeepers and others who hired out coaches when an opportunity presented itself that would enable them to make some profit by it. These were known as interlopers and have also come down through the centuries as jobmasters, private hire and minicabs. For as long as there has been a licensed trade, there has also been an unlicensed one working quiet well and prosperous without any recourse to a licensing system.

By February 1637 the 'ancient coachmen' had received no reply to their petition and they duly presented another on February 11th, 1637. This petition gives a remarkable insight into the kind of thinking at that time, it also shows that contrary to popular beliefs, hackney carriages were not licensed because it was necessary to control men who were overcharging and cheating the public, but because the trade itself wanted control and were willing to pay for it. If the king would grant them incorporation they were prepared to pay £500 to the Exchequer per annum and they would maintain fifty able horses and men well armed to be exercised under the command of who the king should appoint. (2)

Almost two years later, Mr. Secretary Coke, writing to the Lord Keeper on May 12th 1639 said, "his majesty hath commanded me to signify to you and the Lord Privy Seal that conceiving the incorporation of coachmen will be no public grievance his pleasure is that you will pass the grant without stop or hindrance". For some reason it all came to nought, the coachmen were neither incorporated or made the subject of any kind of legislation at that time and it was not until 1654 that the thread becomes visible again; this time the coachmen were petitioning Oliver Cromwell.

They appealed to Cromwell's regard for the army, "we have from the beginning of the wars been ready to serve with our horses in the artillery train under the Lord Essex", prudently omitting the fact that they had some years earlier offered a similar service to Charles I. The petition also referred to the fact that, "the late Parliament had read our Bill twice but the house was dissolved". (3) This was a reference to the 'barebone' Parliament, so called because one of it's members was Thomas 'Praise God' Barbon. This Parliament had been dissolved by Cromwell on December 12th 1653. The next Parliament was the first of Cromwell's Protectorate and one of it's first Acts was to provide legislation setting up the Fellowship of Master Hackney Coachmen on similar lines to other trades in the city such as the Watermen and the Billingsgate Porters.

Though the act itself was to remain in force for only three short years, it was to lay down the pattern for every subsequent Act of Parliament concerning hackney carriage vehicles until the present day. From such humble origins London's present public transport; buses, taxis, Green Line and coach services have all descended. In fact, "the reader who will examine the record of the Commonwealth from the standpoint of economic and social development, will find in these troublous years the beginnings of many institutions of our own time". (4)

The Act of June 1654 related to persons owning hackney coaches "in the City of London and Westminster and six miles about from the late lines of communication".

AN
ORDINANCE
For The
REGVLATION
OF
Hackney Coachmen
IN
LONDON
And the places adjacent.

Fryday June 23. 1654.
ORdered by his Highnefs the Lord Protector and His Council, That this Ordinance be forthwith Printed and Publifhed,
Henry Scobell, Clerk of the Council.

London, Printed by *William du-Gard* and *Henry Hills*, Printers to His Highnefs the Lord Protector, 1654.

Title page of Cromwell's Ordinance 1654.

This was a reference to a chain of defences erected around the city and Westminster before the civil war in 1642 from Vauxhall to the Elephant and Castle, then via Aldgate to Oxford Street, Marble Arch, Hyde Park Corner and back to the river at Vauxhall.

The number of coachmen to be licensed was restricted to two hundred and the act named the first thirteen overseers, to who was entrusted the task of choosing the remainder. Each man admitted to the Fellowship was required to pay £2 toward defraying the expenses of the company. The Court of Aldermen in the City of London to whom overall control was entrusted, were empowered to make additional bye-laws concerning the distribution of coaches among the coachmen, the places of standing, the fares and the penalties for disobedience according to the provisions of Cromwell's ordinance, "provided that nothing therein contained do extend to the prejudice of coaches commonly called stage coaches, coming to or coming from London". (5)

(1)

Pack Mayor. Tueſday the Second day of January, 1654.

ORdered, That ſuch of the Rules and By-Laws made by this Court in purſuance of the late Ordinance for Regulation of Hackney Coachmen, and approved by His Highneſs the Lord *Protector* and the Council, as are of moſt concernment to be preſently and publickly known, be forthwith Printed, that all perſons concerned may take notice thereof, and act according to the ſame Rules, being now to be put in ſtrict execution without further warning.

TO the intent there may be no exaction, ſtrife or debate about the hire of Coaches for time to come; It is Ordained, That no perſon or perſons of the Fellowſhip of Hackney Coachmen ſhall require, take or have any greater rate or prices then is hereafter ſet down and expreſſed; that is to ſay, for the hire of a Coach, Caroach or Charret with four Horſes, twenty ſhillings a day; and

A for

Explanation of dates:
To avoid any misunderstanding it must be pointed out that Cromwell's Ordinance is dated 24 June 1654, whereas the rules and Bye-laws for the regulation of the hackney coachman, which were drawn up by the Court of Alderman on the authority of Cromwell's Ordinance, are dated 2 January 1654. The apparent discrepancy in the dates is due to the fact that the Court of Alderman counted the New Year as commencing on Lady Day, the Feast of the annunciation on 25 March, thus what should have been 2nd January 1655 in today's calendar appears as 2nd January 1654 in the Court of Alderman's Official calendar.

Part of the Rules and Bye-Laws drawn up by the Court of Alderman as a result of Cromwell's Ordinance, 1654.

The common practice of paying fares at this time was by the day for journeys that exceeded six miles from the boundaries of the City of London and Westminster. When laying down the fare scale the Court of Aldermen had accepted the principle for a coach drawn by four horses; twenty shillings a day and for a coach and two horses; ten shillings a day. A limit of thirty miles was set for a coach and four horses and twenty miles for a coach drawn by two horses. These distances only applied between March and October, for the six winter months it was reduced to twenty miles and ten miles respectively, "excepting the Sussex Road, which being wont and hardest for travelling shall be travelled so far only as is reasonable or shall be agreed by the coachman on hire".

Within the six mile limit of the Lines of Communication a different fare structure applied, "that is to say sixpence a mile forward and sixpence back". The coachman could charge one shilling per hour waiting time after the first hour and if more than three passengers were carried he was allowed to charge sixpence for each additional passenger. Typical fares were:-

"From the Guildhall to Temple Barre or any part of Chancery Lane, Gray's Inn or other place of like distance, not above 12d. From Westminster to Whitechapel or the like place or thereabouts 2/6d. From the Old Exchange to Whitechapel or the like distance or place 12d".

Provision was made for coachmen who refused to be hired, or pretended to be hired when they were not, who misbehaved by, "uncivil carriage or uses reproachful or railling words". The overseers had authority to try a coachman for the first two offences but for a third offence he had to appear before the Court of Aldermen who were able to withdraw a man's licence if he were found guilty of a serious offence.

By October 1654 the Fellowship was formed and the overseers had appointed one Humphrey Powell as their attorney-at-law and two Beadles, William Howard and Richard Justice. (6) These appointments seem to suggest that the business of the Fellowship was conducted with regularity, that records were kept and a written account which would have been necessary to conduct the affairs of a company two hundred strong. Yet, apart from the day to day recordings in the Court of Aldermen's Reportories on matters affecting them and the Fellowship and the accounts in State Papers touching events between the Guildhall, Parliament and the Fellowship, nothing else seems to have survived.

Considerable evidence exists to prove that a proper working relationship was carried on between the Aldermen and the Fellowship. On January 30th 1655, John Saltmarsh, one of the original overseers was tried before the Court of Aldermen for demanding more than the proper fare for a journey from the Royal Exchange to Hoxton. He was found guilty and removed from his position as an overseer and one William Dunstan was appointed in his place.

In March 1655 the Aldermen passed a bye-law forbidding hackney coachmen from working on a Sunday unless they could prove before a Justice of the Peace that such work was necessary. On November 5th 1655 the Court of Aldermen heard a complaint from the overseers that seven members were refusing to pay their quarterage; no reason was given and the seven were expelled with seven others being appointed in their place. (7)

From then until September 1656 nothing further appears in the Aldermen's records, then in that month the entire body of the overseers was ordered to appear before the Aldermen, who accused them of not taking a hard enough line with their fellow coachmen. The overseers were reminded of their oath and that they were,

"to govern by the laws of the Lord Protector and not by their own inclinations". The overseers promised that in future, "we shall be more just and follow the bye-laws and anyone now at liberty we shall punish accordingly".

By January 1657 the situation had not improved and the overseers were removed en masse and were replaced by thirteen others, among them was one Henry Earle. (8) By the following month the impasse between the Aldermen and the Fellowship was such that the Aldermen sent six of their number to see Oliver Cromwell. Their leader, Sir Thomas Wynne was entrusted with the task of explaining to Cromwell the events of the preceding months. He complained of the actions of the coachmen and their overseers, overcharging on the part of the former and mismanagement, bribery and corruption on the part of the latter. They further accused the overseers of being incapable of governing according to the Protector's Act of June 1654 and they called upon Cromwell to disband the Fellowship, "or to confine them to the bounds or limits, whatever else he did, some remedy must be found for all these evils". (9) It is to the State Papers of the period we must now turn to find out what had been the cause of all the trouble.

An ordinance of September 2nd 1654 stated, "that ex-soldiers of the Parliamentary forces were to seek trades on return to civil life". As far as this order related to London, the ex-soldiers were to be given preference, next to 'ancient coachmen' when applying for a hackney coach licence. It appears that the overseers had been ignoring this order, it had reached the ears of Cromwell who issued an order on January 3rd 1656:-

"To the Lord Chief Baron, Recorder of London and Alderman Tichborne, to enquire into allegations that certain persons of the late kings party are allowed to be hackney coachmen and others who have served Parliament are not allowed to keep hackney coaches. You are to enquire of a Cavalier, now a hackney coachman of St. Martins-in-the-Field parish, who had entered into bonds". (10)

Though there is no trace of any answer to this order of Cromwell's his subsequent actions seem to indicate that the allegations were upheld. Then, on July 18th 1656, a petition signed by a John Sanderson was presented to Cromwell on behalf of the hackney coachmen. Attached to this petition was a certificate signed by eight Justices of the Peace, to the effect that several of the overseers had broken the bye-laws of the ordinance of 1654 and had, "dismissed honest and well affected coachmen and daily troubled them to their utter ruin". The petitioners begged speedy relief "with leave to labour for our living".

The overseers denied the charges made against them but Cromwell was not satisfied and he ordered the Lord Mayor and the Aldermen to undertake an inquiry into the affairs of the Fellowship and the following points were to be considered.

1. That the present overseers are disaffected.
2. That they have unjustly suppressed the petitioners.
3. That they have admitted Cavaliers.
4. They have allowed others, not admitted, to keep coaches. (11)

At the same time, without waiting for the results of this inquiry, Cromwell ordered, on July 30th 1656 that all proceedings against John Sanderson, Jackson and Smith who had petitioned Cromwell on July 18th 1656 should be suspended. By August 19th 1656 the result of the enquiry ordered by Cromwell was published; it's findings were summarised thus:-

"Whereas the ordinance of 1654 ordered all persons admitted to the Fellowship to pay 40 shillings to the cost of their admission to the company, the overseers compel a payment of 50 shillings to £5 though they themselves have only lately paid. The ordinance limits the number of coaches to two hundred but there are three hundred and many more would not have set up if the overseers had done their duty. There are numerous cases of John Bray (treasurer) accepting bribes to admit persons to drive who should not be driving. There are cases of the overseers speaking out against the Protector and government and said they were resolved to keep out the Parliamentary soldiers". (12)

The overseers repudiated this report and John Bray vehemently denied taking bribes. He acknowledged receiving £800 in fines but said, "the money was used in the affairs of the Fellowship, I had none for my own use". They further excused themselves for admitting more than the original two hundred coaches by saying that they thought two hundred and fifty could be licensed. As the number to be licensed was clearly laid down in the ordinance of 1654 it is hardly likely that they would have been unaware of it. It would appear that they had given membership of the Fellowship to those other than ex soldiers, hence the charge that they had admitted Cavaliers.

On September 24th 1656 Cromwell suspended the bye-laws and by so doing encouraged large numbers of unlicensed coaches and soon the streets were crowded in a free for all. The Aldermen, in an effort to stem the tide of chaos, drew up bye-laws of their own under powers vested in them by a charter granted to the city by Edward III in 1342. This only gave them jurisdiction in the city within the walls, the Ward of Farringdon Without, Portsoken Ward, roughly corresponding to the area known today as Aldgate, and Southwark, which had been made a Ward of the city during the reign of Edward VI. The lucrative areas of the Strand, Whitehall and the Temple and other parts of Westminster and Middlesex were still open to all-comers.

Tichborne  Mayor.

Tueſday the twenty ſixth of May 1657.

Whereas the late Ordinances touching Hackney Coaches and Hackney Coachmen within the City of London and Places adjacent, are annulled and made void by authority of Parliament from and after the Twenty fourth day of June now next enſuing: And it is by experience manifeſt that by the ſaid Coaches ſtanding and peſtring the Streets, the Common paſſages are hindred and made dangerous, and a great diſturbance and annoyance thence ariſeth and manifold inconveniences are occaſioned to Inhabitants and Paſſengers: This Court therefore doth hereby annull and make void all grants or Lycences made or Granted at any time heretofore by this Court, by virtue of the ſaid Ordinances, to any Perſon or Perſons for the keeping or imploying of any Hackney Coach or Coaches and horſes and all rules and Orders touching or concerning the ſtanding and Regulating of the ſame; And doth further Order that from and after the ſaid Twenty fourth day of June no Hackney Coachman whatſoever nor ſervant to any Hackney Coachman ſhall ſtand or remaine in any the Streets, Lanes or Paſſages of this City with his or their Coach or Coaches and horſes ſo as to annoy or incumber the ſame, Upon Paine to be ſtrictly and ſeverely proſecuted and puniſhed according to Law, And all Conſtables and other Officers and Miniſters within this Citie and Liberties whom it may concerne are Required to be ayding and Aſſiſting in their ſeverall places, whereby ſuch as ſhall wilfully offend in the premiſes may be apprehended and brought before ſome Juſtice of the Peace of the ſame City and thereupon may be proceeded againſt according to the demerits of the offendors, And to the end that all perſons Concerned may take notice hereof and not think to excuſe themſelves by pretence of ignorance, Coppies of this Order are to be diſperſed and affixed in all convenient places of this City and Liberties.

Sadler.

Printed by *James Fleſher*, Printer to the Honorable City of *London*.

Following Parliaments Order in May 1657 revoking the act of June 1654, the above proclamation was issued by the Court of Alderman.

In an attempt to restore some kind of order the Lord Mayor and the Aldermen appealed to Cromwell to remove the suspension of the bye-laws, which he did on December 2nd 1656. (13) Cromwell instructed the Aldermen that they were to "consider the complaints of those who were accused by the overseers, redress them and the affected overseers and replace them with honest men".

It was as a result of these instructions from Cromwell that the Aldermen carried out the dismissal of the overseers which we have already seen and the subsequent dispatch to Cromwell of Sir Thomas Wynne and the Aldermen in February 1657. However the bitterness and bad feeling had gone too far and the different factions could not be reconciled. On May 15th 1657, Cromwell made an order revoking his ordinance of June 1654 thereby disbanding the Fellowship. (14) Thus the experiment begun three years before, had ended in failure; what had gone wrong?

First, it would seem that Cromwell and his Council, the Mayor and the Aldermen of the City of London and the overseers of the Fellowship were all motivated to some extent by political and religious bigotry. Secondly, the overseers were undoubtedly using their position to extract money for the privilege of owning a hackney coach licence. This greed was connected to a natural desire to limit the licences to men who had been connected with the trade for some years. They represented the intrusion of newcomers, i.e., Parliamentary soldiers, and there seems little doubt that this was a major cause of the friction.

Another problem was that the Act of 1654, by restricting the number of coachmen to two hundred, yet allowing the Court of Aldermen via it's powers to make bye-laws to increase the number of coaches to three hundred, made a hackney coach a valuable commodity by virtue of the limitation on the number of people who could own them. What was originally granted for only the cost of joining the Fellowship, became an investment. This made it desirable to own one and was a major cause of most of the problems surrounding the events between 1654 and 1657.

Following the disbandment of the Fellowship the hackney coachmen were forced to go back to the old way of working, from the yards of the principal inns dotted throughout the city., By 1660 they were again venturing out into the open. By now Cromwell was dead, the Commonwealth was ended and the monarchy had been restored with Charles II on the throne. Because of the encroachment of the coaches onto the streets, Charles II issued a proclamation on October 18th 1660 "to restrain the excessive numbers of hackney coaches in the City of London and Westminster. They are therefore forbidden to stand in the streets and may only be hired from a yard or stable". (15)

That not a great deal of notice was taken of this proclamation is evident from an entry in Samuel Pepys diary, "notwithstanding that this was the first day of the king's proclamation against coaches coming onto the streets to stand to be hired, yet I got one to carry me home".

References used in Chapter Three

1. State Papers Domestic 1636/7 Charles I p.35 (GRL)
2. Ibid. p. 436
3. Ibid. p. 109.
4. Story of the King's Highway, Sidney & Beatrice Webb.
5. Acts of the Inter-regnum (GRL)
6. Rep 63 folio 241 (GRO)
7. The references referring to John Saltmarsh, coachmen working on Sundays and the seven members refusing to pay their quarterage are respectively Rep 63 folio 257; Ibid folio 261b and Rep 64 folio 24 (GRO)
8. Rep 65 folio 37 (GRO)
9. Ibid. folio 45
10. State Papers Domestic 1655/6 pp. 94/95 (GRL)
11. Ibid. 1656/7 pp. 26/27 (GRL)
12. Ibid. p. 75. (GRL)
13. Ibid. p. 180 (GRL)
14. Rep 65 folio 114b (GRO)
15. Biliotheca Lindesiana. (GRL)

Chapter Four

"Journeys into remote parts"

Of all the different facets of public and goods transport that make up the history of travel in Britain, none has captured the imagination more, than that of the stage coach. Stage coaches are said to have begun about 1640 though there is no record of any regular service until 1657. These earlier journeys were probably of a spontaneous nature performed by the hackney coachmen during the course of their normal work. One such journey was that of a Dr. Clark in 1641, who was summoned from London to Woburn Abbey when the Duchess of Bedford was taken ill with smallpox. This journey was by hackney coach and the fare of £2.5.0. was at the rate of 1/- a mile. (1).

Early references to long journeys by coach are few. Those there are were almost totally connected with official business, such as the journey from London to Gravesend by the Spanish Ambassador in 1610. In 1625 a communication from the Privy Council to the Constable of Dover Castle, showed that it was possible to travel from London to Dover by coach despite the bad state of the road. This was on the occasion of a visit to this country by Henrietta, daughter of the King of France in April 1625. The Privy Council's order required the Constable of Dover Castle to see that, "all waies be thoroughly mended and made safe". (2)

A similar order by the Privy Council was made in September 1625 and a Sir Andrew Kith, a gentleman of the king's Privy Chamber, was entrusted to supervise the journey of the Swedish Ambassador from Southampton to Hampton Court, where the royal family were staying. Because of the plague that was raging in London it was not possible to hire hackney coaches and the Mayor of Southampton was required to use his own coach and "those of other gentlemen on such an important occasion as the king's service".

In 1652, during a visit to this country of the Dutch, Spanish and Portuguese Ambassadors, thirty hackney coaches were hired to transport them to and from the official functions they attended including several trips to Windsor. The coaches used today by foreign ambassadors on their way to present their credentials at St. James's Palace had very humble origins. In 1651, Parliament, mindful of the need to regularise this use of coaches, ordered, on the report of Sir Gilbert Pickering, the setting up of a state coach service. An initial sum of £100 was provided for a coach with crimson velvet furnishings and carrying the arms of the Commonwealth. The coachman, a Mr. Gay, was to be dressed in livery as were the footmen. It was first used to meet Oliver Cromwell after the battle of Worcester in 1652. (3)

There appears to be no record of a coach journey at this early period during the winter months, no doubt because the roads were impassable for coaches during the winter. Indeed the general state of the roads in England at this time was a national disgrace. It seems probable that a road of sorts went northwards from London to York and from London to Chester. Bath and Bristol were served by what passed as a road during the Tudor period, though by our standards were more like trackways, which in winter or after heavy rain were often impassable. It is no coincidence that the expansion of coach travel led to better roads at the same time, both begun during the Commonwealth period which resulted in the turnpike roads and the acts to control them.

In 1637 John Taylor wrote his Carriers Cosmographie (4) in which he listed the activities of some two hundred carriers who delivered goods all over the country, among these carriers were three entries relating to coaches. "The wagon or coach from Hartefourd town doth come every Friday to the 'Four Swannes' without Bishopsgate". He then mentions the wagon or coach that came every Friday to the 'Bell' in Aldersgate Street, but significantly, "a coach and wagon from St. Albans cometh to the 'Bell' in the same street, the like coach is also there for the carriage of passengers every Tuesday".

A carrier's long wagon, seen here at the Tabard Inn, Southwark, c. 1670. Of the type in which passengers travelled before stage coaches.

Taylor uses the words coach and wagon synonymously but he also identifies them separately. It appears that in general, little distinction was made between these early vehicles. Sir Walter Besant says, "long wagons were used for all long journeys by road and stage coaches did not appear until 1660". But Cromwell's ordinance of 1654 says, "provided that nothing herein contained shall be to the prejudice or restraint of the coaches commonly called stage coaches, that journey into remote parts".

In 1648 John Taylor, that great protagonist of the coach, rode from London to Southampton in the vehicle he had so often decried, was it perhaps the same service as was advertised in the Public Advertiser of May 1657 as "Christopher Crane, lyeth at the 'Rose' at Holborne Bridge with a hackney coach, and goes forth constantly every Friday to Southampton, every passenger pays fifteen shillings for his passage". (6)

Although there is little documentary evidence of the activities of stage coaches between John Taylor's account in 1637 and his journey to Southampton in 1648, there must have continued some kind of regular service as indicated by Cromwell's ordinance of 1654. In September 1655, the Court of Aldermen ordered that stage coaches were not to pick up passengers in the City of London unless they were travelling beyond the city limits "to remote parts". This was necessary to protect the hackney-coachmen, for stage coach fares were approximately 2d. a mile while the hackney coach fare within the city was 1/- a mile.

In April 1657 during the last days of the Fellowship, the known modus operandi of regular stage coaches was first begun by William Dunstan, Henry Earle and William Fowler, who set out to provide a regular service between Chester and London, a distance of 182 miles, with the novel experiment of changing horses every day. Their advertisement in the Mercurius Politicus of April 9th 1657 read:-

"For the convenience of passengers from and betwixt the citties of London and Westchester, there is provided several stage coaches which go from the 'George' Inn without Aldersgate upon every Monday, Wednesday and Friday, to Coventry in two days for twenty shillings, to Stone in three days for thirty shillings and to Chester in four days for thirty five shillings and from thence to return upon the same days; which is to be performed with much ease to the passengers, having fresh horses every day". (6)

The following month they advertised in the Public Advertiser of May 1657, the departure of a coach to Coventry on Mondays only, the fare being reduced to ten shillings and passengers were asked "to give timely notice at the house aforesaid". For two years, until April 1659 nothing is heard of the new venture, then, in the Mercurius Politicus of April 7th 1659 there appeared the following advertisement.

"These are to give notice, that from the 'George' Inn without Aldersgate

Street, goes every Monday and Thursday a coach and four able horses, to carry passengers to Chester in five days, likewise Coventry, Coleshill, Litchfield and Stone, or to Birmingham, Wolverhampton, Shrewsbury, Newport, Whitchurch and at Holywell, at reasonable rates, by us who have performed it for two years.

William Dunstan
Henry Earle
William Fowler". (7)

Within the space of two years they had increased the number of destinations from three to eleven, which included all the important centres in the Midlands, though it had added an extra day for the journey to Chester. This was quite an undertaking for those early years for not only had they increased the number of towns served by their coaches, they had also established new routes.

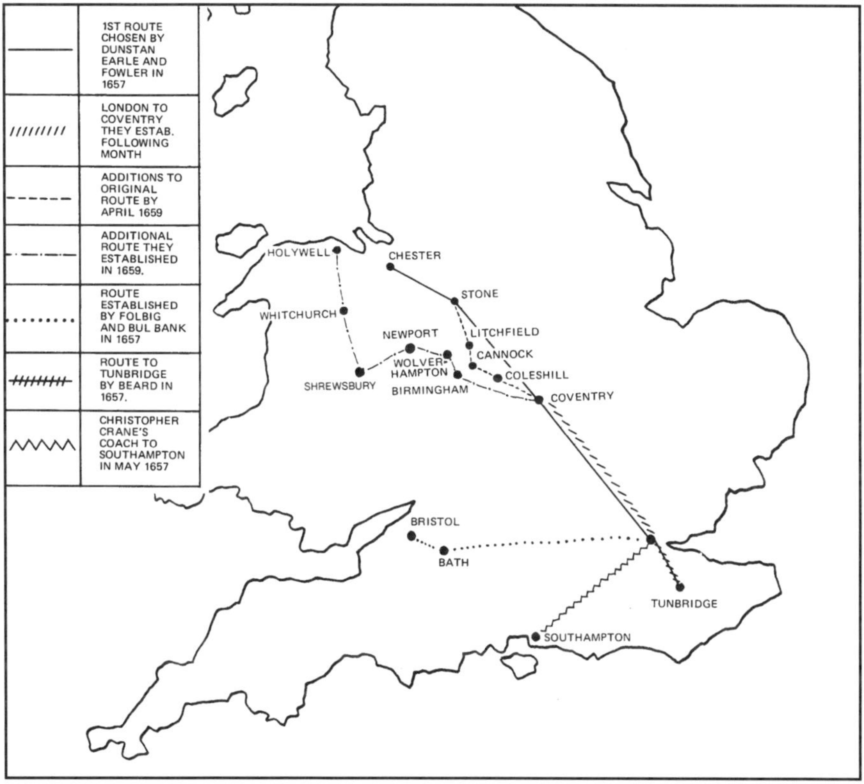

Towns in England served by stage coaches 1657 - 1659. *Map 1.*

The season for travel on these long journeys was from the end of April until the end of September, because the roads became unfit for travel as winter advanced. This is an important point to bear in mind, for when the service was discontinued during the winter the men who drove the stage coaches had to seek employment elsewhere. But who were these men who had started what was to become the most glamorous of all forms of travel? Why did they choose 1657 as the year to begin their operations?

William Dunstan and Henry Earle were two of London's first licensed hackney coachmen and both of them were at one time overseers of the Fellowship of Master Hackney Coachmen. William Fowler was almost certainly a hackney coachman as well, but as his name does not appear during the period of the Fellowship it can only be said he was a coachman with certain reservations. Being as they were so closely involved in the events between Parliament, the Court of Aldermen and the Fellowship, they were well aware that the days of the Fellowship were numbered. They fully realised that when it came, it would mean going back to the old ways of working, from the yards of inns and various stables in the city, without the protection of the law. They were of course well aware of the potential of the 'long stage', indeed, they may very well have been among those coachmen who had for some time been operating "to remote parts".

Why did they choose Chester as their main destination? For centuries, Chester had been the main port for North-West England, situated at the head of the River Dee. It's position here was chosen by the Roman XX Legion, as a fort which could dominate the approaches to North Wales, it's future from then onwards had been of a military nature. Staunchly royalist at the time of the civil war, it was at the time of this story, the main military centre for the shipment of men and arms to Ireland.

Between the reign of Henry VII and Cromwell, Chester's importance as a port had declined because of the silting up of the River Dee. Cromwell's re-conquest of Ireland created a flow of men and goods between the two countries to such an extent that Parliament authorised £3,000 for the purpose of improving the excise revenue and port facilities at Chester. (8) Here then must have been one of the busiest routes in the country. The traffic in passengers and goods would have been considerable, especially as people were being encouraged to settle in Ireland. A regular coach service must have been very welcome to women and children and the infirm, who would otherwise have had to use the laboriously slow 'long wagon', or made the journey by horseback.

But what of Dunstan, Earle and Fowler? William Dunstan was a licensed hackney coachman with licence number 396, he is listed as "a stage coachman to Chester, a sufferer and an ancient hackney coachman". This is from a list of men and women who were licensed to own but not necessarily drive, a hackney coach in 1662. (9) Henry Earle's name was not on this list but it is included in a list of names in the Guildhall Record Office, of all those men and women who had been licensed by an Act of Common Council in 1682. (10) We already know that Henry Earle was licensed between 1654 and 1657 when he was for a short while an overseer of the Fellowship.

In De Laune's Anglia Metropolis, written in 1690, the Shewsbury stage is shown as being owned by Fowler, Earle and a Widow Holloway, (11) whose husband was John Holloway with licence number 214. William Dunstan's name does not occur again and he had either severed his connection with Fowler and Earle, or he had died. Apart from the Shewsbury stage, they now operated one to Litchfield but there was no mention of Chester or any of the other towns originally served. They were however running carriers wagons as well as coaches and by this time they had become a fairly large concern.

In 1753, "Fowler's original stage to Shrewsbury" was still running at a fare of one guinea inside and half a guinea outside. An advertisement of 1774 said, "the proprietors of the original London to Shrewsbury stage announce guard rails for passengers carried on top". If this firm was indeed descended from the original trio, then perhaps their spirits rode with it.

Dunstan, Earle and Fowler were not the only hackney coachmen to operate stage coaches and it does seem as if there was some kind of concerted plan to commence operations following the end of the Fellowship. The Bath and Bristol stage was begun by Roger Bulbank and Henry Folbig a month after the debut of the Chester stage. Henry Folbig was also a licensed hackney coachman with licence number 207 (12) and in 1683 he was still licensed with the same number. He lived in Brewers Yard, close to where the Vintners Hall is now. Their coach ran from the Coach and Horses Inn. Various successors to this inn stood at the corner of Upper Thames Street and Queen Street, the last one, owned by Charrington's Brewery was destroyed in the blitz on London during the 1939-1945 war.

In 1662 the Bristol coach was operated by William Drew, a supernumary coachman who was licensed to drive a coach belonging to Richard Burpitt of Harts Horn Lane in the City of London. The Tunbridge Wells coach was run by a Robert Beard who was also a supernumary coachman, licensed to drive a coach belonging to a Christopher Lewthwaite. Both are described in the list of 1662 as, "ancient hackney coachmen, not in arrears of rent". The significance of all these men licensed to drive as supernumaries is now apparent, as the stage coaches only operated during the summer, they simply went back to driving hackney coaches in London during the winter.

In the spring of 1658 even more stage coaches began to operate, though as no names are given it is not possible to say with any certainty that these coaches too were run by London's hackney coachmen. The Mercurius Politicus of April 1658 carried an advertisement announcing stage coaches on the Exeter and Great North Road. As they started from the same 'George' inn in Aldersgate Street, it is possible that Dunstan, Earle and Fowler were involved for we know that they were running coaches here in 1659.

For towns on the Great North Road, the fare to Stamford and Newark in two days was twenty shillings. Doncaster and Ferrybridge were reached in four days, the fair being forty shillings. York was reached in the evening of the fourth day for forty five shillings and what must have been a bargain if one survived the journey, "to Edinburgh for £4 apeece".

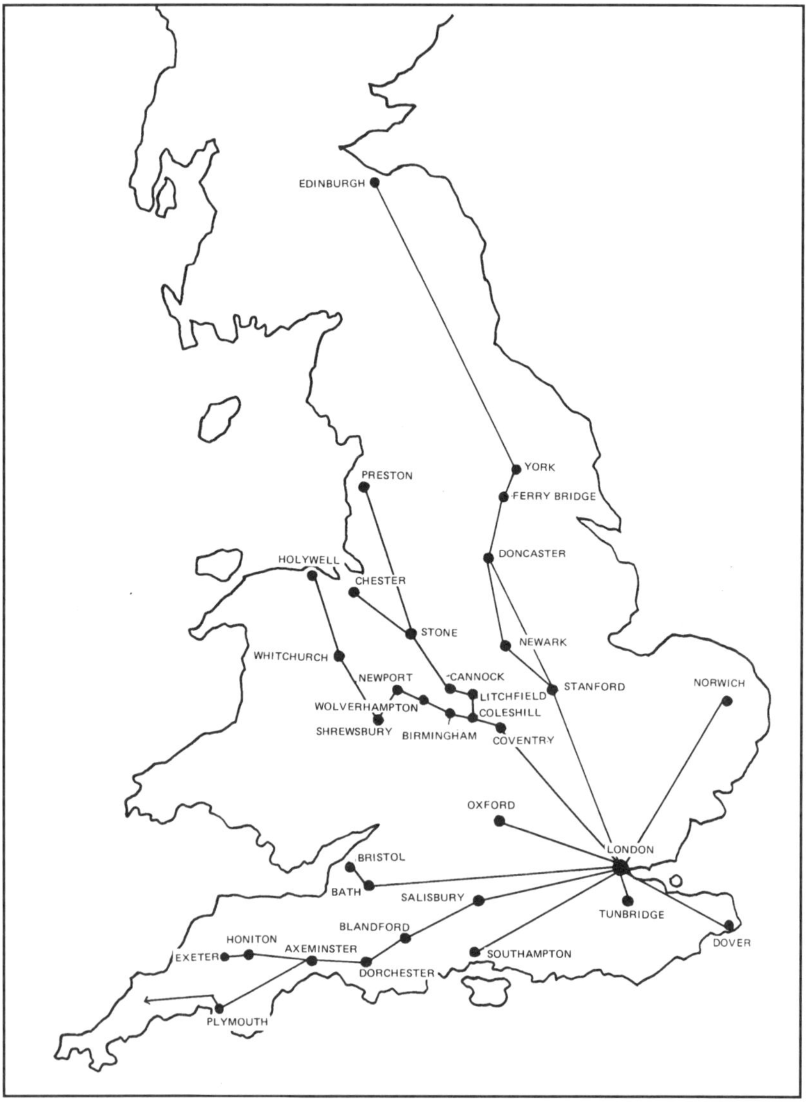

Towns in England & Scotland served by stage coaches by 1661. Map 2.

A regular stage was running between London and Oxford in 1661 and from an account by William Gibbes to his father Alderman Henry Gibbes, there was a daily coach between London and Reading at a fare of seven shillings. In 1663 a coach was making the journey from Preston to London and it appears from an account by one Edward Parker that it was not a pleasant ride, "my journey was noe waie pleasant, being forced to ride in ye boote all the waye". (13) The journey he said cost him thirty shillings but so upset him that he resolved never to make the journey again.

Travel by stagecoach suffered a set back during the plague and fire years of 1665 and 1666. Of all the coachmen involved from 1657 to 1665 only Fowler, Earle, Folbig and Drew appeared to have survived the Great Plague. Even had the coachmen been prepared to carry on during the plague, others it seemed were anxious to prevent them as is evident from a statement issued by the authorities in Norwich.

"From this daie all ye passage coaches shall be prohibited to go from ye citie to London and come thence hither, also ye common carts and wagons". (14)

This sort of action was probably undertaken by other authorities and it is more than likely that little coaching was carried on during the plague. In the Great Fire the following year, all the stage coaching inns, with the exception of the 'George' in Aldersgate Street were destroyed and several years were to elapse before full operations could be resumed.

By the time the coachmen were ready to resume operations, some degree of opposition had arisen against stage coaches, on similar grounds which had earlier been levelled at hackney coaches. The interests of a large number of people had been unfavourably affected by the increase in stage coach travel. Many people from sheer stupidity and short-sightedness were disposed to attack them and it was argued that this method of travel would be harmful to the breeding of horses and the art of horsemanship. Some thought that the Thames, which had long been a nursery of seamen, would cease to be the main thoroughfare from London to Windsor and down to Gravesend. Others thought that Saddlers, Innholders, Farriers and other companies in the City of London and elsewhere would all suffer from the increase in the number of coaches. (15)

It was feared that numerous inns at which mounted travellers had been in the habit of stopping, would be deserted and that the new coaches were too hot in summer and too cold in winter. Complaints were made that the coaches arrived so late at an inn that it was too late for supper and left so early in the morning that there was little time for breakfast. On these grounds it was seriously recommended that no public coach should be permitted to have more than four horses, to start for a destination more than once a week, or to travel more than thirty miles in a day. It was hoped that if these regulations were adopted, all, except the lame and the sick would resume the old way of travelling - on horseback. (16)

A great part of this attack against stage coaches was conducted by a John Cresset, in much the same way that John Taylor had attacked the hackney coach, but Cresset was to meet with no more success than did Taylor some thirty years earlier.

Much to Cresset's disappointment, coaches were encouraged. The increase in trade alone made it worthwhile, for travel by coach was an outward sign of the opulence that was synonymous with the expanded trade, "there being one hundred coaches for each one we had formerly, which is a convincing argument for riches". (17)

Many of the old coaching inns throughout the country today can trace their development back to the 17th century. Some of those inns gave an indifferent service but many were excellent. The White Hart at Alton was described by John Taylor during his coach journey from London to Southampton as having "a good meate, a table with salt on" indicating that the landlord was something of a trencherman and knew how to cater for travellers.

England at this time contained numerous inns of varying degrees of size and comfort, where the floors were swept clean and the sheets smelt of lavender. Here, the traveller would be met with a blazing fire, a jug of good ale and a selection of fish or meat dishes, all at a reasonable charge. One such inn, the 'Lion' at Liverpool charged 6d. per head for a meal which consisted of veal cutlets, pigeon, asparagus, lamb and salad, apple pie and tarts.

At the other end of the scale was the inn at Windsor where Moritz was offered a room, "which much resembled a prison for malefactors". On his departure, the chambermaid stood at the door and asked to be remembered, "yes, yes", he said, "I shall long remember your most ill mannered behaviour and shameful incivility", and he gave her nothing. (18) The innkeepers, so it was said, were not like the innkeepers on the continent. There the landlord was a tyrant. In England he was the servant.

Towards the end of the 18th century, however, when the mail coach was the epitome of coach travel, passengers began to meet a decline in the standard of service. This was not so much the fault of the landlords but of the Post Office. They made it one of the conditions of travel that not more than twenty minutes could be taken for a meal. Consequently very few people were able to get a bowl of soup and a hot meal in the stipulated time and many a traveller paid for a meal that he could not finish.

It can be seen from Map number three that the concentration of travel which occurs now in South East England was beginning to emerge by 1690. Twenty five small towns and villages within fifteen miles of London were served by a daily coach service. Of these, Brentwood, Clapham, Hampstead, Croydon, Romford, Uxbridge and Barnet are a sample of those places that during the next two hundred and fifty years were to be engulfed by the growth of London. Some forty towns over thirty miles distance from London had a regular stage coach service. Lincoln, Stamford, Newark and Grantham were well served by five coaches a week. Exeter, Gloucester, Halifax and Leeds were served by three coaches. (19)

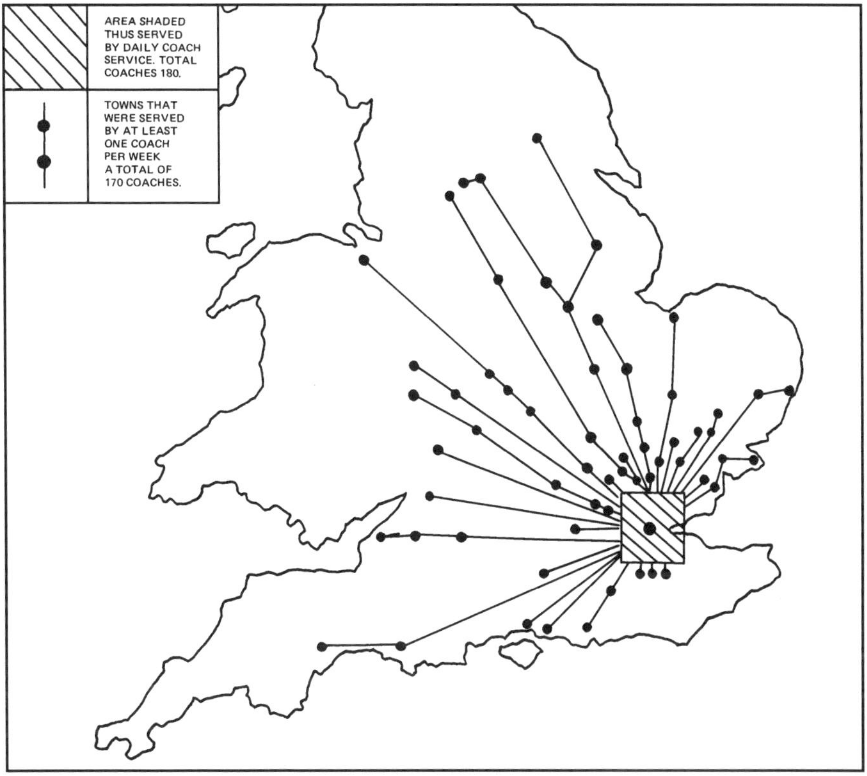

Towns in England served by frequent stage coaches in 1690. *Map 3.*

Nearly all the stage coaches operating in 1690 were owned by individuals. Thus we have the Stamford and Newark coach owned by "the widow Warren" and "John Godsiff goes to Saffron Waldren from the Blue Boar at Aldgate". The Bridgnorth coach was owned by a Hugh Garrat and the Widow Foster, who lived in Southwark, owned the Dover coach. The York coach was triple venture, owned jointly by a Mr. & Mrs. Gardner and Henry Halden, while the Widow Twitty owned the Worcester coach. It would seem that both the Widows Twitty and Foster were the wives of former hackney coachmen, appearing in the list of 1685 as "No. 96 Joyce Twitty" and "No. 182 Elizabeth

Foster". (20)

Many of the stage coach owners' named in De Laune's list, published in 1690 are identical to the Court of Aldermen's list of 1685. Some indeed go back to Cromwell's ordinance of 1654. Many of them are the names of widows of coachmen who were formerly licensed. This strong thread of family connection probably lasted until 1831 when limitation ended. Even then the widow of a horse cab proprietor could still take over her former husband's licence, as can a taxi proprietor's widow today.

Whilst acting as stage coaches they had to conform to the Hackney Coach Commissioners bye-laws, which meant that they could not pick up or set down within the area of the Bills of Mortality, unless passengers were travelling beyond the area of the Bills, or had been picked up outside that area to come into London. In 1694 stage coaches were made the subject of separate legislation by Parliament but this act contained an error which was successfully interpreted by the stage coach operators that they were to be licensed for one year only at a cost of £8. (21)

This respite was only temporary but does not concern us here. We are only interested in them whilst they acted as stage coach owners, although they were in fact licensed hackney coachmen, and their early story has never been told before. Consequently, the originators of the English stage coach have never received the credit to which they were entitled, but to William Dunstan, Henry Earle and William Fowler goes the distinction of inaugurating a service which lasted well into the 19th century.

References used in Chapter Four

1. Life in a Noble Household. G.S. Thompson.
2. Acts of the Privy Council, 1625 p 3. (GRL)
3. State Papers Domestic, 1651/2. (PRO)
4. Carriers Cosmographie, John Taylor. (GRL)
5. Stage Coach and Mail Days of Yore, G.C. Harper.
6. Mercurius Politicus, April 9th 1657. (A.N. 94) (GRL)
7. Ibid. 1659.
8. State Papers Domestic, 1656/7 pp. 134/5 (PRO)
9. A84 No. 57. (GRL)
10. Misc. MSS 213. (GRO)
11. A 32 No. 57 (GRL)
12. A 84 No. 56 (GRL)
13. Stage Coach and Mail Days of Yore. G.C. Harper
14. State Papers Domestic, 1665.
15. Rep.78 folio 3. (GRO)
16. Letters to a Postmaster. John Cressett. (816M 12) (Brit. Mus.)
17. The State of England Considered, 1694. (1029 H4 2-60) (Brit. Mus.)

18. History of the Cost of Living, p 157. John Burnett. (Pelican)
19. Stage Coach and Mail Days of Yore. G.C. Harper.
20. References for owners of stage coaches. See A32 No. 57 (GRL)
21. Statutes of the Realm. 5th & 6th William & Mary C22. (GRL)

Chapter Five

"To his majesty's most royal consideration"

In 1662 Charles II's Cavalier Parliament passed another act for the better control of London's hackney coachmen. When the contents of the Bill became known, the coachmen who had formerly been licensed under Cromwell's ordinance of 1654, petitioned Parliament asking that the licenses should be in force for the period of time the act was to run. They also requested that the widows of the coachmen licensed should have the benefit of the licences during widowhood and that no one should be allowed more than one licence and of the four hundred licences to be granted, 'ancient' coachmen should have first preference. (1)

The act became law on May 1st 1662, (14th Charles II C11). During the committee stage of the Bill some concern had been expressed by Members of Parliament that the number of coaches was to be fixed at four hundred. If such was the case they said, "then the four hundred coaches proposed would not be sufficient for the needs of the gentry". Despite these doubts, the number of coaches to be licensed was set at four hundred.

The original idea of again placing the coachmen under control of the Court of Aldermen was dropped in favour of appointing a board of Hackney Coach Commissioners, who were to be directly responsible to the Treasury Lords. The fee for a licence was fixed at £5 per annum and between 1662 and 1679, the period the act was in force, the treasury received £34,000 by way of revenue. A fare of one shilling a mile was to be charged and a coachman who demanded more than the legal fare could be fined up to ten shillings. Provision was made that the horses to be used were not to be less than fourteen hands high, thus ensuring that only mature horses were used to pull the heavy coaches.

If, as it has been said, Cromwell's ordinance of 1654 had set the pattern for all future acts of Parliament, then the act of 1662 confirmed it. Some of the clauses contained in that act, such as demanding more than the legal fare, appear in existing hackney carriage legislation in exactly the same form. By contrast, however, penalties are much lower now, in real monetary terms, than they were then, and enforcement of the law today is nowhere near as strict.

The act of 1662 was to run for a period of seventeen years, at the end of which time Parliament was to review the situation. However, in 1679 the

Whigs and the Tories were engaged in a bitter struggle for supremacy, for the Whigs were trying to carry through Parliament the 'Exclusion Bill' that would have prevented James, Duke of York, Charles II's brother, from succeeding to the throne on Charles death. The Whigs wanted the Duke of Monmouth, Charles II's 'natural' son to succeed his father, for he was a protestant, whereas James was a Roman Catholic.

As a last resort, unfortunately for London's hackney coachmen, Charles II decided to prorogue Parliament, thereby preventing the Whigs from carrying out their intentions. When the act of 1662 expired a few months later, Parliament was not sitting and as a result, there being no legislation to the contrary, hundreds of coaches were offering their services on the streets of London and Westminster.

During the intervening years (1662-1679) licensed coachmen had formed themselves into an association known as the '400'. (2) Run on similar lines to the old Fellowship, it was an early form of trade union, with a secretary to look after it's affairs. They were to some extent fairly well organised for a struggle that was to last until 1687 to restore them to their original status that had existed under the act of 1662.

Early in April 1680 they petitioned Parliament to restore them to their former position and a Bill for that purpose was prepared, read and sent to committee but before the committee could make any report, Parliament was again prorogued and afterwards dissolved, putting an end to their efforts. Almost immediately the '400' petitioned the king in council offering to pay £5 per annum for each licence,, "so long as we are restrained to '400' and no more". They were told that His Majesty had some thoughts of calling a Parliament soon, when the matter would be given full consideration.

The King however did not call another Parliament. Events then moved to the City of London, for as the '400' were unable to gain any satisfaction from the King or Parliament they looked toward the Lord Mayor and the Aldermen to assist them. Two years had passed since their last unsuccessful petition and during that time they had been involved in several discussions with the city authorities through their secretary; one Robert Murray. There were two reasons why the Aldermen were prepared to deal with the association. First, they were concerned at the many confrontations between members of the '400' and the interlopers, often coming to blows and involving other citizens. Second, this time the coachmen were prepared to pay for the privilege of securing for themselves the sole right to ply for hire in the City of London and it's liberties.

Robert Murray was successful in his negotiations with the Aldermen and consequently an Act of Common Council was passed on May 1st 1682. (3) This was at considerable cost to the '400', for Murray's fee alone was £200 plus five shillings per annum for each licence as long as he remained their secretary.

In addition they paid £500 to the Chamber of Commerce and another £500 to officers of the Knight Marshall, who guaranteed that only members of the '400' would be permitted to take up fares between Charing Cross and Whitehall.

In Cornhill.

Near the *Standard*, Three.
Near St.*Michael's Church*, Three.
From *Finch-Lane* End to *Sweethings-Alley*, Three.
From *Caſtle-Alley* to the Lower End of *Cornhill*, Five.
Againſt the *Stocks-Market*, Two.
In Great *Lombard-Street*, Four.
On *Dowgate-Hill* near *Skinners-Hall*, Two.
In Old *Fiſh-Street*, Two.
In *Coleman-Street*, Four.
In *Aldermanbury*, Two.
From *Guildhall* to *Cheapſide*, Six.
In *Great Wood-Street*, Two.
In *Milk-Street*, Two.
In *Newgate-Street*, Two.
From *Newgate* to St.*Sepulchres Church*, Two.
On Eachſide of *Fleet-Ditch*(void of the Great Street) Two; being Eight in all.
In the *Old-Baily*, Six.

Some of the Hackney Coach stands authorised by the Act of Common Council, 1682.

Later the '400' claimed that they were never allowed the monopoly of this lucrative stretch of road because the interlopers paid as much, if not more to the Knight Marshall and as it was beyond the jurisdiction of the city authorities, nothing could be done about it. Robert Murray continued to be their secretary long enough to obtain £450 plus fees for obtaining licences, "but for all this he badly neglected our business, failed to attend our meetings and seldom came near us except to collect his money".

On April 23rd 1685, James II was crowned in Westminster Abbey. A few days later Robert Murray called a meeting of the '400' and informed them that the king had granted to Lord Culpepper the right to licence hackney coachmen and Culpepper had put £1,000 into the Privy Purse. Only those coachmen who were prepared to pay a sum of money (unspecified) would be granted a licence. In any case Murray said, the number of coaches was to be increased above four hundred. However, Murray told them, he could prevent this happening if the '400' signed an agreement to the effect that not only would they have to pay him five shillings a licence as before but an additional ten shillings for every licence he could obtain for them by virtue of an Act of Parliament.

The '400' rejected this proposition for several reasons but principally because the agreement did not restore the number of coaches to '400', "which if it did not, then we cannot pay £5 per annum and live". Though the '400' never seemed to doubt Murray's intentions, Lord Culpepper cannot be fitted in to such a plan from any other source. The whole story seems to have been a complete fabrication on Murray's part, designed purely as a means to extract money from the '400'.

IT is Ordered by the Right Honourable Sir *James Smyth* Knight, Lord Mayor, and the Court of Aldermen of the City of *London*, That Wm. Swaine of the pariſh of St. Buttolph Biſhopsgate for and during the ſpace of One Year, to be accounted from the Firſt day of *May*, One thouſand Six hundred Eighty five be, and is hereby Licenced to keep a Hackney-Coach within this City and the Liberties thereof, purſuant to an Act of Common-Council, Made, Enacted and Paſſed the Thirteenth day of *March*, 1682. that the ſaid William Swaine conforming himſelf to the Rules in the ſaid Act of Common Council ſet down and preſcribed: And that the Number (391) be the Mark and Figure to be uſed by the ſaid William Swaine upon ſuch his Hackney-Coach. In Witneſs whereof, the ſaid Lord Mayor and Aldermen have cauſed the Seal of the Office of *Majoralty* of the ſaid City to be put to theſe Preſents. Dated the 27th Day of April 1685. and in the firſt Year of the Reign of our Soveraign Lord *JAMES* the Second, by the Grace of God of *England, Scotland, France* and *Ireland*, KING, Defender of the Faith, &c.

The licence issued to William Swaine one of the original '400', 1685.

Parliament sat again in May 1685 and the '400' duly presented another petition, but this time there were others. The interlopers were petitioning for six hundred coaches to be licensed. A Mr. Cadman petitioned for another hundred and Chelsea College also wanted a hundred coaches, "to be made available for the common good". These petitions were all referred to a select committee under the chairmanship of Sir Christopher Wren but before any progress could be made Parliament was adjourned until November 1685.

The '400', realising that all their efforts had come to nothing and that it was a forlorn hope to expect Parliament to solve their problems, and with more and more interlopers coming onto the streets, decided to approach the Earl of Rochester, who was at that time Lord High Treasurer of England. Their application was sponsored by Robert Brent and Essex Strode Esquires and John Cresset, Thomas Herbert and Robert Knott who were described as gentlemen. (4)

In part, their application stated, "that if his majesty would licence the '400' and issue a proclamation suppressing the interlopers, they would pay £2,000 per annum to his majesty". This attempt failed when the Attorney General declared, "it is my opinion that the king could not legally issue such a proclamation unless it could be proved that coaches in excess of four hundred constituted a public nuisance". (5)

There now occurred a break in the deadlock that the '400' had desperately been searching for. On the basis of the Attorney General's statement they charged all the interlopers before the Grand Jury of Middlesex as being a common nuisance and during the Michelmas term of 1686 the Grand Jury presented to the Court of King's Bench sitting at Westminster:-

"That four hundred coaches driving for hire about the Citties of London and Westminster and suburbs thereof, were sufficient to serve the subjects needs and that all coaches supernumary to that number were a common nuisance". (6)

For some reason the Attorney General still maintained that the king could do nothing without the aid of Parliament. The Treasury Lords were not satisfied with the Attorney General's decision and they referred the matter to the Solicitor General who gave as his opinion that the king could restrain the interlopers and he accordingly settled the number of coaches at four hundred.

While the '400' had been involved in this litigation, those who opposed them were pushing their own claims for extra licences to be granted. Meanwhile the '400' had dispensed with the services of Robert Murray, who, they believed, had secretly been working against them. Annoyed at his dismissal Murray offered his services to the interlopers, who accepted his offer. He then set about using all his means to destroy the brat of his own begetting, viz, the Act of Common Council passed in 1683, which had given the '400' the right to ply for hire in the City of London. By doing so he hoped to gain for the interlopers the same rights and privileges that the act had conferred upon the '400'.

Murray's arguments for the interlopers were based on three points. First, the size of London and Westminster had greatly increased during the twenty five years since the act of 1662 had been passed. Second, that as there were twelve hundred coaches driving for hire, to suppress all but the '400' would have meant ruin for the rest. Finally he proposed that the licence fee should be raised to £6 per annum though he had agreed to charge the interlopers £10 each for any licences he could obtain.

The '400' argued that although the number of buildings had greatly increased and the population also, there were now thirty coaches kept by the nobility, gentry and tradesmen for every one that was kept when the act of 1662 was passed and as near as many Sedan chairs. They affirmed that there were only four hundred coaches licensed to ply for hire, plus six letter coaches. "Nevertheless Mr. Murray would infer and have it believed that because some of the coachmen keep two coaches apiece, beside mourning coaches to attend funerals and great coaches for journeys into the country that all these are driven at the same time though he knows that it is not so". Many of the interlopers let several coaches for hire and followed other trades as well.

The coachmen further affirmed "that is the truth of our case" they hoped it would not be thought stubborn of them that they could not pay any licence money unless their numbers were restricted to four hundred and all others restrained by legislation. After all, if unlicenced coaches were working exactly the same as the '400' without paying any fee, then why not them. Finally, they played what they must have thought was their trump card.

"We have always behaved ourselves as loyal subjects and have been ready to serve the crown, we voluntarily raised two hundred of horse and offered to march into the west in the time of Monmouths rebellion, and did furnish three hundred horses at a days warning to carry down the artillery to Sedgemoor. All of which is most humbly submitted to his majesties most royal consideration and determination".

At last, after eight long years of protracted discussions, arguments, petitions and appeals, James II issued a proclamation from Whitehall on November 25th 1687, restoring the '400' to the position they had previously enjoyed under the act of 1662. This proclamation also appointed five Hackney Coach Commissioners who were empowered to make bye-laws for the day to day administration of the coachmen.

On October 20th 1688 just eleven months after James II proclamation restoring the '400', the king issued another proclamation increasing the number of hackney coaches to six hundred; thus the worst fears of the '400' were realised. The Court of Aldermen in the City of London were furious at what they considered was an affront to themselves and their act of Common Council of 1683, especially so because this latest addition of coaches was made via the Justices of Middlesex. Until 1694 the Aldermen were to regard the extra two hundred coaches as unlicensed and did in fact treat them as such.

At this time Robert Murray emerges again, for he better than most was aware of the possibilities that existed and consequently on January 4th 1689 he petitioned the Aldermen to revive the act of 1683. They duly appointed a committee under the chairmanship of Sir Thomas Stamp to report on the matter and to, "heare and determine all matters of complaynt and difference between the coachmen formerly licensed and Mr. Murray , and if they can, to accommodate the same between them".

By the King,

A PROCLAMATION

For Reſtraining the Number and Abuſes of Hackney Coaches in and about the Cities of *London* and *Weſtminſter*, and the Suburbs thereof, and Pariſhes compriſed within the Bills of Mortality.

JAMES R.

Whereas Complaint hath been made unto Us by divers of Our loving Subjects of the great Grievance and Annoyance, which the multitude of Hackney Coaches lately set up, and now Driven about the Streets of Our City of London and Weſtminſter, and Suburbs of the same, are to them in their respective Trades and Businesses; and also of the great Want of some good Rules and Orders to be observed by all such Persons, as are or shall be permitted to Keep and Drive Hackney Coaches about the said Streets. And whereas the undoubted Power of Punishing, Removing, Correcting and Restraining all publick Nusances, Annoyances and Disorders in the common Streets, High-Ways and Passages doth of Right belong unto Us, and having taken the same into Our Princely Consideration, and being desirous to remove all Grievance and Annoyance from Our loving Subjects, and to provide against the same in the best manner that We can, We have thought fit, in order to the remedying the Mischiefs and Grievances aforesaid, to Constitute and Appoint by Letters Patents under the Great Seal of England, Our Trusty and Welbeloved John Phelipps, Colonel Thomas Napier, Thomas Price, Richard Sheldon, and Jerome Nipho, *Esquires*, to be Our Commissioners for the Licensing Regulating, Ordering, and Governing, according to the Instructions thereunto annexed, all Hackney Coaches to be Let and Driven for Hire about the said Cities of London and Weſtminſter, and the Suburbs

Part of the Proclamation issued by James II restoring the '400' to their previous status. Nov, 1687.

The committee were further empowered to "put into execution the act of common council for regulating the coachmen of this city". (7) The die was cast and the City of London was now in opposition to the king, a conflict that was to end in the King's Bench Division with the defeat of the Aldermen; not because of any decision by the judges but because even the Aldermen were not able to resist the Act of Parliament of 1694 which fully regularised the coachmen's position. Even while the court proceedings were going on, the Aldermen were insisting that all coaches over four hundred were illegal and they actually prosecuted some of those coachmen included in the additional two hundred. (8)

It appeared that Robert Murray had some hopes of securing for himself the position as constable in charge of hackney coaches in the City of London but the '400' were adamant. They would have nothing to do with him. The last act of Murrays concerns another petition he presented to the Aldermen on February 16th 1693. However, realising that the coachmen and Murray were not compatible the Aldermen did not even recognise his petition and appointed one Andrew Tomlyn as Constable of hackney coaches.

Robert Murrays association with London's hackney coachmen had a more particular significance, especially with regard to London's social history, because of their involvement with William Dockra's Penny Post. Robert Murray was, in every sense of the word an entrepreneur, an organiser of business, capable of bringing together capital and labour for a commercial venture. We have already seen how he was prepared to change sides and in his venture with William Dockra this aspect of his character becomes more apparent. (9)

Between 1660 and 1680 not a great deal is known about Robert Murray but his greatest achievement was the Penny Post venture begun in 1680 with William Dockra. A good deal of controversy existed as to whom the credit belongs for the Penny Post, though it was probably Robert Murray's organising ability that built it up. The Post Office Act of 1660 refers to the setting up of a "Postmaster General" and that, "no other person or persons whatsoever shall, from time to time, have the receiving, taking up, ordering, despatching post or sending post; except such letters as shall be sent by coaches or carriers wagons". (10)

It appears that as long as Murray and Dockra confined their activities to the area within the Bill's of Mortality and used coaches, they were acting within the law; though when the act was passed in 1660 such a scheme as the Penny Post had not been envisaged. They begun the Penny Post in March 1680 using as their chief sorting office the former London mansion of Sir Robert Ady in Lime Street in the City of London.

They had devised an ingenious system and a broadside published by them entitled, "a penny well bestowed", set out the places that the post was to serve as, "London, Westminster and all the contiguous buildings and all other places within the area of the Bill's of Mortality". Letters were sent out in summer from six o'clock in the morning till nine o'clock at night and at, "reasonable hours agreeable to the winter season". To the more distant places letters went five times a day every three hours and to places within the city and in "term time for the service of the law business; every hour".

The method involved using the hackney coachmen's 'letter coaches' (11) in which the letters and packets were collected from various well known points such as coffee houses and inns, taken to the office in Lime Street and from there they were despatched by the hackney letter coaches to the various districts.

By the summer of 1681 Dockra was running the business by himself, Murray having left him to become the secretary of the '400', in time to be instrumental in gaining the Act of Common Council in 1683. Dockra's services were now advertised as "delivering to Inns of Court and places of business, in term time or Parliament time, ten or twelve times a day".

Unfortunately for Dockra and the members of the '400' who operated the 'letter coaches', the scheme fell foul of the Duke of York (later James II) on whom the profits of the official Post Office were settled. The Duke of York maintained that Dockra's Penny Post was illegal and he set out to deprive Dockra of his right to run the service. Consequently Dockra was accused of operating beyond the area of the Bill's of Mortality; this he denied in an advertisement published in the London Mercury. (12)

On November 22nd 1682 a 'Mr. John Halke' took out an action against Dockra at Westminster Hall where the law courts were at that time established. Dockra's council insisted on a special verdict but the jury was directed to find a general verdict and William Dockra was deprived of his Penny Post. Lord Arlington, the Postmaster General, saw no reason to destroy so useful and profitable undertaking as the Penny Post. Even while Dockra was petitioning the Duke of York to run the Penny Post under licence, agents of the Post Office were obtaining by threats and promises from Dockra's clerks, copies of his "schemes, methods and rules". Most of Dockra's employees went over to the new Penny Post, "being in fear of those wherewith they were threatened to be ruined, terrified of the great power they were under they durst do not other than forsake the said Dockra's employment".

But what of Robert Murray? In 1687 following his rejection by the '400' he was working as a supernumary coachman and following James II proclamation of that year he applied to the Treasury Lords for the position as Registrar of Hackney Coaches. (13) The '400' were aghast at such a prospect and they successfully petitioned the Treasury that their experiences in the past had shown Mr. Murray to be "base and incompetent" and on no account did they want anything to do with him again. As a result, Murray did not get the position and it went instead to Thomas Herbert, one of the three gentlemen who had assisted the '400'. We have already seen Murray's rejection by the Aldermen in 1693 and from this date Robert Murray slid into obscurity.

A year later the Court of Aldermen were to set their own seal on their departure from the hackney coach scene. The act of 1694 became law on May 10th of that year, a few days later the Court of Aldermen issued the following statement. "Sir Thomas Stamp and Sir Robert Clayton are to propose such rules and regulations of such as shall ply within this city and the liberties, as they shall think fit and they are desired to recommend same to the Commissioners appointed, pursuant to the late act of Parliament". (14)

In 1694 England was at war with France and the government was searching for ways and means to raise money for this purpose. This presented Parliament with the opportunity to control the hackney coach trade on a regular basis and a means of providing a useful contribution to the revenue. The main object of the 1694 act was to raise money, not only from hackney coaches but from other sources as well, "Parliament being sensible to the greate and necessary expense in which your majesties are engaged in carrying on the war against the French king". (15)

Orders, By-Laws, and Ordinances,

For the Good Government and Regulating of the Perſons Licenſed to Keep and Drive HACKNEY-COACHES within the Cities of London *and* Weſtminſter, *and the Suburbs thereof, and within all and every the Pariſhes and Places comprized within the Weekly-Bills of Mortality; made, publiſhed, and declared by* Daniel Blake, Thomas Strickland, Edmund Clerke, Charnock Heron, *and* William Congreve, *Eſqs; Commiſſioners, Authorized and Appointed by His preſent Majeſty's Commiſſion under the Great Seal of* England, *for putting in Execution a late Act of Parliament, Entituled,* An Act for the Licenſing and Regulating Hackney-Coaches and Stage-Coaches. *And allowed and approved, as by the ſaid Act is directed, viz.*

Introduction to the Orders, Bye-Laws and Ordinances authorised by the Act of Parliament, May 10, 1694.

Following the second reading of the Bill on April 5th 1694, a petition was presented to Parliament on behalf of the Cornchandlers, Coachmakers and Blacksmiths, seeking to reduce the number of coaches to be licensed from 800 to 700 and to reduce the proposed initial licensing fee from £100 to £50. The petitioners were afraid that with too many coaches seeking work, the credit extended to the coachmen would be a risk, especially so if the licence fee was set too high. This petition apparently made some impression on the House for the number of coaches was set at 700 and the proposed initial payment of £100 was reduced to £50 plus £4 per annum for each licence; the whole to be in force for twenty one years.

The act did not run it's full term of twenty one years for it was repealed in 1711 and substituted by the 9th of Anne C16. The initial £50 levy was dropped but the annual licence fee was increased to £13 per annum; even so as a means of raising money it was successful. During the seventeen years the act was in force the Treasury received £82,600 and offset against this sum was the £19,368 it cost to run the Hackney Coach Office during the same period leaving a balance of £63,232 to use as the act had directed, to carry on the war against the French. (16)

Within one month of the passing of the act several large payments from the hackney coach receipts were authorised by the Treasury. They included £9,920 to the Navy for victualling, £898 for hemp, guns and wagons for the four Irish Regiments and £7,091 towards the cost of maintaining the army in Flanders, which, between March 25th 1694 and April 22nd 1695 cost the country £99,274.

The revenue from hackney coaches reached out to the New World with the "£100 paid to Captain William Hyde on account of his pay from April 1st 1694 to January 17th 1697 as a captain of one of the four companies in New York". In October 1701 the Treasury directed that £330 be paid to the cost of

The *Hackney Coachmens* CASE.

Humbly preſented to the

Honourable Houſe of Commons

WITH A

Propoſal to Raiſe for Her Majeſty 200000 *l.* *per annum.*

THAT in 1693. an Act of Parliament was made to *Licenſe* 700 *Hackney Coaches*, and Five Commiſſioners appointed to put the Act in Execution; but Three of them (for the Lucre of Bribes) did Licenſe Tradeſmen and others not bred to the Employ, and refuſed to Licenſe the *Hackney Coachmen*; which was prov'd upon them before a Committee of Parliament in 1694, for which they loſt their Commiſſions, and the *Hackney Coachmen* have been forced to hire Licenſes of thoſe People ever ſince, to their great Loſs and Damage, amounting to above 100000 *l.* in theſe Sixteen Years that are Expired; making the major part of the *Hackney Coachmen* to pay 18000 *l.* *per annum*, ſometimes more ſometimes leſs, which has broke and ruin'd ſeveral hundred *Coachmen* and their Families, as well as is a great Loſs to the Crown, there being but 2800 *l.* *per annum* paid into the Exchequer.

That the 700 *Licens'd Hackney Coachmen* ſuffer great Wrong ſeveral other ways; there being many hundreds of *Coaches* and *Horſes* let to Hire, in the Bills of Mortality without Licenſe, likewiſe great numbers of *Shaiſes* and *Hackney Chairs* ſet up of late Years, which pay nothing to the Government, (to the great Loſs of the *Hackney Coachmen* who are forc'd to pay ſuch great Rates for their *Licenſes*); alſo ſeveral hundreds of Short Stages ply within the Bills of Mortality which paid nothing till 1693, when all the Stages in *England* paid 8 *l.* to the King, and they raiſed the Price ſo much to their Paſſengers, that they got 30 *l.* by it, and many of them have kept up their Price ever ſince.

Wherefore 'tis humbly Hoped,

That this *Honourable Houſe* will be pleaſed to give Leave to bring in a Bill for the better Regulating of the 700 *Licenſed Coaches*, (which was Reſolved laſt Winter, as appears by the Votes) and lay a Duty on all *Coaches* or *Coach-Horſes*, *Shaiſes* and *Hackney Chairs*, that are let to Hire within the Bills of Mortality without *Licenſe*; and on all Paſſengers that go in *Stage-Coaches* or *Wagons*, and all Goods carry'd in *Wagons* or upon *Pack-Horſes* (Corn and Meal only excepted) which will, by a modeſt Computation, raiſe above 200000 *l.* *per annum*, to her Majeſty, and the great Oppreſſion that is upon the major part of the 700 *Hackney Coachmen* will be made eaſier.

A petition to Parliament presenting the Hackney Coachmen's case for a better regulated trade. c. 1710.

keeping these companies of soldiers in New York and the cost of building Fort William in Newfoundland had already been met from the revenue raised from hackney coach receipts.

Two more items which show the diversity of use for which the money was used comes from a letter to Robert Walpole when he was Treasurer to the Navy. "The £242 from the hackney coaches is to be paid to Colonel Spottiswood, appointed Governor of Virginia, toward the charge of transporting himself and his family to that colony". A similar payment was made to, "Robert Lowther, Governor of Barbados for transporting himself and his family". Altogether, from May 1694 until June 1711, the Treasury spent £45,676, which, added to the cost of running the Hackney Coach Office during the same period left a balance of £17,586. (17)

Apart from ending the £50 levy and increasing the number of coaches to be licensed to 800, the act of 1711 also licensed Sedan chairs for the first time at a fee of ten shillings per annum. They were at first limited to two hundred with the proviso that 100 more could be licensed the following year if it were thought necessary and this in fact was what occurred. The act was to run for thirty years and did in fact run its full term, raising revenue for coaches and chairs amounting to £337,550. Between 1711 and 1743 the Treasury spent £207,531 and to this sum must be added the cost of running the Hackney Coach Office of £45,127, leaving a balance of £84,892. When this is added to the balance of £17,586 remaining from the years 1694 to 1711 we have a total of £102,477 that appears to be unaccounted for. (18)

What became of it? Provision had been made in the act of 1711 for revenue from hackney coaches and chairs to be placed to the general fund, but in a statement from the Treasury in 1718 describing the contents of the general fund the amount under the heading 'hackney coaches and chairs' was omitted. (19) Neither does there appear to be any treasury records concerning the year 1743 when the act of 1711 expired. The period that this money seems to be unaccounted for was covered by the administration of Robert Walpole. "Walpole was not without his critics and abuse of official patronage was only one of the charges brought against him. Most formidable was the accusation that he was dipping his hands into the public till". (20) Could it be that the money spent on Houghton Hall in Norfolk, with it's magnificent picture gallery was paid for by London's hackney coach proprietors?

References used in Chapter Five

1. House of Lords Papers, 24th March 1661 - 27th April 1662, LJ XI p. 426 (HOLRO).
2. Unless otherwise referenced for corroboration, details relating to the '400' have been freely drawn from Pamphlet 8716 in the Guildhall

Reference Library.

3. Rep. 86 folio 117b (GRO)
4. Calendar of Treasury Books, Vol. 8 pt. 2, pp. 1550/1/2 (GRL)
5. Ibid.
6. Ibid.
7. Rep. 94 folio 85 (GRO)
8. Rep. 97 folios 45, 363 and 395. (GRO)
9. Unless otherwise stated all references to the Penny Post are from William Dockra and the rest of the Undertakers (GRL)
10. Statutes of the Realm, 12th Charles II C35.
11. Pamphlet 8716. (GRL)
12. London Mercury, May 18th 1682. (GRL)
13. Calendar of Treasury Books, Vol. 8. pts. 1/2, pp. 1575/1915. (GRL)
14. Rep. 98 folio 271. (GRO)
15. House of Commons Journals, Vol. 11 p. 148. (HOLRO)
16. Calendar of Treasury Books, Vol. 10. pts. 2/3. pp. 1137, 1195, 1223, 1320 & 1352.
17. All the facts concerning these financial disbursements are from the Calendar of Treasury Books, Vol. 16, pp. 28, 174 and Vol. 24, pp. 436 & 462. (GRL)
18. All the facts concerning these financial disbursements are from the Calendar of Treasury Books Vols. 29/32, pp. 180, 337, 54, 461 and see extracts in appendix F.
19. Ibid. Vol. 34. pt.2, p. 684 and Vol. 32, p. 261. (GRL)
20. Britain's Prime Ministers from Walpole to Wilson, E. Royston Pike. (GRL)

Chapter Six

"The chairmen or slaves of the rich"

(Steele.)

The Sedan chair though so called from the place where it was originally used, did not come to England from France, but from Spain. It was introduced from Madrid in 1626 by Charles I, who, as Prince of Wales had gone there looking for a wife. On the Prince's departure from Spain, Olivarez, the Prime Minister and a favourite of Philip IV, gave the prince, "a few Italian pictures, some valuable pieces of furniture and three Sedan chairs of curious workmanship". (1) On his return to England, Charles gave two of these Sedan chairs to his friend the Duke of Buckingham.

Gabrielle Brown writing to a priest in Spain said, "the whole island is so sharpened against him (the Duke of Buckingham) that even ridiculous toys inflame them with offence. The multitude were bitterly disgusted because, being sickly, he suffered himself to be carried in a covered chair upon his servants shoulders from Whitehall to Denmark House". Despite the hue and cry against the Duke of Buckingham, other wealthy and prominent people soon took to them and employed men to carry them.

The early Sedan chairs were quite primitive by comparison with those that became popular during the 18th century. They had no general ornamentation and men who carried them were dressed almost as plainly. Their dress consisted of a loose smock, knee breeches, stockings and a stout buckled shoe and they wore a cap similar to a jockey's cap. The main support for carrying the chair consisted of a leather harness over the shoulder with a thick leather strap hanging down to the waist with a loop at either end to allow the shaft to pass through.

They are first recorded as being used for public hire in 1630 when a Sir Saunders Duncombe, a close friend of the Duke of Buckingham, successfully petitioned Charles I for a concession to hire chairs to the public for short journeys, "where in many parts beyond the seas, people are much carried in chairs that are covered, wherebye few coaches are used among them". (3) As a result of this petition Duncombe gained a concession to operate Sedan chairs which was to last for fourteen years, during which time he built up a profitable business. During the period of the Commonwealth after the civil war, Sedan chairs were pushed into the background but after the restoration of Charles II they again became popular and though Duncombe's concession had long since lapsed, others were to try their good fortune.

James Haliburton, whose wife's Grandfather was Archbishop of St. Andrews and a former Chancellor of Scotland, petitioned Charles II, "your petitioner prays that your majesty will be graciously pleased by an act of council and your proclamation to prohibit all hackney chairs, save such as shall be licensed by your petitioner". (4) In 1665, Henry Prodgers, who was later to become a Hackney Coach Commissioner also petitioned the king "that unknown persons pretend to that profession and by taking people to bye places do rob them". Prodgers proposed to stop this and also to provide special chairs for diseased people. Neither petitioner was successful for it would appear that too many influential people were engaged in the Sedan chair business and Charles II had no wish to alienate them.

The Sedan chairs were centred mainly around the Palace of Westminster, the Court at Whitehall, St. James's Palace and Mayfair. They were seldom seen beyond these areas because the chairs were cumbersome and heavy to carry over longer distances. They were used just as frequently by men as by women. Hogarth often depicted them in his paintings and in one, 'The Rakes Progress' we see a man of fashion using a sedan chair to attend court. At the time of the dispute between George I and his son the Prince of Wales over the Duke of Newcastle, it is recorded that "the Prince left St. James's Palace in a hackney chair to go to Devonshire House in Piccadilly, accompanied by his wife the Princess, in another chair". (5)

Sedan chairs were to remain in use until the early 19th century and as late as 1810 regulations were still in force in the City of London "that such chairmen who do wait for fares at the Guildhall, do place their chairs in that part of Blackwell Hall Yard which shall be allotted for that purpose". They were to survive much longer in towns such as Edinburgh, Cheltenham and Bath but after their demise as a means of travel many fashionable houses in London kept one standing in the hall or lobby and at least one London restaurant still has one which is used as a telephone booth.

When Sedan chairs first appeared on the streets of London they caused a public outcry, Bassompierre, the French Ambassador at that time recorded, "the popular cry arose that the king was reducing the level of freeborn Englishmen to the level of beasts of burden". (6) Quite a large number of these dissenters, however, managed to swallow their pride when it was realised that there was money to be earned by carrying them and in a comparatively short while they became very popular in London.

By the beginning of the 18th century they had become common place but many changes in their construction had taken place since they were first introduced to Paris by M. de Mortbrun in 1617, where they were known as Chaisses a Porteur. The early box like structure had given way to a much slimmer version, heavily gilded with glass windows, plush velvet lined and hanging curtains for privacy and the livery of the chairmen was almost as grand as that of the chairs they carried. A new version of the Sedan chair was introduced in France in 1688 called the Brouette or Vainagrette, being a Sedan chair on two wheels. It was drawn by a man and was an early form of the vehicle which has survived in the east as a Rickshaw. According to James Reid the Sedan on wheels was introduced into this country in 1768 but that it was not until 1770 that it became generally popular.

However, in the Treasury Papers for 1729/30 there appears a statement from the hackney Coach Commissioners addressed to the Lords of the Treasury, "that chairs drawn by one horse only are of late made much use of within the ten mile limit, which deprives the hackney coachmen of much work". The Commissioners recommended that these one horse chairs on two wheels should only be operated by licensed coachmen. (7) There are many pictures showing hackney coaches and Sedan chairs but very few depict one horse chairs, though a reproduction from Pennant's magazine in the late 18th century appears in Knights London, showing Francis Moore's forerunner of the Hansom cab, a large box like structure on two wheels drawn by one horse.

In 1786 two wheeled chairs drawn by a single horse and used for hire to the public were taxed at five shillings per annum for the licence plus a penny for each mile the carriage travelled. They were not licensed to ply for hire but were in the majority of cases self drive. If they were hired with a driver they could only be used to carry passengers beyond the area of the Bills of Mortality and were required to carry a board affixed to the vehicle to inform the public so. (8) Strictly speaking though, they had passed beyond the stage of a Sedan chair. Although they were never referred to as such they were definitely the first licensed private hire vehicles.

As we have seen Sedan chairs were not subject to legislation until 1711 when they were placed under the authority of the Hackney Coach Commissioners and their numbers were restricted to two hundred, with the proviso that another hundred could be licensed if it were thought necessary. Each chair was required to carry a number that was easily distinguishable to the public in case of any complaint against the chairman and for carrying an unlicensed chair the penalty was £5. When the time came to granting licences, former chairmen or the wives of former chairmen were to have first claim and were, in fact, given twenty days in which to apply for a licence.

A statement from the Hackney Coach Commissioners in June 1711 said, "we are resolved to give the licences for hackney chairs to none but such chairmen as shall bring certificates from their parish officers and we have reserved fourteen licences for the widows of chairmen". Within a year of the hackney chairs being licensed it was apparent that some of the licences had been granted to persons who were not entitled to them and in June 1712 a number of chairmen petitioned Parliament.

"The Commissioners have been pleased to give a licence to several young men that have not been above half a year imployed in the said imployment and to eminent men and women who never did any of the labour themselves, who, having engrossed the licence to themselves to let to foreigners, at such extravagant rates as £6 per annum, by which means we that are inhabitants and ancient chairmen shall be ruined having not so much money to lay down. We do beg and beseech your honours to permit us to carry gentlemen in our own chairs, or that you will be pleased to licence one hundred more". (9)

A view of Pall Mall with St James's Palace on the right showing two sedan chairs being used, c. 1710.

It was possibly this petition that induced the Commissioners to licence the additional one hundred chairs that had been provided for in the act of 1711. The foreigners alluded to in the petition were Irishmen, who eventually predominated as chairmen. In 1726 the question of whether to licence a further hundred chairs arose but a Bill which would have allowed this was defeated in the House of Commons on April 19th 1726 by 158 votes to 96. This was not so much because of opposition to Sedan chairs, as against the remainder of the Bill which proposed to raise a tax on victuallers who sold spirits to be consumed off the premises.

Sedan chairs were never again the subject of legislation and they were not even mentioned in bye-laws drawn up by the Commissioners, of which several are extant. It is perhaps significant that their numbers never exceeded three hundred while those of hackney coaches, already numbering seven hundred when Sedans were first licensed, had almost doubled by the time Sedan chairs went out of fashion, circa 1820.

Writing during the reign of George II (1727 - 1760) De Saussure had this to say of Sedans and the men who carried them. "Near to the palace and in it's vicinity there are three hundred Sedan chairs for hire; like the cabs they are found in the principle streets and thoroughfares. Chairs are very convenient and pleasant to use, the bearers going so fast that you have difficulty in keeping up with them on foot. In the whole of Europe no better or dexterous bearers are to be found and all foreigners are surprised at their skill and strength". (10)

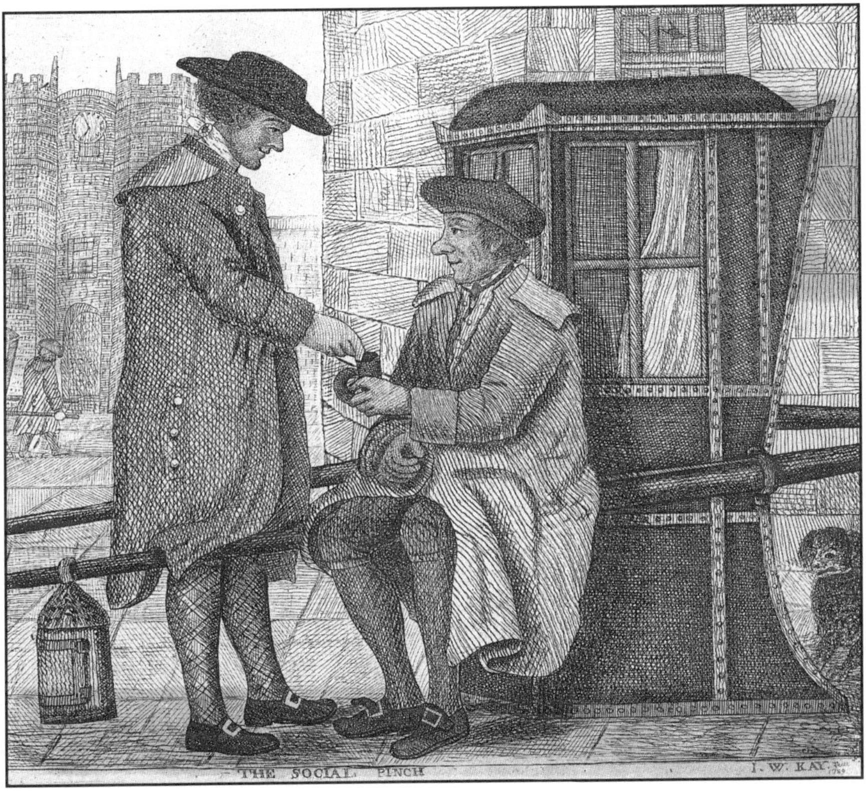

The Court of St James's proved a popular work place for Sedans, as can be seen by this print showing two chairmen resting near to the Palace. c. 1750.

The Irish chairmen in London were notorious for their tipple which on occasions made them extremely disagreeable. A popular doggerel of the time ran, "the drunken chairman in the kennel spurns the glasses shatter and the charge o'er turns". In Edinburgh, however, where there were one hundred chairs by 1738, the chairmen were Highlanders and were more civil; they could be hired for four shillings a day or twenty shillings a week. It is uncertain whether chairmen in London operated on a similar pattern to those in Bath, where Sedans were very popular. There, the chairmen, though licensed would often contract themselves to one family, sometimes serving them for years. Complaints between them were determined by the Corporation who would perhaps suspend or revoke a licence depending upon the charge.

Arguments concerning the respective merits of the Sedan chairs were carried on in much the same way that the merits of transport today is discussed. Not everyone shared De Saussure's view and Sedans were not to everyone's taste. Steele, in one of his Tatler papers said, "the chairmen or slaves of the rich, take up the whole street, while we peripatetics are very glad to watch for an opportunity to whisk across a passage, very thankful that we are not run over for interrupting the machine".

Mathew Bramble, in Humphrey Clinker wrote, "the Valettudinarian is carried in a chair over and above the hazards of being obstructed or overturned by the carriages which are continuously making their exit. I suppose that after some chairmen shall have been maimed or a few lives lost the Corporation will think in earnest about providing a safe and commodious passage". How did a chairman fare if he fell and broke a leg or if he were sick? Who made provision for him and his family if, through no fault of his own, he was temporarily out of work?

That the hackney coachmen had some form of association we have already seen and the wealth of Broadsheets during the 18th century show that they were able to present a united front on many of the problems which affected them. Combinations of workers banding together for the purpose of gaining higher wages was illegal, though as the Industrial Revolution gathered momentum, so too did various movements for improving wages and conditions for those who had lost the revolution. It is not altogether surprising then to find that there were societies to which the chairmen belonged.

At this time they numbered six hundred and they had formed several mutual aid societies that were protected by covenant to give assistance to those of their members who had fallen sick, "and have mutually agreed to contribute for all of them, their wives and their children as shall come to sickness or poverty, to prevent them becoming a charge to their parishes, by allowing them seven shillings a week when sick or lame and sixpence a day if past labour for life; 3 shillings towards such persons funeral and 1 shilling to the widow". (11)

As the 18th century reached middle age and beyond, so the economic expansion from overseas trade and the dawn of industrialisation began to affect the towns and cities of Britain. The increased wealth was to create another class of rich; merchants, wholesalers and bankers etc. Life began to move at a faster pace, imperceptible at first perhaps but a movement that was undoubtedly there. As the towns grew so did the distances travelled and the Sedan chair was not suitable for long distances. They were used less and less though still infrequently used by some members of the aristocracy after the turn of the 19th century until as we have seen they became objects of ornamentation.

References used in Chapter Six

1. Old and New London, Vol. 4, p. 117. E. Walford. (Cassell)
2. Coach and Sedan Pleasantly Disputing. Henry Peachum (1626) (GRL)
3. Old and New London, Vol. 4, p. 117. E. Walford. (Cassell)
4. From records belonging to Lord Bath. (Longleat Library)
5. Calendar of State Papers Domestic belonging to H.M. The Queen.
6. The Evolution of the Horse Drawn Vehicle, James Reid.
7. Calendar of Treasury Papers, 1729/30 p. 24 (GRL)
8. Statutes of the Realm, 25th George III C51 S IV.
9. Broadside 11.76. (GRL)
10. A Foreigners View of England in the reign of George II, p. 165/6. De Saussure (GRL)
11. House of Commons Journals, Vol. 17, p. 433. (HOLRO)

Chapter Seven

A Social Documentary

Birmingham is Britain's second largest city and yet in 1993 only 740 taxis were licensed to ply for hire within the city limits. In 1688 London was much smaller than present day Birmingham yet 600 hackney coaches were licensed to ply there, and by the end of the 18th century when the number of coaches in London had increased to 900, London was still smaller than present day Birmingham. How then did the hackney coaches in London manage to survive and even increase in numbers? Who used them and for what purpose? What standard of living did the coachmen enjoy compared to the rest of the working population? Were they only used by the rich and the criminal fraternity with an extra shilling to spend?

The answer is that they were used by all sections of the community from the richest to the poorest in the same way that taxis are used today. Samuel Pepys used hackney coaches extensively, a perfect example of how the rich and influential used them. For many years he had been content to ride in them and in one period between January 1st and March 31st 1664, he used them on no less than forty one occasions. (1)

He used them for visits to friends, the theatre, coffee houses and on his official business as Navy Secretary. He was particularly fond of taking his wife for a ride in Hyde Park, something that was quite fashionable then. In 1669 he felt the time had come to purchase his own coach and on May 1st of that year he rode in it for the first time. "To the park but full of coaches and dusty, windy and cold and now and then a little dribbling of rain and what made it worse, there were so many hackney coaches as spoiled the sight of a gentleman and so we had little pleasure".

The fashion of riding in Hyde Park became a lucrative part of a coachman's work, but it had it's disadvantages and in 1685 following an incident involving two 'ladies of the town', who drove around the park in a hackney coach insulting all and sundry, which so infuriated Charles II that he instructed William Chiffinch, the head keeper, "not to suffer any hackney coaches to enter Hyde Park". (2) This exclusion was to last until 1687 when the Treasury Lords wrote to William Chiffinch saying, "it is the King's pleasure that the licensed hackney coachmen be permitted to come into the park during the evening and at all other times". From then until 1711 hackney coaches used Hyde Park to considerable advantage but on July 14th of that year, by order of Queen Anne, "hackney coaches are forbidden to use Hyde Park where several disorders have been committed". This time the ban was to last until

1924 when the park was made open to taxis by the Labour Government of that year.

An incident outside Newgate Jail in 1797 serves to illustrate how on at least one occasion they were used by ordinary folk.

"At the execution of John Bryant for rape, before Newgate on Wednesday last, an extraordinary occurrence took place. Between nine and ten o'clock a hackney coach drew up at the prison door in order to convey away the body of Bryant, which being brought out, a violent altercation broke out between two parties in the crowd, each headed by a woman, as to which was best entitled to the corpse. Upon the body being brought out into the street, the two contending parties seized hold of it, some holding it by the legs and some by the head and arms and contributed to prevent it falling to the ground. After an obstinate contest for half an hour, the deceased was carried into Giltspur Street, where being put into the hackney coach, it was driven off and the population dispersed". (3)

Transporting dead criminals was one side of the coin, carrying dead members of the nobility was the other. On Saturday, November 15th 1712, Lord Mohun and Duke of Hamilton both died as the result of a duel in Hyde Park. Both had gone there alive at seven o'clock in the morning and they both left there dead, carried home in the hackney coaches they had arrived in. The Duke of Hamilton's body was put into the coach driven by a John Pennington, who asked who would pay him. Colonel Hamilton, the Duke's second said "the footman" but Pennington said, "I brought you here as well as my lord and you should pay me", whereupon Colonel Hamilton gave him half-a-crown. (4)

London's hackney coachmen not only drove the living but they also catered for the dead. Apart from the above incident they had always provided hearses and mourning coaches at funerals. By 1714 however, trouble began to occur at funerals with unlicensed coaches and Parliament was forced to intervene by passing an act, part of which read, "if such hearses and mourning coaches did not carry an official hackney plate, or if it displayed a false one, it would be deemed out of hand to be illegally plying for hire - penalty £5". (5)

Before the act of 1714 only a bye-law made by the hackney Coach Commissioners had restricted all but the licensed coachmen from attending funerals, but a statement from the hackney coachmen in 1711 accused the Commissioners of fining several licensed coachmen for attending funerals with un-plated coaches, with fines up to £10, yet at the same time allowed others who were not licensed to attend funerals with no action being taken against them. It would seem that this action of the Commissioners induced Parliament to bring in the act of 1714.

In 1784 another act strengthened the coachmen's position still further, stating, "that after September 4th 1784, any person driving a mourning coach or hearse within five miles of Temple Bar within the City of London, without a number properly affixed thereon, may be summoned before the Hackney Commissioners and fined £5 and that although no express hiring shall be proved it shall be deemed and adjudged driving for hire unlicensed". (6) The act of 1831 (1st & 2nd Will. IV c 22) which repealed all former legislation did not contain any word about funerals. There was no longer any restriction on coaches other than hackney coaches attending funerals and gradually undertakers began to use coaches of their own and the two trades of morticians and cabmen grew apart.

Funerals were only one facet of the hackney coachmen's work. They also performed many tasks for the government of the day. There was the occasion when the coachmen used their horses to transport the artillery from London to the Battle of Sedgemoor during the Monmouth Rebellion for which they subsequently claimed they were never paid. (7)

On Thursday, October 10th 1695, King William III arrived at Margate in the Royal Yacht 'William and Mary', accompanied by a squadron of English and Dutch men o' war, under the command of Sir Cloudesly Shovell. The king and his retinue stayed overnight at Canterbury and completed the journey to Kensington Palace the following day. In January 1696, the Treasury issued the following order, "to the Master of Horse, to the unsatisfied order in his name, for the extraordinary expense of the stable, to whit, £1,000 in part of what is owing to the hackney coachmen who attended his majesty's arrival from Holland in the Margate Roads and those who waited upon him in his progress".

William and Mary arriving at Kensington Palace in the state coach with their retinue travelling behind in hackney coaches. 1695.

The coachmen had submitted a bill for £2,000 for the Margate venture and this had been agreed by Henry Ireton, Master of the King's Horse. They were, however, to wait until August 1702 for the balance of their money and even then they were not paid in full. In July 1702 they petitioned Queen Anne "for payment of the debt due to them, amounting to £1,054". Subsequently, an order was made the following month, "to pay hackney coachmen £880.16.6. for debts in stable for service to the late king".

In 1706 during the visit of the Moroccan Ambassador, the Treasury spent £55 for the hire of hackney coaches from May 1st until August 3rd and a further £22.15.0. on the occasion of the ambassador's journey to Windsor to see the Queen. Altogether between 1706 and 1710 the Treasury spent £444.17.0. for the hire of hackney coaches on official business for the government of the day. (8)

We have seen how apart from chance availability, spontaneous hirings on the street and from coach stands appointed for that purpose, the coachmen also had their regular work at funerals, services to the government, their participation in stage coach work and as we shall see later, how they were extensively engaged in the short stage coach network (See Chapter Eight). But what sort of living standards did they enjoy? To what extent did their living standards compare with other workers in London?

An almost total lack of records concerning the earnings and expenses of hackney coachmen make it difficult to arrive at a definite comparison with other trades. However, some items are known because they affected everyone who owned a coach and horses. The cost of food, rent, clothing and fuel etc., has been well set down by Dorothy M. George in her book, 'London life in the 18th Century', from which a number of the following facts have been freely drawn. Set out below as far as can be estimated is the sum that would have enabled a hackney coachman to run his coach and horses and maintain his family for a year.

	£ s d
Hire of licence	30. 0.0.
Stabling for three horses	26. 0.0.
Cost of one horse per annum	10. 0.0.
Cost of corn for three horses	26. 9.0.
To renewing coach every five years	10. 0.0.
Repairs to coach and harness etc.	9. 0.0.
	£111. 9.0.

The cost of a horse is for a bay gelding in 1750. Though most coachmen would have carried out some repairs themselves, they would have from time to time, required the services of a wheelwright and a blacksmith. With regard to the cost of keeping himself, wife and two children, every item can be authenticated.

	£ s d
Rent	13.10.0.
Cost of Food	36. 0.0.
Cost of clothing	10. 0.0.
Extras, including amusements, beer, coal and lighting	15. 0.0.
	£74.10.0. (9)

From a budget presented to the Justices at the Quarter Sessions in 1779 on behalf of journeymen saddlers, it emerges says Dorothy M. George that they required a salary of £74.4.0. This compares favourably with the coachmen's £74.10.0. yearly wage and making his gross annual takings £185.19.0. This amount had to be earned in 325 days bearing in mind that a hackney coachman could only work one Sunday in four. Assuming that he did work 325 days he would have required to earn nearly 11/6d a day; would this have been possible?

If we take into account that every act of legislation between 1662 and 1767 had laid down that, "no driver of a hackney coach shall presume to take more for his hire in and about the Citties of London and Westminster or within ten miles thereof, above the rate of ten shillings for a day, reckoning twelve hours to the day", the estimate of 11/6d per day would seem to be in reason. After 1767 the amount he could earn in a day was increased to 12/6d.

This, of course, does not take into account tips which even then were in the region of twopence for a fare up to two shillings and fourpence for a fare of four shillings. Tips then would have added at least another shilling a day to his takings, bringing his personal income up to around £90 per annum. This meant that the hackney coachmen were probably amongst the highest paid of any group of workers in London, at least until the early 19th century. In the late 17th and early 18th centuries it was not unknown for a coachman's family to have a servant. (10)

A hackney coachman's wage was often supplemented by his wife working, and taking in washing was a common form of such work, though others aspired to a higher kind of employment. The wife of one hackney coachman, by name, Roberts, kept the 'Feathers' inn at the Broadway, Westminster and a public house of that name still stands there today. Wages, of course, differed from county to county. In South-East England a labourer's wage varied little between 1720 and 1793 and seldom rose above one shilling and three pence a day, £20. per annum.

In London there was no shortage of people who used hackney coaches. In 1688 it was estimated that there were some 84,000 of the 'middling classes' in London. Many observers expressed surprise that such a small population could support so many shops who specialised in tea, coffee, furniture and apothecaries. A new development in the 18th century was the appearance of "ready made" tailors and shoemakers, though their products were often of an inferior quality.

A detail from a print shows hackney coaches standing in the middle of the road on Fish Street Hill, c. 1799.

By the middle of the 18th century London's population was some 700,000 and was well able to support a growing number of hackney coaches plus the three hundred Sedan chairs and the stage coach network, now over a century old provided a transport service for visitors to and from the capital.

An ever increasing short stage service was catering for the needs of those who were, even at this time, commuting from home to work. Although most shopkeepers still lived over their shops as they had done for centuries, thousands of others, government officers, doctors whose numbers were growing, merchants, the better off shopkeepers and many tradesmen, were now prosperous enough to have a house in the suburbs and were already commuting between home and place of business. (11)

In 1767 the amount a coachman could charge when hired by the day was increased to 12/6d and remained so until 1808. The act of that year abolished the hiring of hackney coaches by the day, henceforth they could only be hired by so much per mile or by the hour. This act also firmly established the principle of return fare. Previously it had been assumed to have been covered by the fare scale laid down. i.e.. "Sixpence forward and sixpence back".

It is necessary to understand that the former practice of the coach owner being the licencee had changed to some extent. Between 1694 and 1711, the initial licence fee of £50 had proved too expensive for many of the former 'ancient' hackney coachmen and they had been forced to relinquish the licence and rent it back; they were known as 'renters'. In turn the 'renter' would often hire out the coach to a driver, so that there was, in effect, a three tier system of licensee, renter and driver. There were, of course, still some owner drivers who retained the original licence and not all renters sublet to a driver and in some cases drove the coach themselves.

This system had several drawbacks. By the 1760's the cost of renting the licence had increased from the £16 charged in 1711 to £32 and this cost was itself the source of many petitions to Parliament during the 18th century. By 1808 these charges, where they were passed on to a driver, were causing some hardship. This, plus the fact that many drivers were reluctant to undertake long journeys for a shilling a mile, induced Parliament to allow return fare to be charged during the day. Previously this had been the perogative of a coachman working between the hours of sunset and sunrise and had become law in 1792. Before 1792 coachmen working at night had been allowed to refuse anyone wishing to travel beyond the Bill's of Mortality or, "the limits of a continuous carriageway pavement". (12)

The increased profitability accruing to the London hackney carriage trade following the act of 1808 heralded the end of the licensee, renter, driver system. More and more licences were acquired by fleet owners and in an appendix to the Select Committee Report into the Hackney Coach Office in 1829, listing twenty larger fleet owners, shows that from a total of 186 coaches and cabriolets only 15 were licensed prior to 1808.

Until the end of the 18th century, complaints against hackney coachmen for overcharging had been few. Indeed many foreign observers, such as De Saussure, had often commented that London's hackney coach drivers were honest. The main cause of overcharging from 1800 onwards was the high rate of inflation, plus the fact that the benefits of the 1808 act had not been passed on to the drivers whose income was related to the basic charge of one shilling a mile, which had kept at the same level for 150 years.

Many prices rose by 50 to 100 per cent between 1750 and 1790 and the economic position of the working man had declined dramatically. The Reverend David Davies recorded that in his own parish of Barkham in Berkshire that the price of cheese rose from 3½d a pound to 6d a pound. Bacon from 6d to 9d a pound. A loaf of bread increased from 8d to 1/2d. Fresh butter from 6d to 1/- a pound and a pair of men's shoes rose from 5/- to 7/6d.

Drivers defrauding their proprietors went hand in hand with overcharging and in the absence of a foolproof device for measuring distance, overcharging and indeed undercharging was relatively easy. Proprietors had to rely upon the honesty of their drivers as to how much they had taken in the course of the days work and although legislation had always been specific on the fare a coachman could charge a passenger, no attempt had ever been made to fix the payment between the owner and the driver. The most simple way to overcome the driver's defrauding would have been for the owner to hire out the coach on a flat rate basis and everything the driver took over and above the flat rate would have been the driver's wage.

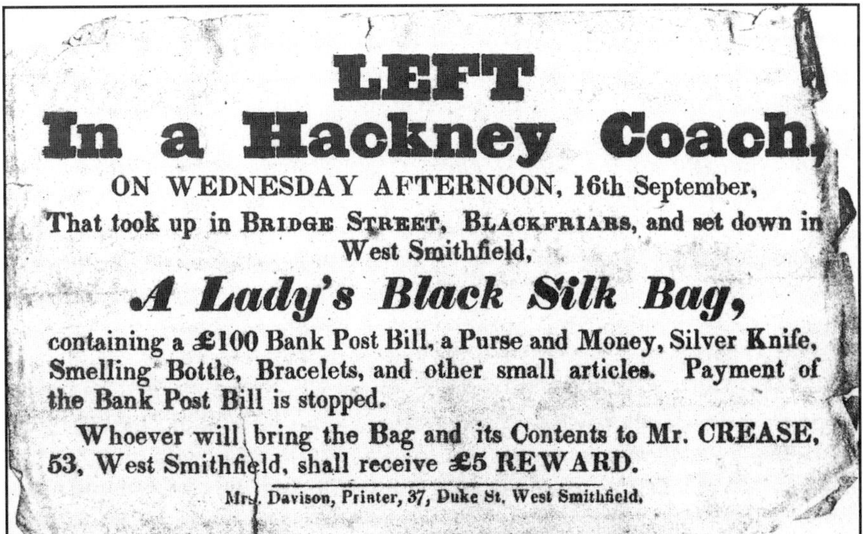

LEFT

In a Hackney Coach,

ON WEDNESDAY AFTERNOON, 16th September,

That took up in BRIDGE STREET, BLACKFRIARS, and set down in West Smithfield,

A Lady's Black Silk Bag,

containing a £100 Bank Post Bill, a Purse and Money, Silver Knife, Smelling Bottle, Bracelets, and other small articles. Payment of the Bank Post Bill is stopped.

Whoever will bring the Bag and its Contents to Mr. CREASE, 53, West Smithfield, shall receive £5 REWARD.

Mrs. Davison, Printer, 37, Duke St. West Smithfield.

The reward offered in this early 19th Century notice would represent approximately two weeks good takings for a hackney coachmen at that period. c 1825.

It is apparent that this system was not worked because by 1814 proprietors were being defrauded to such an extent that they were having difficulty in paying their licence fee. When events reached this stage Parliament decided to deal with the problem, by passing an act which was designed to prevent the coachmen from carrying out these frauds, "wherebye the said owners are rendered less able to discharge their weekly rent due to his majesty on their respective licences". (13)

Accordingly the act provided for a ticket system to be introduced. The public were made aware that they were to ask for a ticket on completion of their journey and no complaint could be made against the driver unless the passenger produced the ticket. The ticket carried the name and address of the owner, the licence number of the coach and at the journey's end the driver was required to fill in the date and the amount charged for the journey. At the same time Parliament also directed that the driver's wage would be easier to calculate if a commission rate of 3s.4d in the pound was fixed, payable from the total amount recorded on the ticket. A penalty of £3 and one month in the House of Correction was the punishment meted out to any driver found guilty of defrauding his employer.

Almost immediately after the act was passed it was evident that it was virtually unworkable. No one it seemed, had thought to consult the drivers, for if they had they would have been acquainted with the fact that the majority of them could neither read nor write. Those who could were as averse to giving a ticket as Ministers of Parliament are to give a true answer. The government then set about repealing the act of 1814 and in 1815 it was repealed, but what to put in it's place? While the government were in this dilemma, debating the repealing bill, there arose a protagonist, by name John Irving Maxwell, a barrister of the Inner Temple, a Don Quixote, tilting at the Windmills of Essex Street, where the offices of the Hackney Coach Commissioners were located.

During the debate of the Hackney Coach repealing bill, Stephen Lushington M.P., Secretary to the Treasury, suspended the second reading of the Bill. Maxwell congratulated Lushington for his candour which had induced him to suspend the second reading, "that time shall be afforded to collect such information as might make your projected bill a more complete and beneficial system of legislation".

Maxwell's main object was to establish beyond doubt that the Hackney Coach Commissioners were already empowered by existing legislation to make bye-laws necessary to deal with the situation and, knowing that they had this power had failed to exercise their inherent function. Lushington had made known his intention of producing an effective method of regulating hackney coaches and as a result the Commissioners were "suspending licences and committing coachmen wholesale, they have at last awoke from their slumbers and given evident proofs that they do not consider their office to be absolute sinecures". When it became obvious that the act of 1814 was going to be repealed it drew forth the comment from Maxwell, "if we might form any judgement from the present proceedings in Parliament upon this subject, we might be induced to suppose that the interests of the coach owners was everything and the protection of the public nothing".

Whether Lushington was influenced by Maxwell's arguments or not we shall never know but certainly Parliament, recognising that the act of 1814 was unworkable, seemed determined to replace it with a law which had some bite. All reference to the ticket system was dropped but it still remained an offence for a driver to defraud the owner but the sting was in the tail with a fine of £5 for any coachmen found guilty of "demanding more than the legal fare". Also, unattended coaches, whether hired or not, left at a place of entertainment were to be driven away to "a place of deposit" and would only be returned by payment of £5, a precursor of the modern police car pound. (15)

However, extortion and fraud were never the sole prerogative of the drivers. Figures supplied by the Home Secretary in 1852 show that during the previous year there were 423 cases where proceedings were taken out by drivers against passengers for bilking, i.e.. defrauding the driver of his fare. Out of these, 185 cases were proved and ten were dismissed. The number of convictions under this class of summons bears a low proportion to the number of proceedings taken, because these cases are frequently settled out of court. The number of proceedings taken out by persons against cabdrivers in the same year were 358 taken out and 183 convictions obtained. (16) Bearing in mind that a cabdriver would not have been given the same opportunity to settle out of court, it would seem that passengers had the edge over drivers for villainy.

*See chapter eight 'Short Stage'.

References used in Chapter Seven

1. Samuel Pepys Diary, edited by H. Wheatley, Bell, London. (GRL)
2. Sate Papers Domestic, March 1685. (PRO)
3. Evening Mail, November 10th, 1712. (Brit. Mus. Col.)
4. Flying Post, November 15th/18th 1797. (Brit. Mus. Col.)
5. 1st George 1st.
6. 24th George III C27, Sec. 3.
7. Pamphlet 8716. (GRL)
8. For the events surrounding the services to William III and the money due to the hackney coachmen see - London Gazette, October 10th, 1695; Calendar of Treasury Books, Vol. 10. pt. 3, p. 1289 and pt. 1, p. 557; Vol. 17 pt. 1, pp. 56, 319 and Vol. 28 pp. 443, 451, 461 and 469.
9. Broadside 11.75 (GRL) and a diary of a gentleman in the private

collection of Mrs. Stoppes of Bournemouth.

10. For references relating to the income of hackney coachmen see - 7th George III C 36; Pamphlet 8716 (GRL). For references to tips to coachmen see - a diary of a gentleman in the private collection of Mrs. Stoppes of Bournemouth.
11. For references to relating to the 'Feathers Inn', the population figures and details of professions etc., see - Old Bailey Session Papers 1685 (GRL) and The History of the Cost of Living, John Burnett, Pelican, pp. 171/173.
12. For references in this paragraph see - 7th George III C 36; Acts of the Interregnum, an ordinance for regulating hackney coachmen 1654. (GRL) and 58th George III c 87.
13. 58th George III C 87.
14. Hints for protecting the public and a letter to Stephen Lushington M.P. by John Irving Maxwell (Barrister) 1815. (GRL)
15. 55th George III C 159.
16. House of Commons Session Papers, 1852, Vol. XLI p. 550. (HOLRO)

Chapter Eight

Short Stage

During a Parliamentary Committee of Inquiry in March, 1695 into allegations of bribery and corruption against the Hackney Coach Commissioners, it was revealed that some of the licences that had been granted by the Commissioners contained the words "and elsewhere". Investigations showed that the Commissioners had used these words corruptly in some short stage licences on payment of an unspecified amount, thereby enabling the holders of these licences to circumvent the conditions of the licence. Subsequently, Commissioners Killigrew, Gee and Ashurst had their commissions revoked. (1)

A short stage licence was issued on the condition that it was used to convey passengers to and from the towns mentioned in the licence. In the case of John Mathews mentioned at the inquiry, he was licensed to drive a short stage coach to Tonbridge in Kent, but by virtue of the words "and elsewhere" he performed the work of an ordinary hackney coach, taking up and setting down passengers within the area of the Bill's of Mortality, thereby defeating the intention of the act.

Ever since 1688, when the number of hackney coaches had been increased from 400 to 600, some of their numbers had been forced to seek work beyond the confines of London. Until 1694, there being no legislation to the contrary, these worked as stage coaches and because they generally restricted their operations to towns within a twenty mile radius of London they were referred to as short stage coaches.

The act of 1694 licensed stage coaches as well as hackney coaches and the Hackney Coach Commissioners were responsible for both groups. Section three of the act was badly drafted and it was successfully interpreted by stage coach proprietors as being in force for one year only. Consequently, at the end of the first year, hundreds of stage coaches could work without being licensed. Clearly there was insufficient work for them all, as numerous petitions of the time testify, some swelled the ranks of those working as short stages, while others it seemed were working illegally in London.

In 1708 London's licensed hackney coachmen petitioned Parliament, "that the seven hundred licensed coachmen suffer great wrongs several ways, there being hundreds of coaches let to hire in the Bill's of Mortality who pay nothing". (2) Far from doing anything to alleviate the situation, Parliament licensed another 100 coaches in 1710, which led to another petition in 1711, "that the 100 coaches lately added to the existing 700 may be ordered to perform the short stages around London". There is no evidence to suggest that this was done, though it appears that they agreed amongst themselves to do just this. Sixty one years later, in 1772, as we shall shortly see, Parliament was forced to accept the status quo brought about by it's own indifference.

By 1728 the pattern of short stage coach operation seems to have settled on providing a service to the larger villages and small towns, some ten to fifteen miles beyond the area of the Bill's of Mortality. For example, Brentwood was served by twenty one coaches a week; Brentford with twelve; Dulwich with fourteen; Highgate with fifteen and Romford with twelve. (3) The number of coaches serving Dulwich can perhaps be explained by the presence of the famous college but in that case, Harrow, which was an even more famous public school should at least have had a similar number of coaches calling weekly, whereas in 1728 and later in 1794, Harrow was only served by three coaches.

Romford was and still is an important market town and the number of coaches calling there cannot be considered unusual. Highgate was the Clapham Junction of the north, with many stage coach routes converging there. A passenger bound for a destination in or near London could alight from the long stage coach at Highgate and board a short stage that served smaller towns on branch roads.

A typical short stage coach. This one is waiting at Charing Cross for passengers to Blackheath. Note the parcel boot in the rear, c. 1770.

By 1794 the situation had altered dramatically. From Kent's Guide we can see to what extent the short stage service had increased. Altogether a total of sixty nine small towns and villages within a fifteen miles radius of London were served by short stage coaches, between them providing 4,454 separate journeys a week. Of these towns, twenty three were served by forty or more coaches. Greenwich had a colossal 385, explained perhaps by the presence there of the Royal Naval Hospital and the Royal Observatory. Deptford's 148 coaches can be attributed to the commercial and naval dockyard but by far the greatest number of journeys were made by commuters, as we shall shortly see.

There were three main reasons for such a rapid rise in coach travel between 1728 and 1794, though the latter two spring directly from the first.

1. The Industrial Revolution.
2. The shift of population
3. The improvement of the roads.

It is possible to trace nearly all the development of transport in London to the shift in population that arose because of the Industrial Revolution. As the 18th century drew to a close, London became less industrialised in terms of the means of production, in fact, "the industrial revolution was like a storm that passed over London and broke elsewhere". (4)

The acquisition of territories beyond the seas, i.e., India, Canada, Australia, New Zealand and the West Indies, more than compensated for the loss of the original thirteen colonies on the eastern seaboard of America. As the empire grew, so did the desire of industrialists and merchants to make and sell goods to an ever increasing market. Even the loss of the American colonies did not deter merchants from trading there and, in fact, the first cotton seeds were sent from the Botanical Gardens at Chelsea purely with a view to establishing a cotton industry in the Southern States.

The result of this trade, centred as it was in London, began the transition from what had been predominantly a residential city to a centre of trade and finance. The Bank of England had been established in the city since 1694 and the Royal Exchange since the days of Elizabeth I. As London had for centuries been the pivot for trade in the British Isles and the continent, it was natural that world trade should be conducted there. It was not achieved overnight and the story of the change is a story of it's own. It concerns us because of the shift in population and the effect the migratory movement of it's citizens had on short stage and hackney coaches.

The laissez-faire policy of governments during the 18th century led, at one extreme to the loss of the American colonies while another result of this policy, as it affected domestic issues, was a total lack of transport coordination even though it was a target for taxation. It was not until 1764 that Parliament was forced to intervene in the short stage coach operation. The hackney carriage acts only covered the area within the Bill's of Mortality, whereas the short stage coaches who were licensed hackney coaches, were, for the major part of the time, working in Kent, Surrey, Middlesex and Essex. The act of 1764 made it possible for the judiciary of those counties to treat offences committed by coachmen as if they had been committed in London. (5) But it was the act of 1772 that firmly established the position of those hackney coachmen who were working as short stages.

"And whereas a great number of persons licensed to use and keep for hire hackney coaches; do regularly use and employ them as short stage coaches to and from towns and places in the neighbourhood of the Cities of London and Westminster and the Borough of Southwark. Doubt has arisen whether by the laws now in force relating to hackney coaches, such persons who are licensed in the general form are not compelled to do the work of ordinary hackney coaches. Therefore, the Commissioners shall not fine or punish any licensed hackney coachman or his driver for refusing to carry out the ordinary course of his work, as long as he regularly uses his coach for stage work and has displayed a board notifying the public that it is a short stage coach". (6)

The previous year (1771) the number of coaches had been increased from 800 to 1,000, of which increase the majority were no doubt committed to working as short stage coaches. This in turn induced the government to recognise that short stage working was in fact an extension of the ordinary work of the hackney coachmen. Thus was sown the seeds of what was to become the London Transport bus undertaking.

The birth of the City of London that we know today meant an exodus of the poorer folk first. The land their houses occupied was cheap and easy to acquire. Even cheaper accommodation was provided for them, not too far away, where they could still walk to work. They settled in the expanding districts of Shoreditch, Bethnal Green, Stepney, Clerkenwell, Finsbury, Islington and Southwark. These areas were for the greater part to become slums, the build up of the working class districts south of the river was not so rapid because of the tolls charged to pedestrians crossing the Thames bridges.

By 1833 the migration of the inhabitants had reached such proportions that for the week ending March 8th 1833 some 194,390 people entered the City of London between 6 a.m. and 6 p.m., many of whom were walking to work. The same census revealed the entry of 10,262 cabs and carts, plus 2,550 two horse carriages, the majority of which appeared to be short stage coaches and omnibuses.

In 1700 the population of the City of London within the walls was 139,300 by 1847 it had fallen to 50,306. By comparison the population outside the city walls rose from 130,000 in 1700 to 171,445 in 1847. But the depletion of the city parishes is best illustrated by the figures for St. Giles Cripplegate, whose population in 1700 was 42,600 but by 1801 had fallen to 11,446 and in 1847 was only 7,185. (7) It can be seen that although the population within the City of London declined by 88,994 the population in the outer parishes only rose by 41,445, less than 50 per cent.

The population of the inner parishes of the City of London began to decline about 1730, with the sharpest drop recorded between 1780 and 1801. One reason for the rise in the outer parishes, being less than 50 per cent of the decrease of population of the inner parishes, is probably due to the fact that between 1730 and 1780 the number of burials exceeded baptisms by 206,011. But between 1780 and 1830 the position had been reversed with baptisms exceeding burials by 66,840. (8) There is another reason, quite a large proportion of those leaving the inner parishes settled further away in towns and villages not covered by the population figures for London.

Not all the population in the outer parishes had come from the depleted inner parishes. The East End of London received a large influx of Europeans, mostly Jewish, fleeing from the progroms of Russia, Poland and Lithuania etc. In 1801 the population of Whitechapel was 23,666. By 1847 it had risen to 71,350, predominantly of foreign extraction. (9) There would appear then to be evidence of a large rise in the population of districts around the City of London, the needs of many with regard to travel were served by the short stage coaches.

Both short stage and long stage coaches came under the purview of the Hackney Coach Commissioners as far as the regulations governing them were concerned but the tax on them both resulted from the revenue acts on carriages in general and was known as mileage duty. For long stage coaches licensed by the Commissioners to carry eighteen passengers or more, $3^1/_2$d a mile was levied on every mile the wheels turned, whether the coach carried it's full complement of passengers or not. On the other hand short stages were taxed at $1^1/_2$d a mile and the inequality of this will be seen.

The police committee of the City Corporation were responsible for the allocation of coach stands in the city and the coaches were only allowed twenty minutes to wait for passengers. Failure to observe this, carried a penalty of forty shillings. By 1825 there were sufficient stands to accommodate 421 short stage coaches, ranging from a stand in Moorgate for three coaches to another in Gracechurch Street where 106 coaches stood. (10)

The majority of these coaches were owned by large firms such as Chaplin & Co. who ran coaches from several points in London and who owned between 1,300 and 1,500 horses and 164 coaches. In 1834 this company had a gross income of £500,000 and Chaplin was a Member of Parliament for Salisbury and chairman of the South Western Railway. Two more of the larger firms were Horne & Co. of the Golden Cross Inn at Charing Cross and Shermans of the Bull and Mouth in St. Martin's le Grand, and who between then owned nearly 2,000 horses and over 200 coaches.

At the other end of the scale was "Thomas Ives of Ealing who drives his own coach three times a day to London, at half past eight in the morning, afternoons at half past one and evenings at six". A Mr. Grint operated a coach from Wandsworth which left the 'Spread Eagle' at 8.45 a.m. for Gracechurch Street, returning to Wandsworth at 10.30 a.m. It left Wandsworth again at 5 p.m. for the same destination, arriving back at Wandsworth at seven in the evening. The fare for the six mile journey was one shilling in the morning and one and sixpence for the return journey later in the evening, though the average fare for short stage coaches was 3d a mile. The majority of short stage coaches carried twelve passengers, plus parcels etc., which were picked up and delivered by the driver for an ex gratia payment. (11)

Who were the people who provided an estimated 1,000 coaches with sufficient passengers? In 1801 the district of Bow in East London had a population of 6,594 and was served by 84 coaches a week. By 1847 the population had increased to 37,060 and though some of these worked in Bow and others worked in the nearby Millwall and Royal Group of docks that were then under construction, large numbers travelled to work in London.

As with the coaches operating from Ealing and Wandsworth at peak times in the morning and evening, so a similar pattern existed in all the districts around London. It seems reasonable to assume then that the majority of those travelling were going to work and if we also assume that they worked six days a week, they would have paid on average 15/- per week on fares. Obviously, they were not ordinary working people who could not possibly have afforded the luxury of travel to work each day, they were middle and lower middle class merchants, the larger shopkeepers, etc., affluent enough to have moved into what was then open country. It was the dawning of the commuter age.

Though Bow itself lay beyond the area of the Bill's of Mortality until 1840, the boundaries of the Bills did reach as far as the western edge of the parish. Until 1831, when the question of short stages picking up and setting down within the area of the bills was resolved, only passengers travelling to Bow or beyond could have boarded the stage that left from Gracechurch Street. Any intermediate destination could only have been reached by ones own coach or by hackney coach. It was this last factor which increasingly from 1800 onwards, gave rise to the charge of monopoly against the hackney coaches that in part, was responsible for the act of 1831.

The demise of the short stage coach was not to be the same as the long stage coaches that were replaced by the rapid growth of the railways, though as regards to some of the routes that followed the river, there was some degree of similarity. Steamboats, which paid no tax, were beginning to attract people to travel on the river; a reversal of the situation that had existed during the 17th and 18th centuries, when people forsook the river to ride in coaches. However, to dismiss the decline in travel by coach purely as a result of the railways is not good enough, just as important was an error in taxation that placed coaches, both long and short on an unequal footing with their rival - steam.

The 1822 Stage Coach Act (3rd George 4 C95 ss 1/2) had altered the flat rate mileage duty to 1d per mile for one horse, 3d a mile for two horses and 4d a mile for three horses or more. It also, for the first time allowed twenty passengers to be carried if they were a one class fare, providing the coach was drawn by three or more horses. It was this clause that enabled George Shillibeer to begin his omnibus service in 1829, from the Yorkshire Stingo in Marylebone Road to the Bank.

The taxation of rail travel at this stage was one eighth of a penny per mile per passenger, whereas by coach it was one farthing per passenger, double that paid by the railway. The number of passengers charged on the railway was according to the number of passengers carried, while on the coaches, the number of passengers taxed was according to the number specified on the licence. During the Committee of Inquiry in 1837, Mr. B.W. Horne, managing director of the firm Horne & Co., said, "the duties paid on coaches licensed to carry passengers was 3d a mile, every mile the coach ran and such a state of things could not last long". (12) Hence the efforts of the coach trade to place both coach and steam on an equal footing with regard to taxation.

The Committee of Inquiry advised the total removal of all taxes on road travel (travel by steamboat was already free of tax) to destroy the existing inequality. Unfortunately, neither the Committee's report or the advice of Sir Robert Peel that "there should be no inequality of taxation for horse travel", was acted upon and the old system, being found to produce such a good income was continued. The act of 1842 did reduce the level of duty payable by coaches to 1½d a mile though the tax was still paid on the vehicle irrespective of the number of passengers carried. The railway tax was fixed at five per cent of all fares actually received and steamboats were still left free of tax.

In June 1829 George Shillibeer began his omnibus service from Marylebone Road to the Bank of England in the city, the kind of service that was working quite well in Paris from where Shillibeer seems to have got the idea. His choice of route was dictated to him. First, his starting point lay beyond the area of the Bill's of Mortality. Second, the 'New Road' as it was then called but what is now the Marylebone, Euston, Pentonville and City Roads, had recently been freed from tolls to encourage it's use as a by pass around London. Third, the area around his starting point was rapidly building up into a residential area, populated, in the main by, middle class folk who could afford to ride to work in the city.

There was, however, one obstacle that Shillibeer could not overcome. As soon as his omnibus reached St. Pancras Church, it came within the area of the Bill's of Mortality and it could not pick up any additional passengers and remain within the law. In 1829 a Select Committee of the House of Commons was set up to investigate the London hackney carriage trade in relation to the restrictions it placed on short stage coaches and the new omnibus service. One of it's main findings was that the clause in the 1815 Hackney Coach Act, which prohibited short and long stage coaches from picking up passengers within the area of the Bill's of Mortality, ought not to be re-enacted. (13)

In 1831 the entire recommendations of the committee were included in an Act of Parliament that was to come into effect on January 5th 1832 (See Appendix A). It stipulated that until January 5th 1833 only the 1,200 original licenses were to be issued and that they were in the first instance to be made available to ancient coachmen or their widows. After that date all limitations on licences were to be removed and the former clause prohibiting long and short stages from picking up and setting down within the area of the 'Bills' was not re-enacted; so were the streets of London thrown open to all-comers.

What had really occurred to change a system that had been built up over a period of 171 years, ever since the act of 1662 had established the principle of control by Hackney Coach Commissioners? On June 13th 1828, the Duke of Wellington who had been Prime Minister since January of that year, wrote to the Hackney Coach Commissioners asking them to licence an additional 300 coaches and cabriolets on behalf of a Frederick Gye. The Commissioners replied on June 16th 1828 that the existing law did not permit them to licence more than 1,200 coaches and cabs and that the quota had been taken up (See Appendix C and D). They also pointed out that to put some 300 coaches and cabs on the road would require a joint stock company with a capital of £60,000. (14)

We must now turn our attention to Frederick Gye, who, in 1828 was the Member of Parliament for Chippenham in Wiltshire and a Parliamentary colleague of the Duke of Wellington. Some few years earlier Gye had won £30,000 in a state lottery for which he had the contract to print the tickets. This he used to start in business as a tea and coffee merchant, after a venture into the wine business had not met with success. In 1821 he entered into partnership with a William Hughes and between them they purchased Vauxhall Gardens from the Tyers family for £28,000. (15)

This project was an immediate success with receipts reaching £29,000 in 1823. During 1827 and 1828 their spectacular presentation of the battle of Waterloo, received public acclaim for it's authenticity, complete with horses, foot soldiers and set scenes. Did the Duke of Wellington assist Gye and Hughes? It seems very likely. It is also strange that not long after, the Duke of Wellington was making representations on behalf of Gye, trying to obtain hackney coach licences for him.

Then there is the question of the £60,000 required to operate the 300 coaches and cabs. Successful as Vauxhall Gardens were, Gye was not making sufficient money to have that sum at his disposal. Who then was his financial backer if such was the case? In the light of the foregoing it is not unreasonable to assume that it was the Duke of Wellington. That the 1831 act was looked upon as a measure of reform is certain but reform means different things to different men and in light of Wellington's opinion on reform "that as long as I hold any station in the government of the country, I will always feel it my duty to resist such measures when proposed by others". (16) But not perhaps when proposed by himself.

For some years prior to the Select Committee of 1829, Parliament had received a number of petitions from disgruntled proprietors, both hackney and short stage. Among these was a petition from George Green of Clerkenwell and Charles Saggers of Holborn who were later to appear before the Select Committee. Part of their petition read:-

"Will the House take into consideration the little benefit that the Hackney Coach Office has to the public and that it may be dispensed with altogether as a useless and oppressive establishment without benefit to the country, revenue or the public".

A prominent petitioner was George Shillibeer. He twice petitioned the Treasury Lords who had the ultimate authority to issue licences. His petitions were presented on November 3rd 1827 and January 23rd 1828. He was refused on the grounds that there was no legal authority for granting them for the limit on the number of hackney carriages had been reached on both occasions. He complained most bitterly to the Treasury Lords in his second petition that his first had been rejected while he had been in Paris in November 1827. Yet while he had been away, their Lordships had granted twenty licences to two persons, who were unnamed, and who Shillibeer alleged had built their cabriolets on his design, saying "I am prepared to prove it to your Lordships" (See Appendix E and F). (17)

In the petition of November 3rd, Shillibeer refers to a separate seat for the driver of his cabriolet, which on the existing cabs was placed next to the passengers with the driver sitting in the open over the offside wheel. In his second petition, Shillibeer is proposing to build his cabriolets "upon an improved principle". Frederick Gye's plan for an improved cabriolet also contained ideas similar to those expressed by Shillibeer, some two years previous to Gye's proposals. There appears to be no record of any patent taken out by Shillibeer for his "improved principle" which showed a lack of discretion on his part which perhaps allowed others to steal them.

In the event, Shillibeer did not get any cab licences and as a result he turned his attention to the omnibuses he had seen in Paris. There was nothing very novel about the operation of Shillibeer's omnibus, the use of such a vehicle had been possible since the stage coach act of 1822, yet no one had rushed to take advantage of it and neither would Shillibeer have done so had he been able to have obtained cab licences.

A list of applicants for hackney carriage licences between 1825 - 1830. George Shillibeer was one of those refused on the grounds of 'no vacancies'. Note also the application from William Gye M.P. for 300 coaches.

DATE.	NAME of APPLICANT.	BY WHOM RECOMMENDED.	NATURE of APPLICATION.	CAUSE of REFUSAL.
1825 to 1829:	George Hollis	Mr. Monies	For a Cabriolet	
—	Morris Martin	Lord Falmouth	ditto	
—	Thomas Brewster	Mr. Bainsbridge	ditto	
—	Joseph Jacobs	General Leigh	ditto	
—	James Whitcomb	Mr. O'Reilly	ditto	
—	Archibald Caddell	Marquis Conyngham	ditto	
—	J. Hard	Miss Cartwright	ditto	
—	Robert Eaves	Mr. Dine	ditto	
1829:	John Youard	Mr. Youard	ditto	
—	Samuel Stear	Mrs. George Banks	ditto	
—	John Cook	Lord Strathmore	ditto	
—	Edward King	Duke of Clarence	ditto	No Vacancy.
1827: 16 October	W. B. Clark	Referred from the Treasury	For 25 Cabriolets	
16 November	George Shillibeer	ditto	For 19 ditto	
23 November	George Moravia	ditto	For 20 ditto	
21 December	William Fawcett	ditto	For 3 ditto	
1828: 7 March	John Damm	ditto	For 50 ditto	
1830: 6 May	Joseph Tillett	W. Smith, esq. M. P.	Several Cabriolets	
	Number of Applications for Cabriolets refused		150	
1828: 15 February	Martin Tucker	Referred from the Treasury	For 30 Carriages with four wheels and one horse	
—	George Morton	ditto	For several ditto	No legal authority for licensing them.
3 April	Abraham Van Oven	ditto	For 25 ditto	
5 May	William Walker	ditto	For 100 ditto	
13 June	William Gye, esq. M.P.	ditto	For 300 ditto	
	Number of Applications for One-horse Four-wheeled Carriages refused		455	

Hackney Coach Office, 8th June 1830.

Edward Jesse,
Thos Marrable,
Edward Gwatkin,
Commissioners.

Despite the clause in the act of 1831 to the effect that only the ancient coachmen and the widows of former coachmen were to be licensed until January 1833, Shillibeer did gain his cab licences and operated them from stables in Penton Street, Islington, on the site where the Public Carriage Office now stands. On March 27th 1832, George Shillibeer and twenty one other cab proprietors petitioned the Court of Aldermen in the City of London thus:-

"We pray for extra cab ranks in Fleet Street, Cheapside Cornhill and the Bank, which are at present occupied by your petitioners new but natural enemies, the omnibus, to the great injury and entire exclusion of your old and tried friend the hackney carriage". (18)

George Shillibeer's sojourn in the omnibus trade had indeed been very brief.

It was not only pressure from people wishing to obtain hackney carriage licences that spelled the end of the Hackney Coach Office. London was growing and the restrictive legislation which prevented the increase of hackney coaches and cabs and which curtailed the activities of the short stage coach and the omnibus had to end. New roads with better surfaces were under construction and at the same time more roads were being freed from tolls, which had a restrictive effect upon transport for the movement of passengers and goods. The turnpike gates and toll bars became more and more irksome to an ever increasing population and from about 1825 the movement for their abolition grew, especially in London.

A toll reform committee was organised and a campaign begun to persuade Parliament to free the roads from tolls. Some notable early successes were to have considerable impact, as we have seen with Shillibeer's omnibus using the 'New Road'. The Hollywell Gate in Shoreditch was the first to go along with the gate at the 'Yorkshire Stingo' in Marylebone Road in 1829. These were followed by the toll gates in Kentish Town, Newington Causeway, Camberwell, Kennington and Lambeth in 1830. Three new bridges across the Thames had been built between 1816 and 1819. They were Vauxhall, Waterloo and Southwark, including the widening of many approach roads from the north and south giving easier access to the bridges. Unfortunately, all these bridges carried a toll of 1/2d for pedestrians which meant that a labourer living south of the river would have been required to pay the equivalent of a weeks wages for the right to walk to work, during the course of a year.

Southwark Bridge was the first bridge to be freed of a toll charge when the City Corporation purchased the bridge for £218,868 in February 1868 and gave it to the public "free of tolls for ever". Lambeth, Vauxhall, Chelsea, Albert and Battersea Bridges were made free of tolls in May 1879. The opening of these bridges was marked by a ceremony, held on Queen Victoria's birthday, by the Prince and Princess of Wales, when they drove across Lambeth Bridge "festooned with garlands, flags and streamers". (19)

From January 5th 1832 short stage coaches and omnibuses were able to pick up and set down passengers anywhere along the route they were licensed for. Bishopsgate and Gracechurch Street were still the main departure points but these slow and rather cumbersome vehicles were gradually to be replaced by omnibuses, smaller than those used by Shillibeer, carrying up to fifteen passengers and drawn by two horses.

Competition was extremely fierce. Shillibeer himself was made bankrupt and his partner, William Norton committed suicide following his heavy financial losses. There were many omnibuses and it was a cut throat business. These were the very people who had clamoured for an end to the hackney coach monopoly because they said, "it stifled competition". Soon, they themselves were trying to stifle competition and were "curbing it amongst themselves on London's busiest routes". The 1831 act had ended one monopoly only to sow the seeds of another, even larger monopoly.

Within the space of a few years the transition from short stage to the omnibus had been rapid and the coaches had given way almost entirely to the omnibus design. In 1825 there were 418 short stage coaches departing from the City of London, by 1834 following the end of the hackney coach monopoly there were 293 short stage coaches and 232 omnibuses. It would appear that the omnibus was replacing the short stage but not adding greatly to the number of vehicles. By 1839 there was a dramatic change with 825 vehicles comprising 625 omnibuses and 200 short stage coaches. T. Ives of Ealing, previously mentioned as driving his own coach, now owned two coaches and his father, James Ives owned one. R. Blore & Co. was the largest single owner with thirty omnibuses and there were 262 individual owners of omnibuses and short stage coaches. (20)

By the middle of the 19th century, the growth of the omnibus trade in London had attracted the attention of the Paris Omnibus Company and in conjunction with some of the larger proprietors in London the Compagnie Generale des Omnibus des Londres was formed. This company made available huge investments of French capital in December 1855 and the London General Omnibus Company was registered in London. The buying out of those London proprietors willing to sell did not start until January 1856, when they received £510 for each omnibus sold.

The former London proprietors who included MacNamara, and Wilson who owned the 'Favourite' omnibuses, in company with several others, after selling out for huge profits, were appointed to run the L.G.O.C. and these former proprietors now found themselves running the largest omnibus undertaking in the world. The French shareholders were under the impression that the operation in London would be run as in Paris, where the French company had been granted a monopoly by Napolean III to run for thirty years. There was to be no monopoly for the L.G.O.C. until well into the 20th century and in fact the French company met considerable opposition from such people as Thomas Tilling and Ball Bros. who refused to come to terms with the L.G.O.C. (21)

With the formation of the L.G.O.C. in 1856, London saw the beginning of a monopoly that was to give the capital the finest transport system of any capital city in the world. Though as we look at London's bus service today it is difficult to imagine that it has grown from such humble origins as to be part of a fraud set up by corrupt Hackney Coach Commissioners in 1695 and later developing from London's licensed hackney carriage trade.

References used in Chapter Eight

1. House of Commons Journals, Vol. 11 p. 261.
2. Broadsheet 11.67. (GRL)
3. Review of London, Berridge. (GRL)
4. New Statesman, March 21st 1925.
5. 4th George III C36.
6. 12th George III C49.
7. London Life in the 18th Century. Appendix C. D.M. George. (GRL)
8. Ibid.
9. Ibid and The (Inner London) Register Generals Weekly Returns con tained in the History of London (Supplement) J. Loftie. (GRL)
10. Number of Short Stage Coach Stands, PAR Book 4, pp. 91/93. (GRO)
11. Pigots Land and Commercial Directory and Edwardes Companion from London to Brightelmstone 1801. Minet Library, Lambeth.
12. Parliamentary Papers 1837, Vol. 20 pp. 2/21. (HOLRO)
13. Reports and Returns (Hackney Coaches) 1819-31 (26) (GRL)
14. Ibid. See appendix.
15. DNB Vol. 8 p. 851. (GRL)
16. British Prime Ministers, Walpole to Wilson. G. Pike. (GRL)
17. For reference to Green and Saggers see House of Commons Journals, Vol. 85 p. 346. and to George Shillibeer see - Reports and Returns (Hackney Coaches) 1819-31 (26) appendix 18. (GRL)
18. Rep. 236 folio 377 (GRO)
19. Turnpikes and Tollbars Vol 2. H. Searle. (GRL)
20. See History of London Transport, Barker & Robbins, Vol. 1. (GRL) and Robson's London Directory 1839 (19th Edition) (GRL)
21. For a detailed account of London Transport see History of London Transport, Vols. 1/2 (GRL)

Chapter Nine

From Hackney Coach Office To Public Carriage Office

From 1662 until 1831, apart from the years 1679 to 1683, all London's public road passenger vehicles were controlled by the Commissioners at the Hackney Coach Office. Beginning with hackney coaches in 1662, the licensing of stage coaches was added in 1695. (1) Sedan chairs followed in 1711 and the short stage coach service, as we have seen, was an extension of the service provided by the hackney coaches. Despite the overall control by the Coach Office there is no evidence to suggest, that any effort was made to plan or make provision for an integrated passenger transport system. Each group under the control of the Hackney Coach Office made its own way, often in conflict with the other groups.

The division of transport necessary for an integrated system were all there. Sedan chairs for short journeys in the centre, the hackney coach as a short haul vehicle for journeys in the centre and up to their compellable limit, which varied from six to ten miles at different times of the year. The short stage coaches performed the journeys to and from towns and villages within generally a radius of twenty miles from London and the long stage coaches to towns and cities beyond the area of the short stage coach operation. We cannot be too critical because now, more than 300 years later, we still have no fully integrated passenger transport system.

The choice of the name 'Commissioner' was not coincidental, as all those men appointed by the administration to run government departments were known as Commissioners. During the latter half of the 17th century Improvement Commissioners were set up in various towns and they were known as Police Commissioners. The first of these were those appointed to control London's hackney coaches. Their office was in Scotland Yard and they became known as the Commissioners of Scotland Yard. (2)

Scotland Yard was so called because it was the former site of a palace for the reception of the kings and queens of Scotland when visiting London. Margaret, Queen of Scotland, sister of Henry VIII and the widow of James I of Scotland, was the last royal personage to occupy the palace. The buildings were eventually absorbed into the Palace of Whitehall until its destruction by fire in 1695.

Scotland Yard was divided into two parts at this time, the inner yard was situated where Whitehall Place is now and the outer yard, where Great Scotland Yard now runs. The two Scotland Yards were separated by a row of buildings and the Hackney Coach Office was located in the outer yard in premises that were owned by a Mr. Mackbury, at a rent of £50 per annum.

The Hackney Coach Office remained in Scotland Yard until 1694 when it moved to Surrey Street off the Strand. A Royal Warrant was issued in June 1694; "To create and erect an office to be called the office of the Receiver of Hackney Coaches and to constitute John Hawkins in that office with a salary of £100 per annum". (3) John Hawkins held this office for a year, when he was replaced by Edward Wharton, Goldsmith, in 1695. The Hackney Coach Office was to occupy this site until it was destroyed by fire in 1771. Following the fire it was moved to Somerset House and in 1815 it moved back to Essex Street, only a few yards away from the former site.

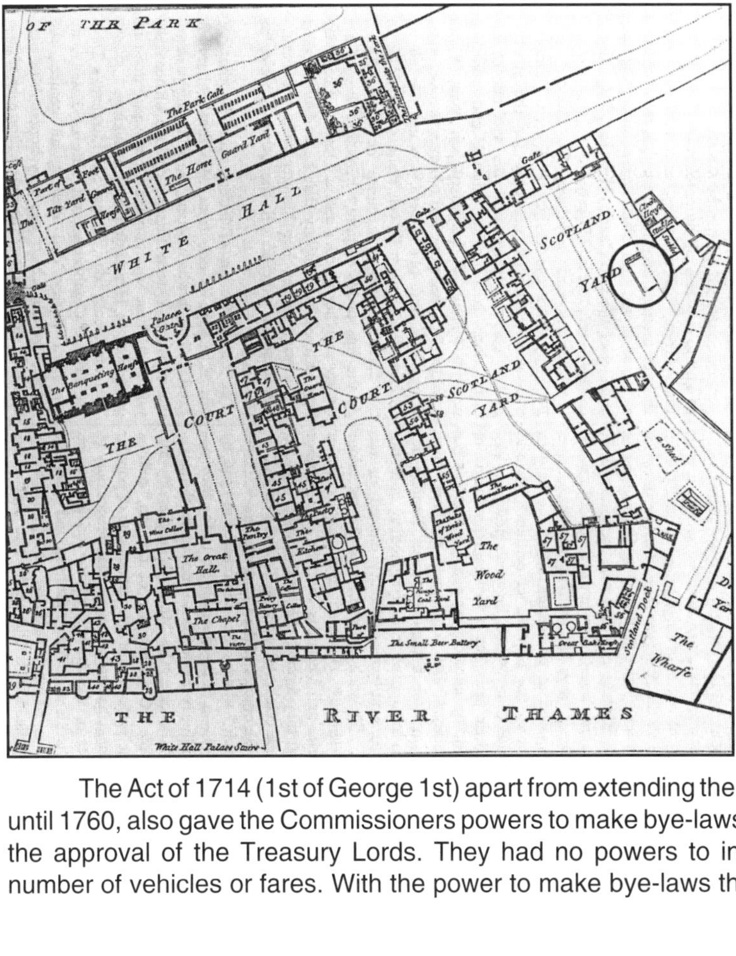

This map shows the Hackney Coach Office in the outer Scotland Yard (circled) standing in isolation, c. 1688.

The Act of 1714 (1st of George 1st) apart from extending the Act of 1711 until 1760, also gave the Commissioners powers to make bye-laws, subject to the approval of the Treasury Lords. They had no powers to increase the number of vehicles or fares. With the power to make bye-laws the Commissioners also had the power of enforcement, which, judging by the number of petitions to Parliament, they seemed to have carried out in an arbitrary fashion.

From a Broadsheet in the Guildhall Library we find that the coachmen were dealt with quite summarily by the Commissioners. In 1714 they convicted a Mr. Weaver, Mr. Mathews and a Mr. Tucker forty shillings each, on the evidence of a footboy, because they were unwilling to go from Aldgate to Mile End for nothing to fetch a fare. On another occasion they fined a Mr. Stokes 2/6d, though he maintained that the legal fare was 3/-. A driver of a Mr. Lucas was fined 10/- for a similar offence and Commissioner Charnock Heron told Mr. Lucas afterwards: "We sit here to punish who we please and not to dispense justice". (4) There was no right of appeal except to Parliament, hence the numerous petitions throughout the 17th, 18th and 19th centuries.

The bulk of the work carried out by the Hackney Coach Office was performed by the staff under the commissioners. In 1694 they numbered seven, viz, a clerk, a registrar, two messengers, two streetkeepers and a housekeeper. The streetkeepers duties consisted of carrying out spot checks on the coachmen and their vehicles. These duties are still carried out today by officers of the Public Carriage Office. In 1727 a James Cook who was appointed as a surveyor, had his duties defined as: "To take care of the Hackney Coach Office, to attend to the Commissioners on board days, to take in complaints against coachmen and Sedan chairmen, to give orders for new plates for those worn or lost and to measure disputed distances". (5) His salary of £40 per annum was enhanced with a measuring allowance of £20.

The total expenses of funding the Hackney Coach Office from 1694 to 1695 were £1,198, and its staff was constituted thus:-

Commissioners Gee, Ashurst, Villiers, Overbury and Killigrew at a salary of £100 per annum	£500.
Edward Wharton, Receiver General	£62.
Anthony Mackendale, surveyor and Housekeeper	£40.
Charles Bolton, clerk	£50.
George Eades, Michael Brown, messengers, at £30 each	£60.
Joseph Tomlinson, Richard Colton, streetkeepers	£50.
Office rent	£38.
Items. Coal, lighting, paper and books etc.	£398.

The duties of Anthony Mackendale the surveyor, varied considerably from those of James Cook who was appointed thirty years later. (6)

The first Hackney Coach Commissioners were appointed in 1662 under the Act of that year (14th Charles II C2). This Act was primarily concerned with the repair of roads and the construction of sewers, and the money raised from licensing hackney coaches in London was to be used for this purpose. In John

Evelyn's diary under the date of 14th May 1662, we find:-

> "To London, being chosen one of the Commissioners for reforming the buildings, wayes, streets and incumbrances and for regulating hackney coaches".

Little remains of any records of that time except that we know from an original licence issued to William Huggins in December 1678, that the commissioners at that time were Samuel Maidwell, Henry Prodger, Philip Burton, J. Mytton and Philip Bulstrode. These commissioners were located at Scotland Yard.

On 7th March 1676, a petition was presented to Parliament on behalf of: "Charles Taunton, Gilbert Jennings, Ambrose Neal and Henry Alder, on behalf of themselves and other licensed hackney coachmen, complaining of exactions and abuses committed by the present commissioners for licensing hackney coachmen". (7)

After some deliberation it was resolved by the House to appoint a committee who were to examine the complaints made against the commissioners. This committee included Sir Thomas Clarges, Sir John Birkenhead (the Rhyming Cavalier), and Sir Edmund Jennings. Their deliberations will never be known because their findings were destroyed in 1834, by the fire which consumed three quarters of the Palace of Westminster.

However, in the state papers for July 1676 there is a document concerning the appointment of new commissioners and that: "His majesty is pleased to have the commissions renewed and to have his own servants put in and people of good quality". (8) The new commissioners were those who appeared in the licence of William Huggins in 1678. Another document, in the British Museum headed: "The Case of the 400 Coachmen 1676", appears to be the petition presented to Parliament by the hackney coachmen. It appears from this petition that the commissioners were accused of depriving 16 coachmen of their licences and some of them had been licensed by Cromwell's Act of 1654.

This could possibly have been their crime! The commissioners had apparently decided that the best way to make "their £200 a year apiece", was to get rid of the Cromwellians and accept bribes from others who took over the licences. The rest of the British Museum document does seem to substantiate this. (9) It is perhaps significant that of the four men mentioned in the petition to Parliament, three of them, Jennings, Alder and Neale were still licensed coachmen in 1683. (10)

The duties of the Hackney Coach Commissioners were both of the revenue and the police. They licensed the owners and the vehicles and were accountable to the Treasury Lords for the revenue raised. Drivers were not licensed until 1843. One of the conditions laid down by the Treasury Lords was:-

> "You are at the charge of the 400 licensed coachmen to prosecute all offenders driving a hackney coach without licence contrary to the King's proclamation" (11)

Between 1714 and 1831 the commissioners obtained a degree of autonomy seldom found in other government departments. Yet, despite this autonomy Parliament became more and more involved, passing a total of 21 Acts between 1760 and 1831, ranging from the abolition of a coach stand in Bond Street, to an Act of 24 pages setting up a ticket system, designed to prevent drivers from defrauding their proprietors. (12) The contents of these Acts could easily have been dealt with by bye-laws drawn up by the commissioners, instead of Parliament spending so much time on purely domestic issues.

The autonomy of the commissioners went so far as to direct, by the Act of 54th George III C147, the drivers earnings, based on a commission rate of 16.5 per cent. The Act was repealed the following year, as we shall see, and the commission method of fixing drivers' earnings was not introduced again until taximeters were made compulsory in 1907.

From 1732 until 1831 two families were to figure prominently in the composition of the Hackney Coach office. These were the Cappers and the Quaifes, the former as Commissioners and the latter family as employees of the coach office. Thomas Quaife was appointed surveyor in 1800 and begun his family's connection with the coach office which was to last until at least 1833.

In 1805 he was working as a Streetkeeper at a reduced salary and his son James Quaife was appointed as surveyor. By 1815 James Quaife had become chief clerk and his son Thomas was employed as a Streetkeeper. By 1830 five members of the family were employed in one capacity or another, Sarah Quaife being the housekeeper, a position she kept until the Hackney Coach Office was abolished in 1833. (13)

By far the most illustrious of all the Commissioners was Francis Capper, who was appointed as a commissioner in 1732. Born in Eagle Street, Holborn in 1698, he became a student of the Inner Temple in 1714 and entered Corpus Christi, Cambridge in 1716. In 1721 he was admitted to Lincoln's Inn and called to the Bar of the Inner Temple in 1722.

His marriage to Mary Bennett in 1725 at Ely House Chapel was performed by his cousin the Reverend Edward Capper. Five children resulted from this union, of which, the second child Richard was to follow in his father's footsteps as a Hackney Coach Commissioner in 1761.

Francis Capper was eminently successful as a lawyer and his rise to wealth and position was rapid. First came his appointment to the Board of Hackney Commissioners in 1732, in 1743 he was made Deputy Keeper of Enfield Chase and invited to the Bench of Lincoln's Inn in the same year. In

1749 he was appointed Master of the Walks and this was followed in 1750 and 1752 as Master of the Library and Dean of the Chapel. His crowning success was his appointment in 1753 to the position of Treasurer of Lincoln's Inn.

Francis Capper, probably the most illustrious of all Hackney Commisioners, 1732. His family figured prominantly in the development of the Hackney Coach Office.

During his lifetime he owned the Manors of Bushey and Garston in Hertfordshire, farms at Hornsey, Totteridge and Islington and property around Lincoln's Inn. Of his five children only Richard survived. The others Elizabeth, Francis, Mary and James died as infants.

His son Richard Capper was born at Bushey in 1730 and was educated at Eton and Balliol College and he was called to the Bar in 1752. Thereafter he followed in his father's footsteps, holding all the positions held by his father. He was appointed to the Board of Hackney Commissioners in 1761 and became Treasurer of Lincoln's Inn in 1788. In 1759 he married Mary, daughter of the Lord Chief Baron, Robert Ord of Lincoln's Inn, by special licence of the Bishop of London at St. Georges, Queen Street, Holborn. He died in 1801. (14)

The cost of running the Hackney Coach Office over the years rose disproportionately, which can best be described as follows:

1695 .... £1,198.0.0.
1730 .... £1,595.0.0.
1745 .... £1,677.0.0.
1809 .... £2,776.0.0.
1822 .... £4,099.0.0.

The difference between the years 1809 and 1822 represents an increase of 48 per cent, on the other hand receipts from taxation had dropped from £28,753 in 1809 to £26,248 in 1822. (15) The major reason for the drop in taxation was the introduction in 1814 of the 'chariot', a one horse, two wheeled cabriolet. These soon became very popular because of their mobility, performing some journeys in half the time taken by a hackney coach. At first only two hundred were licensed but the following year in 1815 another two hundred were introduced. As these chariots were included in the total number of hackney carriages licensed, which then stood at 1,200, their arrival was at the expense of a similar number of hackney coaches which carried a higher rate of taxation.

Taxation on hackney coaches in London had made a significant contribution to the revenue. It also paved the way for taxation on private vehicles. By 1754 there were 4,255 four wheeled and 2,090 two wheeled carriages in London, all privately owned. Each four wheeled carriage paid £4 per annum tax and the two wheeled carriages paid £2, so that the total duty for that year from private vehicles was £22,838. Taken all over the country the revenue raised from taxing private carriages must have been considerable, even Barnstable in Devon contributed £1,204 in 1754 while that for York in the same year was £892. (16)

By 1815 the staff at the Hackney Coach Office had increased to 15, including the five commissioners and a new position of inspector had been created. By this time the coach office was developing along the lines which we are familiar with today. There were regular street inspections of coaches and a form of stop note was issued. One such note was issued to "Mary Roberts, Licence No. 48 (owner) for coach with a bad outside appearance and dirty". On the same day George Hunter, with licence No. 29 (owner) was also issued with a stop note for, "A coach with a bad roof and wheels". (17)

In 1829 the Duke of Wellington, then Prime Minister, appointed a Parliamentary Committee of Inquiry, to investigate the alleged monopoly enjoyed by London's hackney coachmen. It was said that the current legislation was preventing the growth of the omnibus trade and that influential people, such as Frederick Gye, MP for Chippenham in Wiltshire and a very good friend of the Duke of Wellington, were being denied hackney coach licences because of the strictly enforced limitation.

The committee's recommendation that the Hackney Coach Office should be abolished was accepted and after an existence of 170 years it came to end on 31 December 1832. From 1 January 1833 limitation was ended and the sole right of hackney coaches to pick up and set down passengers in the Area of the Bills of Mortality was also ended. The way was now open for the growth of the omnibus trade. (18)

In 1833 the duties of the Hackney Coach Office were taken over by the

Stamp Office. In 1838 the Home Secretary delegated overall control to the Registrar of Metropolitan Carriages, a position newly created. This position was offered at first to Daniel Whittle Harvey, who was at that time Member of Parliament for Southwark, in South London. The office of the new Registrar was 22 John Adam Street, off the Strand and it was from this office on August 15th, 1838, that Harvey wrote to Lord John Russell who was then Home Secretary, expressing reservations about the position. He felt that he would have to resign his seat in Parliament if he accepted any amolument under the crown, saying: "I cannot reconcile the position and remuneration of office to being disqualified from representing the Borough of Southwark, or any other large section of people, in Parliament". (19)

The government under Lord Melbourne had baited the hook but Harvey was not biting. Daniel Harvey was a thorn in the side of the government, he was a prominent advocate of the claims of the Dissenters and had for some time been recognised as the head of the radical party. It was in an effort to be rid of Harvey that induced the Prime Minister to offer Harvey the position of Registrar, in the full knowledge that if he accepted he would have to resign his seat in Parliament. (20) Harvey was waiting for bigger bait and his letter of resignation from the position of Registrar was sent to Lord Russell on January 30th, 1839.

Daniel Whittle Harvey can best be remembered for two reasons. In 1822 he founded the Sunday Times newspaper and having built it up to a good circulation, he sold it for a handsome profit. He was also the first City of London Police Commissioner. By an Act of Parliament in 1839, the Metropolitan Police regulations were extended to the City of London and Harvey had been chosen as the first Commissioner before the Act was passed. This time the government, still under Lord Melbourne, were taking no chances for a special clause was inserted in the Act, making it impossible for a Commissioner of Police to be elected to Parliament while still in office. Harvey now decided that the bait was large enough for he readily accepted the position offered to him.

The London Hackney Carriage Act of 1843 placed London's hackney carriages entirely under the control of the Commissioner of Police. Until then only the proprietors had been licensed but under the 1843 Act the drivers of cabs, buses and the conductors were all licensed. All three were required to wear a metal badge which carried their licence number. These badges were to be worn at all times during their employment or when appearing in a court of law, either as a witness or when they themselves were the subject of prosecution. The Public Carriage Office was also established in 1843 and until the end of the 1939-1945 war, this office was to feature prominently within the Metropolitan Police.

The birth of the Metropolitan Police Traffic Department had its obscure beginning in the London Hackney Carriage Act of 1843. The Commissioner of Police did not take control of all aspects of London's hackney carriage trade in one fell swoop, it was more of a piecemeal takeover. In 1850, there were two police commissioners appointed, Sir Richard Mayne and Captain William Hay. In that year the Home Secretary delegated the duties of the Registrar of Metropolitan Public Carriages to Sir Richard Mayne. His duties appear to have been fairly onerous for on February 24th, 1851, he applied for an increase in his allowance saying: "The granting of licences imposes upon me considerable labour ..... it prevents me from going out of town, even for a short time". (21)

The Metropolitan Police Public Carriage Office in Scotland Yard dating from 1843. Ironically almost on the site of the original Hackney Coach Office of 1662.

The Cruelty to Animals Act of 1849 (12 & 13 Vict. C 92) required Public Carriage Officers to have an intimate knowledge of horses, a point often disputed by proprietors. They were required to diagnose illness and disease in horses, in addition to the knowledge required for carriage inspections, in order to issue the necessary certificate of fitness. The penalties for working unfit horses were severe and there were often disputes between drivers, the proprietors and the inspectors as to whether a horse was fit or not.

Doubts have often been expressed as to when the knowledge of London examinations commenced. It now seems that an early form of knowledge was implemented in 1851 by Sir Richard Mayne. This was confirmed by John Cochran, a cab proprietor and driver, at a meeting of the Society of Arts on June 11th 1869. This meeting had been called to discuss proposals the Society wished to place before the Home Secretary, Mr. H. Bruce, for inclusion in the Bill shortly to be introduced in the House of Commons and which in November became the Metropolitan Public Carriage Act 1869 (32 & 33 Vict. C115). John Cochran also stated that the examination was "hard enough already", though he did not object to the knowledge examinations being: "As strict as possible for drivers for an area five miles around Charing Cross". (22)

The 1869 Act gave the Commissioner of Police additional responsibilities with regard to hackney carriages and omnibuses. New duties were imposed upon the Commissioner:-

1. How the carriages were to be fitted and furnished and the regulation of the number of persons to be carried.
2. The fixing of cab ranks.
3. The fixing of fares.
4. The safe custody of property found in the vehicles.

A new dimension of responsibility occurred when in 1897 the first horseless cab appeared in London, the Bersey electric powered vehicle. In 1903 the first internal combustion engine cab appeared, the Prunel, followed in 1905/6/7 by other makes such a Vauxhalls, Fords, Heralds and Rationals. The late arrival of motor cabs in London, compared with other capitals such as Paris and Berlin was because the speed limit of 12 mph was not increased to 20mph until 1903. By 1906, the introduction of 500 Renault taxis were imminent, when new 'Conditions of Fitness' for motor cabs were introduced. In 1903 there were over 11,000 horse drawn cabs licensed in London, 7,449 Hansom cabs and 3,905 four wheeled 'Growlers'. Within ten years the Hansoms were reduced to 386 and there were 1,547 'Growlers'. (23) These facts alone show the massive changes which had to be undertaken by the Public Carriage Office.

Following the passing of the 1903 Motor Car Act, a Royal Commission was appointed. It's main recommendation was: "That a Traffic Advisory Board should be set up. Such a board would enable traffic matters to be considered as a whole". This part of the report was not acted upon, but in 1909 under the Police Act of that year, a fourth Assistant Commissioner was appointed, redistributing the ACs duties in traffic matters.

That which affected the Public Carriage Office was headed Civil

Business. This included a responsibility for the operation and control of the Public Carriage Office and the Lost Property Office. The head of the department was known as Assistant Commissioner, Civil Business, AC"B". The new department was to be responsible to Assistant Commissioner 'B', Mr. Frank Elliot and it came under the control of Mr. Suffield Mylius, a civil staff member and Superintendent Arthur Bassom, who was in charge of the Public Carriage Office, designated as B3. It was administered from the 'Bungalow' at Scotland Yard, a small building detached from the main building. A Chief Inspector who was also attached to HQ was responsible to Superintendent Bassom for the supervision and efficient operation of the twelve passing stations.

The Hackney Carriage Office, adjacent to Scotland Yard from which the trade was administered. The cabriolet shown was a special vehicle used just for driving tests, c. 1897.

The HQ staff consisted of four inspectors, eleven clerk serjeants, fourteen assistant clerk serjeants and sixteen assistant clerk constables, under the immediate command of a sub-divisional Inspector. Their duties included the knowledge of London examinations, applications for examinations, vehicle licences, mechanical unfitness, taximeter fittings, drivers (taxi and bus) and bus conductors licences, summonses, street accidents, omnibus schedules, fare tables and the photographing of applicants for licences. The Public Carriage Office kept the register of all foreign cars temporarily in use in England.

For the purposes of administration the Metropolitan Police area was, at that time, divided into twelve areas, each of which had a 'passing station'. These were located at Rochester Row, Hunter Street, Harrow Road, North West Fulham, Paddenswick Road, Bow, Camberwell, Peckham, Brixton, Kentish Town, Richmond and Golders Green. Apart from dealing with the day to day matters of licensing, they were also responsible for traffic conditions in their respective areas.

Assisting the 'passing stations' in their work were a number of sergeants who were divided into two categories, one dealing with technical matters and the 'Conditions of Fitness' and the other dealing with enquiries connected with drivers, conductors, proprietors, licences and lost property.

The sergeants could gain entry to the Public Carriage Office without having specialist knowledge. Promotion to the rank of inspector within the branch could not be achieved without obtaining either a certificate issued by the approved Polytechnics, in motor engineering and construction, or a certificate from the City and Guilds of London examinations. Having passed the technical examinations, it did not automatically qualify a serjeant for promotion, as he still required the Assistant Commissioner's approval before he could be made an inspector.

The early 1920's still found traffic in and around the West End in a chaotic state and ever increasing demands were made on the Public Carriage Office branch B3, to deal with congestion and its regulation. The situation was aggravated by the so called 'pirate' buses, cruising the London General Omnibus Company's more profitable routes. This general struggle for more trade, to the detriment of the traffic flow, was not helped by the absence of stopping places for buses, allowing passengers to be picked up and set down at will. Cruising cabs were also blamed for causing some of the congestion. Although it was recognised that cabs cruising looking for passengers was caused by insufficient cab ranks, very little was done to increase the number of ranks until the mid 1930s.

One of the first tasks of the Public Carriage Office B3 branch was to fix stopping places for buses and increasingly up to 1933 to place restrictions on empty cabs plying for hire. This required legislation known as the Cruising Cab Orders, a source of constant annoyance to the London cab trade. In 1923 the Commissioner of Police announced the appointment of Superintendent Bassom to act as Director of Traffic Services, to advise on remedial measures connected with the movement of traffic.

In 1924 the London Traffic Act was passed, it was to have a profound effect on all the bodies having an interest in the problems of London's traffic. Under the Act, a committee known as the London and Home Counties Traffic Advisory Committee was set up, under the chairmanship of Lord Ashfield, then chairman of the London General Omnibus Company. It was this committee that was responsible for the abolition of 'pirate' buses by 1933 and for the Cruising Cab Regulations, enforced by the Public Carriage Office, which curtailed the activity of London's taxis, in favour of the L.G.O.C. until the outbreak of war in 1939.

In 1926 Superintendent Bassom died. Although his loss was keenly felt, he had, during the five and a half years with the Public Carriage Office B3 Department, more than played his part. He had however lived to reap some of the reward due to him for his untiring work. In addition to receiving the OBE and the KPM, he was also awarded the Road Transport (Passenger) Gold Medal by the Institute of Transport, just two months before he died. No doubt as a mark of respect, it was decided not to fill his position after his death and his duties were absorbed by AC'B; Mr. Frank Elliot.

The considerable growth in traffic and the introduction of motor patrol cars in 1930, resulted in an increase in work carried out by the police, placing an ever increasing burden on the staff of the Public Carriage Office, who then numbered 126 police officers. The passing of the London Passenger Transport Act in 1933, led to a complete revision of the work carried out by the Public Carriage Office. The duties relating to Public Passenger vehicles was transferred to the Traffic Commissioners and they became responsible for the licensing of buses, trams, coaches and trolley buses, which at that time number 10,507 vehicles. When the Public Carriage Office took over in 1870, there were, excluding cabs, only 1,268 public passenger vehicles.

At the same time the opportunity was taken to streamline the Public Carriage Office. One effect of the reallocation of work and the revision of the Public Carriage Office, was reduction in the number of staff and 37 police officers were returned to normal duties. The licensing of bus drivers and conductors still remained the responsibility of the Public Carriage Office until 1984 when that duty too was transferred to the Traffic Commissioners.

Two years after the newly streamlined Public Carriage Office could feel proud at what had been achieved with 37 fewer staff. During 1935, 18,545 bus drivers and 16,679 conductors had been licensed and 11,587 taxi drivers. Of the latter group 20 were horse cab drivers and three of those still drove Hansom cabs. A total of 438 applicants passed the knowledge of London test, compared with 310 in 1934.

1935 was a year of several firsts for the London cab trade. Previously the drivers licence had been renewed annually, but in 1935 licences were issued for a period of three years, which is still the case. The Suburban knowledge commenced in 1937 and the drivers with this restricted form of licence were issued with a yellow badge.

A new type of chassis was also approved and eight body designs were certified as 'types' in connection with the new chassis. Some of these bodies were streamlined and incorporated special ventilated window, a full length driver's door, concealed return indicators and other up to date features. In order to assist the public to identify unhired cabs, a specially illuminated sign was fixed to the front of the top canopy. The enamelled fare plate formerly displayed inside the cab was replaced by a fare table contained in a glass frame.

Before 1885 the Public Carriage Office of the Metropolitan Police was located at 4 Whitehall Place, then in that year the famous building known the world over as Scotland Yard was built and some 2,500 tons of granite was used in its construction. All of this granite was quarried and dressed by prisoners at Dartmoor: "An economic arrangement somewhat suggestive of the manner in which the Pyramids were built". Here the Public Carriage Office remained until 1927, when, as a result of the expansion we have seen, a new police building was erected at 109 Lambeth Road (dungeon as well!). On October 3rd 1966 the Public Carriage Office moved to 15 Penton Street, Islington, the former site of the stables and yard where George Shillibeer had moved from Bury Street, Bloomsbury, to run a fleet of hackney carriages in 1832. (24)

Despite the deplorable drop in standards generally in the post war period, the standard set by 300 years of continual licensing have always been kept. The London cab trade would not have it any other way. The Public Carriage Office is a unique institution and most probably there is no other body in the world quite like it. Perhaps it is not generally realised that though licensing of London's hackney carriages commenced in 1654, since May 1694 licensing by Parliament has been continuous. Long may it be so. (25)

References used in Chapter Nine

1. 5th/6th William & Mary 1695 C22. GRL.
2. Scotland Yard. J. Moylan, GRL.
3. Calendar of Treasury Books Vol.X. Pt.3 p 601. PRO.
4. Broadsheet 11.75 GRL.
5. Calendar of Treasury Books Vol.X. Pts.2/3, pp 1137, 1195, 1223, 1320
6. For details of HCO costs till 1822 see Calendars of Treas. Papers (Misc) Expired Commissions; Hackney Coaches etc. PRO
7. House of Commons Journals, March 30th, 1662, HOLRO.
8. State Papers Domestic July 1676.
9 British Museum 1865 CM 28.
10. Misc. MSS 213. gro.
11. Calendar of Treasury Books, Vol.3 PT.3.pp 1550/1/2. PRO.
12. 54th George 111 C147. GRL.
13. Appendix Nos. 5/6, The Establishment of the Hackney Coach Office. SC(HCO) 1830 R&R Vol.26 No.1.GRL
14. The facts concerning Francis Capper and his son Richard are from the private papers of Mr. I Capper, London SW1
15. Treasury Papers (Misc) Expired Commissions, Hackney Coaches

etc. PRO.

16. (Treasury Papers) Registers, plates etc. No. 1. PRO.
17. Reports & Returns (Hackney Coaches) 1819-31 GRL.
18. Ibid.
19. Extract from a letter to Lord John Russell from DW Harvey House of Commons Session Papers, Vol.9. HOLRO.
20. DNB. Vol.9. GRL.
21. PCO Records.
22. Journal of the Society of Arts June 11 1869. pp 576/580.GRL.
23. See Taxicabs - A Photographic History by Philip Warren & Malcolm Linskey 1976. GRL.
24. Reportories of the Court of Aldermen 236 folio 377. a petition from George Shillibeer.
25. Details contained in this chapter from 1843, unless otherwise stated, are drawn from Acts of Parliament referred to in the text; An Abstract of Laws Relating to Proprietors, Drivers and Con ductors of Public Carriages within the Metropolitan Police District and the City of London and its Liberties. 1910. The History of the Traffic Department of the Metropolitan Police 1969 by Chief Inspector K. Rivers, in the possession of the author. Metropoli tan Police Reports 1935/6. Departmental Committee on Motor Cabs - Reports and Minutes of Evidence 1911. GRL. And various documents in the possession of the author.

Chapter Ten

"The Hansom cab is the Gondola of London" *Disraeli.*

Ever since 1853 the design and construction of public carriage vehicles in London have been governed by strict Conditions of Fitness, laid down by the Commissioner of Police, based on the advice of technical committees of civilian experts. Formerly and up to 1945 these conditions applied to London's buses, horse drawn and mechanically propelled. Today, the Commissioner's responsibilities extend only to London's taxicabs. This principle of assuring that passenger carrying vehicles had to be specially designed and constructed for the safety of the public has it's roots set centuries ago.

In 1555, rules for the construction of boats used by the Thames Watermen, stipulated that all wherries were required to be 12 feet six inches long and 4 feet 6 inches broad amidships. In the 17th century similar construction regulations were introduced for hackney carriages. For example in 1678, a licence, number 321, granted to William Huggins stated, "no gelding, horse or mare to be used in the coach under the size of fourteen hands high, according to the standard; the perch of which coach is to be ten foot long and to have cross braces before and not to be braced down, but is to hang upon a level and not with the hinder part being higher than the former part thereof". These conditions were restated in 1697 by the Hackney Coach Commissioners and again in 1732. (1)

Between 1625 and 1700, seventeen patents were taken out which sought to improve the safety and design of coaches. In January 1625, Edward Knappe declared, "divers newe waies and means by which coaches and other carriages maie be made to last and contynue longer to goe and be kept mayntenyed with less charge". He was proposing that the axles should be made of "iron, brass or steele". He also described what possibly could have been the first handbrake, "the coach is fitted with a device wherebye the coachman, without comyng from his box shall in every descent of grounde keepe the hinder wheels from turnynge soe as the carriage shall goe downhill with noe more hurt or danger to the passenger or horses than in playne grounde". (2)

The advancement of ideas was taking shape in the minds of inventors. They had the basic structure of a box on wheels, now they were setting out to improve it. Springing was of paramount importance and so were other safety factors such as the release catch if the horses became uncontrollable, invented by Edward, the Marquis of Worcester. In 1664 the forerunner of the hansom cab, probably one of the safest horse drawn vehicles ever built for carrying passengers, can be seen in a patent taken out by one Abraham Hill of "a coach with two wheels upon one axletree, haveing a seate or chaire sett high upon two shafts or perches, one end resting on the axletree, the other upon the horse". (3) Though this particular vehicle appears not to have been built.

By the turn of the 19th century coachbuilders were looking at ways of building lighter vehicles, capable of being drawn by one horse yet light enough to combine a greater speed with safety. The chariots introduced into London in 1814 and 1815 were a step in the right direction but a big improvement came with the construction of twelve cabriolets by a Mr. David Davies and shared between three London proprietors in June 1824. Painted yellow and black they were a distinct improvement on their predecessors, the chariots, and their shape quickly earned them the nickname of 'coffin' cabs. In a short while they became extremely popular, especially as they were a third of the normal fare. They have been immortalised in the following verse.

"In days of old when folks got tired,
a hackney coach or a chariot was hired;
but now along the streets they roll ye,
in a shay, with a cover, called a cabriolet".

The French name of cabriolet was quickly shortened to 'cab' and has remained with us ever since.

Hansom's original cab which is substantially different from the cab associated with his name, 1834.

The growing popularity of the new cabs alarmed the hackney coachmen. They jeered at them and prophesied that they would be short lived. They were soon to abandon this attitude and endeavoured to transfer their own hackney coach licences to the cabriolets. By 1832 the number of cabriolets had only reached 165. Two years later after the ending of the hackney coach monopoly the number of cabriolets had reached 800. (4) In 1832 a Mr. Edward Boulnois, the son of William Boulnois, a well known London cab proprietor, introduced a new cab onto the streets of London; two wheeled and closed in, the driver sat aloft in front. The door of this cab being in the rear, it presented some passengers with the opportunity of alighting before the journey's end. It quickly became known as the "bilker's cab" and needless to say it was to have a short life.

The removal of limitation in 1833 was to have a dramatic effect upon the future development of horse cabs and following the Boulnois cab came the first early Hansom. On December 3rd 1834, Joseph Hansom registered his Patent Safety Cab, a vehicle which was later to revolutionise passenger carrying vehicles plying for hire. (5) Prior to this, Hansom had been associated with a Dempster Hemmings of Hinckley in Leicestershire as a manager of Hemming's affairs, which included banking, coal-mining and landed estates. It was Hemmings who persuaded and most probably financed Hansom's project.

The main principle of Hansom's design was the cranked axle coupled with unusually high wheels, with the body slung low to the ground. This meant less wear and tear and fewer accidents. Hansom sold his rights in the cab for £10,000 but never received a penny of the money. In 1839 when the company ran into trouble they called Hansom in to manage it's affairs and after putting the company on it's feet, he received £300, which was all the money he ever earned for his work on the cab.

Forsaking the London cab scene, he turned to architecture in which profession he had been apprenticed and where he was to follow a distinguished career. Among the buildings he designed were Birmingham Town Hall, Plymouth Cathedral, the church of St. Francois de Sale in Boulougne and St. Walburgh's church in Preston, Lancashire, whose spire of 306 feet was at that time the tallest, built since the Reformation. Joseph Hansom died in London at 399 Fulham Road in June 1882 aged 79 and he is buried in the Catholic Church of St. Thomas of Canterbury, in Ryleston Road, Fulham. (It is a quirk of history that the Hansom cab carried his name, for certainly the vehicle which is common to most people as a Hansom cab, bears little resemblance to the cab which Hansom patented.)

Hansom's carriage was very similar to a carriage invented by Francis Moore a well known coachmaker who lived in Cheapside in the City of London in 1771. The wheels of which were eight feet high and the body, constructed of wood, was slung low, with the driver sitting on top in front. (7) It did bear a strong resemblance to the cab later patented by Hansom and which caused quite a stir when he drove it from Northampton to London in 1834. Like many other inventors, Francis Moore was before his time and some sixty five years later, his carriage, or something very much like it, turned up as Hansom's patent safety cab.

In 1836 the secretary of the Two Wheeled Cabriolet and Two Wheeled Carriage Company was John Chapman. He recognised the defects in Hansom's design and he made improvements to the vehicle approaching that which is familiar to us today. A patent was granted to Chapman and his backer Gillette, on December 31st, 1836. Chapman placed the drivers seat in it's now familiar position at the rear, the sliding window was introduced and the framework under the cab was constructed to rest on the ground when the cab tilted forward or backward. (8)

The company that owned Hansom's cab quickly purchased Chapman's and Gillette's patent and soon some fifty of the new Chapman Hansoms were out on the streets. Such was the success of Chapman's cab that other proprietors wanted them and soon, imitations almost identical to the real ones began to appear. To avoid any legal consequences they painted the words "not Hansom's patent safety cab" on the side in the belief that it would prevent prosecution. In this they were mistaken because the patent holders were determined to protect their rights. In every case taken the company were successful but because for the greater part, the losers were 'men of straw' they could not recover their damages, they were forced to stop litigation and as soon as they did, pirate owners dispensed with the word 'not'.

When the Hansom Cab Company took over Chapman's patent they still continued with the words "Hansoms Patent Safety Cab" painted on the side, so that the public could recognise that the cab belonged to the same company as the cab that Hansom had patented. Thus Hansom's fame should really have gone to Chapman. Few people could tell the difference between Chapman's cab and the many imitations, though the drivers could and they treated the pirates with contempt. They called them 'shofuls' a word of Jewish origins meaning counterfeit. Many Jewish drivers worked for the original company and they conferred this term on all vehicles which infringed Hansom's and Chapman's patents. The word 'shoful' eventually became the slang word for a Hansom cab and was used extensively during the 19th century.

At the same time the Chapman's cab appeared on the streets also saw the introduction of another type of carriage. Built by the same Mr. Davies, the builder of the first cabriolet in June 1824. Constructed to carry two passengers inside and one next to the driver, on a seat which projected from the body of the main carriage, which was closed in. Within a year or so Mr. Davies had made several improvements to this carriage, which was completely closed in with all the passengers sitting inside and at first it was known as 'the covered cab'. This was the vehicle which was to become known as the 'growler', whether because of the noise it's wheels made on the cobbled streets, or because of the disposition of the driver, is a matter for conjecture.

An early Victorian version of Chapman's "Hansom's Patent Safety Cab" later redesigned by the Forder Company, c. 1841.

It was this carriage that Lord Brougham was so pleased with and in 1840 he instructed his coachmaker, a Mr. Robinson of Mount Street, Mayfair, to build a similar carriage with some refinements, notably a shorter wheelbase with the driver's seat nearer to the body. Hence the 'Brougham', the earliest private four wheeled closed carriage to be drawn by a single horse. (9)

The Hansom cab and the 'growler', or to give it it's correct name, the Clarence, were to reign supreme in the London cab trade until they were ousted by the internal combustion engine. Before the dawning of that age, however, the Hansom was to undergo another change. The man responsible was Henry Forder of the Forder Cab Company, Wolverhampton. His alterations were to make the Hansom cab probably the finest horse drawn carriage in the world at that time, the cab to which Disraeli referred to as "the Gondola of London".

By far the most important of Forder's improvements was the re-introduction of the straight axle. This he achieved by cutting away the body of the cab under the passenger's seat at an angle of forty five degrees, sloping to the floor where the passenger's feet rested. He also raised the driver's seat so that the cabby sat some seven feet off the ground, his weight counterbalanced by the shafts, gave a perfectly balanced vehicle. In addition, as the weight was taken off the horse it was possible to attain a greater speed which, in certain conditions could be as high as 17 m.p.h.

Forder's improvements were the direct result of action taken by the Royal Society of Arts, under its chairman, Lord Henry Lennox M.P. In May 1869 the society sent a deputation to see the Home Secretary, Henry Bruce, to discuss certain aspects of the London cab trade. Lord Lennox told the Home Secretary:-

"The attention of the council has been drawn to the bad state of London's cabs during the exhibition in 1862. As the society had been responsible for the exhibition it felt some responsibility towards thousands of foreigners visiting London who had been the victims of a disgraceful cab system. In 1867 the council had passed a resolution urging the Home Secretary to bring in a Bill for regulating hackney carriages in London". (10)

The Home Secretary assured the delegation that the government was introducing a Bill in the current session of Parliament and that their points would be taken into account. The society was not content to let the matter rest there. Parliament could perhaps command a better cab system, but it could not command a better cab, so the society announced it's own plans in that direction.

Previously on July 2nd 1868, the society had decided to award it's gold and silver medals for various types of hackney carriages for two persons, open and enclosed and for the best hackney carriage for four persons, either open or closed or both. The response was not very fruitful and the offer was dropped. In 1872 they revived the idea after being told by cab proprietors that they were not willing to incur expense unless cash prizes were offered. The society withdrew it's medals offer and substituted cash prizes instead. They were £60 for the best improved cab of any description, £20 for the next best two and £10 for the next two. The conditions were that the cabs had to be ready for the exhibition at South Kensington in 1873 and that the judges must be satisfied that the cabs had been working on the streets of London for the previous three months though this was later reduced to one month.

In June 1873, the society announced the names of the judges. They were the Duke of Beaufort, Lord Arthur Somerset, Major General Earley Wilmot, Lord Alfred Churchill and Colonel Henderson, the Commissioner of Police. To give the judges some professional status they also included a coachbuilder, a cab proprietor and a cabdriver, all three were unnamed.

Sixteen different vehicles were entered but the judges could not find an outright winner. Therefore, they decided that four of the entries were worthy of sharing the prize money between them. They were C. Thorn of Norwich; Mr. Lambert of 66 Great Queen Street, Holborn; Forder & Co., of Wolverhampton; and Messrs. Quick and Mornington of 8 Netherwood Street, Kilburn. The following Saturday these four cabs were lined up at Marlborough House for inspection by the Prince of Wales. So impressed was he with Forder's cab that he ordered one from the company for his own use.

The Royal Society of Arts was pleased with the outcome of the exhibition and in 1874 they told members of the society "that the offer of prizes for improved cabs had attracted numerous competitors. The council believes that the competition had successfully directed attention to the subject and that an improved class of vehicles will result". Some twenty years later the society were to pride themselves with the fact that the Hansoms introduced by Forders had, with other improvements, proved to be the most popular vehicle ever used in the cab trade.

Hansom cabs being built at Messrs. Forder & Co works in Wolverhampton. The Forder cab became the most popular vehicle ever used by the cab trade, c. 1897.

In June 1875 the society announced details of a special exhibition which was to be held at Alexandra Palace. This time £200 was offered for the best cab and to find the driver with the longest employment, who had never been charged with cruelty, or being drunk, insolent or guilty of reckless driving; an impossible task if the columns of Punch are to be believed. Forders won this prize outright with the cab of the kind supplied to the Prince of Wales. (11)

As late as 1894 a Mr. Thrupp of Maida Vale in London, offered prizes for the best designed cab on four wheels, which was probably an attempt to do for the 'growlers' that which the Royal Society of Arts had done for the Hansom. They were to carry two or more passengers with luggage, the hood was required to fold and the driver had to sit in front. Durability, simplicity and economy of construction were all points to bear in mind. Thirty designs were received and they were exhibited at the Carriage Bazaar in Baker Street.

But it was too late. The age of the motor vehicle was upon them. Karl Benz's first production car was already a year old and the writing was on the wall for horse drawn cabs. By 1905 Hansoms and 'growlers' were diminishing at the rate of 600 a year and the days of the horse drawn cab were over. By 1908 the transition was such, that a linkman's one blast on a whistle for a Hansom cab was now used to call a motor cab. The public had taken to the new cabs, "recent reports of the companies owning them show that they are being run at a substantial profit and a much larger number of motor cabs will soon be on the streets. The promoters are now busy appealing to the public for the necessary money". (12)

References used in Chapter Ten

1. See - History, Origin and Progress of the Watermen's Company. H. Humerous. (GRL) and A Licence granted to William Huggins of the parish of St. Andrews, Holborn, in 1678. (GRL) and Orders, Bye-laws and Ordinances 1697/1732. (GRL)
2. British Patent Specifications of Coaches, No. 31. Vol. 98. (GRL)
3. Ibid. March 1664, No. 143.
4. House of Commons Session Papers, March 1852. (HOLRO)
5. Alphabetical Index of Patents and Inventions. (No. 6733) (GRL)
6. DNB Vol. 8. p. 1194. (GRL)
7. Gentleman's Magazine, October 1771 and Knight's London, Vol. 2. p. 357. (GRL)
8. Alphabetical Index of Patents (No. 7266) 1817-1852. (GRL)
9. Carriages and Coaches, R. Strauss. (GRL)
10. Journal of the Royal Society of Arts, Vol 17. May 1869. p. 410/459. (GRL)
11. For reference to the events surrounding the Royal Society of Arts and the exhibitions see - Journals Vol. 10. pp. 433, 859, 921; Vol. 22 p. 6; Vol. 23 p. 213.
12. Ibid. Vol. 44 November 1908.

Chapter Eleven

"Behind the facade of Victorian respectability"

While Parliament could command a better cab system and the Royal Society of Arts could command a better type of cab, neither could command a better way of life for the drivers. If past history reveals anything it is that any advances made by London's cab trade have been in spite of Parliament and sometimes in direct opposition to it. The events of the preceding chapter concerning the development of the Hansom cab, does not reflect upon the conditions of work and the living standards of men living and working in conditions almost feudal by comparison of those of a century later.

Following the end of limitation in London it was the ambition of many thousands of the unemployed "to get on a cab". Among those who succeeded were men from all walks of life, "costermongers, jewellers, clerks, broken down gentlemen, footmen, pickpockets, burglars, housebreakers, many ex policemen and shopkeepers etc". (1) Henry Mayhew writes of "one of the old fraternity of hackney coachmen, who had, since the decline of his class, prospered by devoting his exertions to another department of business". This would seem to suggest that many undesirables entered the trade after 1831.

The turn over of drivers was high, bearing in mind that they were not licensed until 1843, even so, once convicted few proprietors would ever employ them again. Many of these former drivers, known as 'bucks' from the habit of "giving out buck" as they call it, between themselves, would frequent the larger cab stands trying to earn a few shillings "rubbing up". i.e. polishing the brasses on the cabs and moving them up on the stand as a vacancy occurred. Some 'bucks' were employed by 'long' night drivers to drive the cab for a few hours while the regular driver rested and though these 'bucks' were rogues, many of them pimps, and petty criminals, who would rob one another as well as an unsuspecting passenger, they were extremely honest with the drivers. After 1853 each cab stand had a licensed waterman whose responsibility it was to water and feed the horses and move the cabs up.

Very few of the respectable proprietors would allow their cabs to be worked at night, preferring to employ married men who were trying hard to bring up a family on a wage of between 15/- to 25/- a week and whose wife supplemented this wage by taking in washing or needlework. Mayhew estimated that about one tenth of London's cabdrivers "were of the criminal class" and that they lived in London "where ever low depravity flourishes", behind the facade of Victorian respectability. Later, after the 1853 act, the licensing regulations were more rigid and properly enforced and a better type of person was employed as a cabdriver. His status improved considerably and they were much sought after, particularly by young women in service, as suitable husbands.

It was not only the 1853 act which changed the status of the London cabdriver. From about then there was a move towards greater self determination, to shake off the shackles of poverty. It was not just cabmen. This period was the cradle of the trade union movement. People were stirring and they wanted a better way of life. During the next sixty years the London cabdrivers were in a van of the struggle to achieve it.

Strangely enough though, life for the omnibus drivers and conductors was probably as hard for them as it was for the cabdriver by nature of the similarity of employment. The omnibus trade was not organised as a trade union until 1911 and only then as a result of the efforts of the London cabdrivers trade union. Omnibus drivers and conductors only had two hours off every alternate Sunday, while the horses were rested one day in four. One driver who asked for time off to go to church was told, "you can go to church as often as you like and we can get a man who does not want to go there". (2)

There appears to be only one account of the hackney coachmen defying authority prior to 1853. This was on the occasion of George III's coronation in 1761. Then, the hackney coachmen and the Sedan chairmen demanded the right to charge a higher fare during the period of the coronation because householders and shopkeepers were charging up to five guineas for a seat at a window on the processional route. The Privy Council were enraged at this effrontery and issued a proclamation accusing them of entering into an illegal combination not to work unless their request for exorbitant rates was granted. Unless they worked and discharged their duties "without making exorbitant demands they will be proceeded against with the utmost severity". (3)

The coachmen and chairmen refused to comply with the proclamation and still refused to work unless their request for higher fares was granted. With so many foreigners in London for the coronation it could have proved embarrassing if the Privy Council had used force; so they decided to use tact. A well known Sedan chairmaker was approached to act as mediator and he persuaded the coachmen and chairmen that numerous influential people had assured him that they would voluntary agree to pay extra if the coachmen and chairmen worked normally during the coronation. This, in fact, was what occurred and by all accounts they reaped a golden harvest.

Almost a hundred years was to elapse before London's cabmen were sufficiently organised to challenge authority again. This time it was against the harshness of the law and it's application by the police. Early in 1853 a cabdriver was charged with demanding more than the proper fare. The passenger said the journey was three miles but the driver claimed it was five and as it was beyond the limit of four miles from Charing Cross he could charge extra. The driver was found guilty and sentenced to one month's imprisonment. However, his case aroused considerable public sympathy. The distance was measured and found to be seven miles, completely vindicating the driver. (4)

The Times of February 16th, 1853, commenting on the driver's sentence, was mounting a campaign "to fix the cabby" as they called it and a few days later under the heading "The dirty cabs of London" criticised them for being "slow, dear, dirty and in poor condition" and complaining of extortion by the drivers. On March 5th, Sir Richard Mayne the Metropolitan Police Commissioner, issued an order forbidding the cabmen, during the course of their employment, from smoking and drinking and that they were to sit on the 'box' at all times and were not to converse with one another. To make sure that these regulations were carried out police constables were appointed to enforce the order. (5)

Two weeks later the cabmen held a meeting in St. Martin's Hall, Long Acre, to protest at the new regulations. James Scully, Chairman of the London Cabdriver's Trade Union, which had not then long been formed addressed the meeting. His opening remark that "one could often see bank clerks, shopkeepers and merchants in the dock at the Old Bailey but no one had ever seen a cabdriver there", was greeted with rapturous applause which was taken up by an overflow meeting outside. A resolution condemning the Commissioner of Police and telling cabmen not to allow themselves to be "ridden over roughshod" was passed unanimously.

They called upon the proprietors to select one day "preferably wet" and keep all the cabs off the street for what was an "unconstitutional interference with the rights of British cabmen". The Times was alluded to as having been bought by the omnibus lobby. A few days later a letter to The Times said, "the cabmen's attitude bears materially upon the comfort of almost every inhabitant of this great metropolis belonging to the middle and upper classes". (6)

The drivers resentment had barely died down when Parliament passed the notorious Fitzroy Act (16th & 17th Vict. C33) which, apart from reducing the fare from 8d to 6d a mile, also withdrew the right of cabmen to charge return fare which had previously been allowed where a cab was hired to go beyond the four mile radius of the General Post Office, but only that part of the journey that went beyond the radius. The Commissioner of Police was to have sole discretion as to when a cabdriver's licence was to be revoked and the driver was to have no right of appeal. Drivers still retained the right to refuse to undertake a journey beyond six miles.

The cab trade and the omnibus trade, for this act affected the busmen just as much as the cabmen, were inflamed by this act as were a large proportion of the public. A Mr. E. Bradfield, a well known author wrote, "the reflection is made by men who have learned their profession and trade, not with any intention of throwing discredit on the capacity of the police force, but to show the absurdity of expecting men who are created into a force for the protection of lives and property of her majesty's subjects, being armed with the power to judge and decide on trade questions. The principle of placing any trade or profession in the power of the police establishment is dangerous and opposed to civil liberty". (7)

The Sunday Times of June 12th, 1853, went a stage further and in it's editorial said, "we believe it to be utterly impossible that the Commissioner of the Metropolis can satisfactorily discharge the additional duties the Act imposes upon him, even were he another 'Admirable Crichton' and combined the varied excellencies of that mythical personage, we should still, in defence of human freedom, protest against confiding to a single individual which the history of human nature, from the days of Ceasar to those of the autocrats of Russia, proves to be a source of tyranny and injustice, slavish in principle and mischievous in practice".

The government was not to be moved and the Bill became law. The following day, July 26th, 1853, the entire cab trade came out on strike and not a cab was to be seen. Members of Parliament complained to the Sergeant-at-Arms who asked a Mr. Gamble to provide omnibuses for the use of the members but Mr. Gamble was also a cab proprietor and he refused.

After four days the police broke the strike by allowing unlicensed vehicles to ply for hire but the cab trades action had made an impression on Parliament and an assurance was given that the trades grievances would be looked into. Less than six months later Parliament passed another act (16th & 17th Vict. No. 2 C127) which moved the radius that had formerly been four miles from the General Post Office in St. Martin's le Grand, to four miles from Charing Cross. It also allowed drivers to charge one shilling per mile or part of a mile if the carriage was discharged beyond the radius. Had the centre of the radius been left at the General Post Office more passenger journeys would have been affected by the extra charge for going beyond the radius. But as the majority of journeys went to Belgravia, Chelsea, Kensington, Paddington and Earl's Court etc, by centring the radius on Charing Cross, fewer journeys went beyond the radius. The new act also reduced the licence revenue tax from ten shillings a week to one shilling a day, so in nearly every respect the strike had been a success.

Apart from another brush with authority in 1867 a reasonably peaceful period lasted until 1894. The strike which broke out that year had been smouldering for years with considerable bitterness between driver and proprietor. Because of the conditions of work during the 19th century and the onerous laws the drivers worked under, the cab trade was probably more oppressed

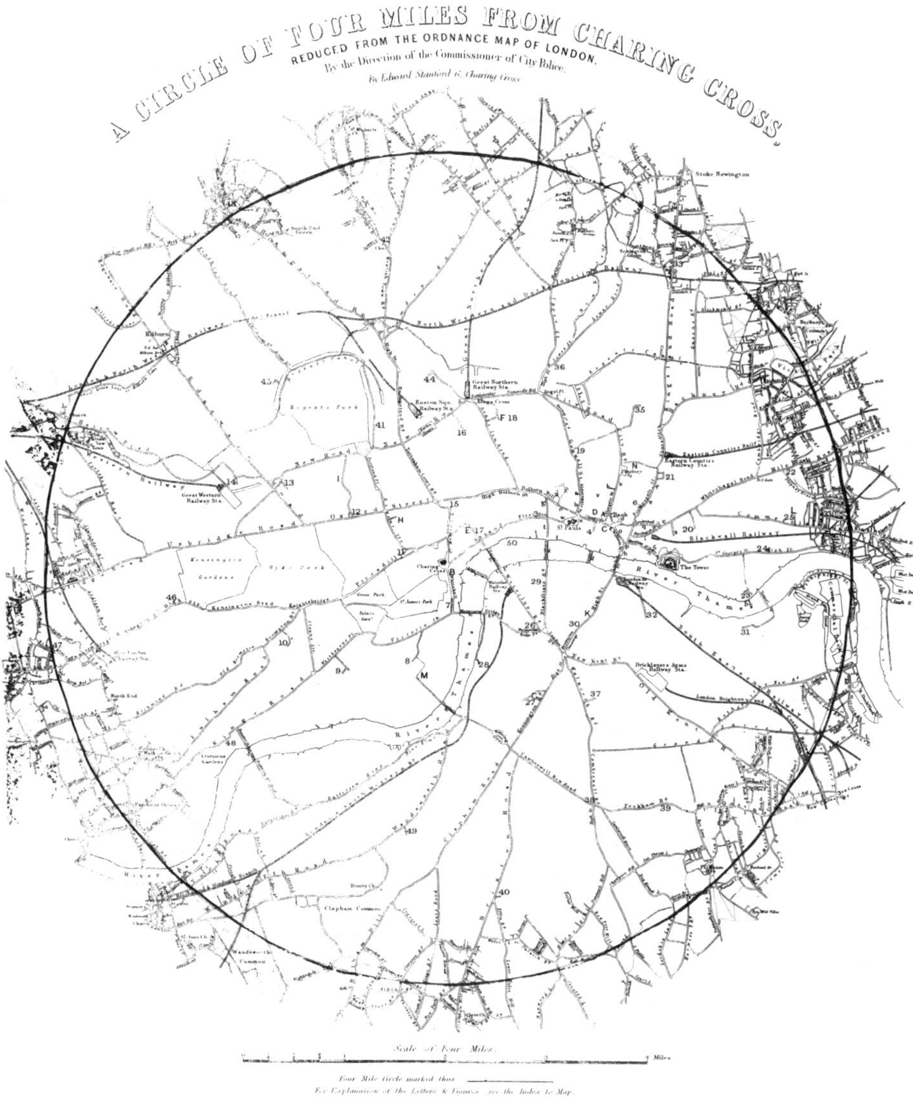

The 1853 Act transfered the four mile radius from St Martin's le Grand in the City to Charing Cross thus fewer cab journeys went beyond the radius.

than any other.

A great deal of ignorance surrounds the subject of London's cabmen during the 19th century. Drivers were bailees and had very few rights under the hackney carriage laws and although basically those laws are still in force today they are interpreted much more liberally. The hiring of cabs by drivers was linked to a contract where the driver agreed to pay a certain sum, which, prior to 1894 was usually six shillings a day plus a shilling 'yard' money. Until that agreement had been formally cancelled he was required to pay that sum whether he worked or not, even though his cab remained in the yard where it was available for another driver.

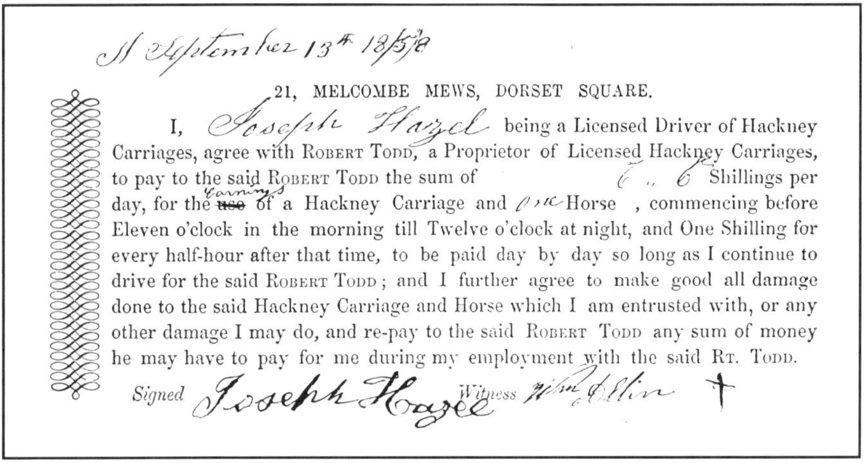
11 September 13th 1858

21, MELCOMBE MEWS, DORSET SQUARE.

I, Joseph Hazel being a Licensed Driver of Hackney Carriages, agree with ROBERT TODD, a Proprietor of Licensed Hackney Carriages, to pay to the said ROBERT TODD the sum of 6 „ 6 Shillings per day, for the ~~use~~ earnings of a Hackney Carriage and One Horse, commencing before Eleven o'clock in the morning till Twelve o'clock at night, and One Shilling for every half-hour after that time, to be paid day by day so long as I continue to drive for the said ROBERT TODD; and I further agree to make good all damage done to the said Hackney Carriage and Horse which I am entrusted with, or any other damage I may do, and re-pay to the said ROBERT TODD any sum of money he may have to pay for me during my employment with the said RT. TODD.

Signed Joseph Hazel *Witness* Wm. Ellis †

A proprietor's contract with a licensed driver for 6 shillings 6d per day for the hire of a cab and one horse. Note the driver also accepts liability for any damage to the vehicle, 1858.

The evils of this flat rate system of working can best be seen from the figures of the police courts. From January 1st 1861 until July 1862 some 477 cabdrivers were committed to prison for failing to pay their proprietors. The term of imprisonment varied from three days to twenty four days, the minimum and the maximum allowed by the act of 1853. These sentences were passed for defaulting on sums of money ranging from four shillings to forty two shillings and sixpence. The act of 1853 was the main cause of the trouble. Before the act when the fare was 8d a mile a driver could earn up to twenty five shillings a week for a fifteen hour day. When the act reduced the fare to 6d a mile he could only manage to subsist but the proprietors still wanted the same daily rate for the cab as they had when the fare was 8d a mile. (8)

It is a long time since a London cabdriver was sent to prison for a breech of the hackney carriage acts but during the 19th century many of them were. The majority of them sojourned in Surrey County Gaol which formerly stood in Newington Causeway in Southwark. This building served as a gaol from 1791 to 1879 and it was after watching the execution here of Mr. & Mrs. Manning, for murder in 1849 that Charles Dickens wrote to The Times protesting at "the scenes of horror". London cabmen's familiarity with the gaol earned it the sobriquet of 'Keen's Hotel'.

Probably the worst period for the cabmen was between 1853 and 1869 when the Commissioner of Police had absolute authority. A system which was both vexatious and despotic. A police inspector examined all horses used in cabs in London and there was no appeal against his decision. He was not popular and many people thought it strange that he was not a veterinary surgeon and they doubted his ability to pronounce on the condition of a horse.

In a case at Bow Street Magistrate's Court in 1864 in which two well known veterinary surgeons were pitted against this inspector, the cab proprietor was heavily fined. Even had the case gone in his favour his triumph would have been short lived, for an order, signed by the Commissioner of Police a fortnight before the court hearing had been presented to the proprietor requiring him to withdraw the horse from work. (9)

Because of the terrible conditions of work, several religious orders gave assistance to cabmen and it was largely because of these religious groups that a move was made towards a six day week for cabmen. In 1853 this was helped by the reduction in licence revenue to one shilling a day per plate thus it was possible to have a six day plate and seven day plate, the former being white and the latter were blue. The number of six day plates increased each year providing proof that more and more drivers were determined to have one day off a week. This feeling was so intense that many drivers paid the proprietors who would not have a blue plate a full week's money in order to gain a day of rest, until they were compelled by poverty to discontinue the practice. From a total of 4,002 cabs in 1856 there were 774 six day plates. By April 1864 there were 2,025 six day plates from a total of 5,704 cabs. (10)

Many drivers were dishonest men with a propensity to defraud the proprietor if they could. Others were completely honest and respectable men who often could not obtain the money required of them. Some proprietors distinguished between the good and the bad but in general the proprietors dealt harshly with all drivers who would not or could not pay. "Injustice was often done to many men who would have done well in any calling; for magistrates seldom had any notion of cabdrivers as anything but a monster of iniquity and accordingly treated them 'a la Judge Jeffreys': "The unsupported testimony of the police, discredited when a member of the upper classes is the subject of it, is always accepted as conclusive evidence against a cabdriver". (11)

Because of the terrible plight which many cabdrivers found themselves in and the harsh conditions under which they worked, several remedial agencies were at work on their behalf. Foremost amongst these were the protection societies of which there were several in London. Their object was to combine together the respectable men engaged in the cab trade and provide them with legal and other assistance to protect them from injustice. No member was 'protected' more than four times a year and this assistance was not given to any driver who attempted to overcharge by more than sixpence. Meetings were generally held at midnight so as to give everyone a chance to attend.

A higher position was occupied by the cabmen's clubs of which five existed in London. These were formed in 1859, the first was at Paddington, formed as a Penny Bank with social and bible class meetings given by a Mr. W.C. Bennett, a missionary to the cabmen. There were some 1,000 members during the early years of the clubs but they had declined by the 1870s due to the widespread poverty of the cabmen. Each club had its benefit society and initially there were coffee and reading rooms and facilities for religious services.

At the King's Cross club, regular bible classes were held and cabmen's families featured regularly in prayer meetings held outside on the public highway. Religion was difficult as the cabmen's conditions of work were opposed to it. The London City Mission, which still exists today, employed three full time missionaries to give help to cabmen in need and as late as 1965 these missionaries could still be seen at Waterloo and Victoria Stations. It's earliest appointment was in 1843 and it played a large part in forming the Cab and Omnibus Lords Day of Rest Association. The missions main object was to bring comfort to men, "who were long tossed about as shuttlecocks by inharmonious laws and conflicting decisions between the police and the public who are almost compelled to be bad men to remain cabmen". (12)

The London Cabmen's Mission was formed in February 1875, also at King's Cross, under the presidency of Samuel Morley Esq., M.P. The objects of this mission were, "to proclaim the glad tidings of salvation to cabmen and their wives and families; to invite and encourage a regular attendance at the preaching of the gospel, to converse with and give suitable literature to the men while on the ranks, assist the afflicted and distressed and for the moral and spiritual instruction of cabmen".

Five years earlier in 1870, the Cabdriver's Benevolent Association had been formed at 15 Soho Square. It's first president was the Earl of Litchfield and later presidents included the Duke of Leeds, Cardinal Manning, the Earl of Shaftesbury and Lord Carrington. The objects of this association were, "to establish a pension fund to pay an annual pension of £15 per annum for aged or infirm cabmen unable to follow their calling and to promote a fund for granting loans without interest for members requiring aid, on the security of another member of the association".

It was not only religious groups which recognised the appalling conditions that cabmen worked under. In January 1875, a Captain J. Armstrong, editor of The Globe newspaper and who lived at St. John's Wood, sent his manservant out into a blizzard that was raging at the time to engage a cab to take Captain Armstrong to his office in Fleet Street. Returning an hour later with a cab, Captain Armstrong enquired of his servant why he had been so long. He was told that although the cabs were on the rank the cabmen had retired to a nearby grog shop for protection from the weather and were fortifying themselves with mugs of hot cocoa with a nip of rum.

During his journey to Fleet Street, Captain Armstrong reflected upon the events of the morning and later in the day he spoke to several friends who confessed that it had never occurred to them that cabmen were expected to sit 'on the box' in rain, snow, cold and wind waiting for a fare, without any protection from the elements. They decided to donate money for the erection of a shelter adjacent to the cab rank in Acacia Road, St. John's Wood and so was born the London Cabmen's Shelter Fund.

During the next seventy five years, some 47 of these shelters were erected at the larger cab ranks in inner London, though now they have declined to about 13 in number. Many wealthy and influential people including the Prince of Wales and later as King Edward VII subscribed to the fund. One shelter, erected in Old Palace Yard, Westminster, was paid for by members of both Houses of Parliament, the list of subscribers reading like a page from Debrett included the Earl of Aberdeen, the Earl of Rosslyn, Lord Beconsfield, W.J.R. Cotton Esq., M.P. and Colonel R.J. Lloyd Lindsay V.C. M.P. (13)

As a result of Captain Armstrong's efforts this was the first cabmans shelter in London located at Acacia Road, St John's Wood, on 6th February, 1875.

At first the shelters had no provision for supplying meals but by 1882, larger shelters were erected which included a small kitchen and hot meals and drinks were provided by the attendant. Many of the shelters in Central London were frequented late at night by well known personalities who would pop in for a cup of steaming hot cocoa and a slice of 'tottenham'. Sir Ernest Shackleton, the explorer, was a regular visitor to the shelter which stood at Hyde Park Corner. Prior to his departure on his last expedition, where he tragically died at sea, the cabmen who used this shelter presented him with a set of pipes and a pipe rack. His letter of thanks to them hung there for many years until the shelter was pulled down to make way for the Hyde Park underpass traffic scheme.

This brief account of the work done by many well known people over a period of some eighty years, who were genuinely seeking to bring some kind of relief to a social class of men, their wives and children, reflects upon the social upheaval in Britain at that time. Was it the work of these agencies that stayed the hand of revolt against the system, which the cabmen themselves related to the intransigence of the cab proprietors? Whether that was the case or not, matters came to a head in 1894, the cabmen were determined that there was need for a change and many drivers expressed the opinion "that a cabman had as much right to be paid for his labour as the master for his capital".

The London Cabdriver's Union called a mass meeting at Bell Street, off Edgware Road and demand was made that the flat rate be reduced from 17/- a day to 15/- a day. Negotiations with the proprietors followed the meeting but they refused to accede to the drivers demands, saying that many drivers only worked a four day week and could well afford the rate of 17/- a day. The union called a second meeting, this time at the Novelty theatre. It was so well attended that an overflow meeting was held outside. A resolution calling for a strike was carried with tremendous enthusiasm by both meetings and the strike commenced the following day. (14)

Owner drivers were permitted to carry on working but they were expected to contribute to the strike fund and allow other drivers to share their cabs. They were issued with different tickets every day they made a contribution to the strike fund and the tickets bore the inscription "working by permission of the union". Other drivers took out barrel organs, or staged impromptu concerts to raise money and one month later the strike was still on. An effort to break the stalemate had to be made and a Board of Conciliation was appointed with both the drivers and the proprietors represented on it, the chief mediator was Mr. H.H. Asquith, Home Secretary.

After several meetings at the House of Commons, Mr. Asquith announced his award, based on a sliding scale throughout the year. For Hansom cabs the rate was ten shillings a day from September 10th to March 26th, rising to sixteen shillings a day from May 14th to July 22nd. For the four wheeled 'growler' the rates over the same period of dates rose from ten shillings a day to thirteen shillings a day. Both Hansoms and 'growlers' carried an extra shilling a day if they were fitted with rubber tyres. Mr. Asquith's rate for a four wheeled cab drawn by one horse was set so low, rising from six shillings a day over the same period, to eight shillings, that the one horse 'growler' rapidly declined except those operated by owner drivers. (15)

The strike had lasted nearly six weeks and Mr. Asquith's award seemed to vindicate the driver's actions, especially with regard to the rate they had formerly paid during the winter months; even so many of them were out of work when the strike ended. Some proprietors, including the Earl of Shrewsbury, one of London's largest cab fleet owners had sold up. The balance sheet of the union showed that £8,202 was received during the strike and that £8,111 was spent until July 24th 1894.

For the Earl of Shewsbury it had been a disaster. The company was formed in 1888 as the "Shrewsbury and Talbot Cab and Noiseless Tyre Company" and the purpose of the company was to "purchase, amalgamate and carry on the business of cab proprietor and job master". The manufacture of steel and rubber tyres was carried out in Manchester. The cabs, Forder Hansoms, were superior in every way and all of them were fitted with India Rubber tyres. Each cab had a coronet painted on each side panel. Because these cabs were quiet by comparison with other vehicles, small bells were attached to the harness to warn pedestrians of the cabs approach.

Though the Earl of Shrewsbury helped considerably to raise the standard of cabs in London, he was regarded with mixed feelings by other cab proprietors, many of whom thought he had ruined the trade. They were also forced to use rubber tyres, an expense not recoverable except by raising the rate to the driver, though the validity of this charge was subsequently upheld by Mr. Asquith. Within the space of six years the venture had ended, though it was not realised then that the demise of the horse cab trade was only a few years away.

References used in Chapter Eleven

1. Mayhew's London, pp. 587/592. Edited by P. Quennell. Spring Books 1969.
2. Ibid.
3. Acts of the Privy Council, 1761. (GRL)
4. Omnibus and Cab, H.C. Moore. (GRL)
5. The Times, March 7th 1853. (Brit. Mus. Col.)
6. Ibid. March 26th.
7. Ibid.
8. The Annals of the Royal Statistical Society. (GRL)
9. London's cabs and cabmen's grievances, Pamphlet 7385 (GRL) quot-

ing Cherry v Emmett, Beeline Newspaper, March 19th, 1864.
10. Ibid.
11. Ibid.
12. Omnibus and Cab, H.C. Moore. (GRL)
13. Records of Cabmen's Shelter Fund administered by the T.G.W.U. (Cab Section)
14. Omnibus and Cab, H.C. Moore. (GRL)
15. Ibid.

Chapter Twelve

Into the 20th Century

"For years to come you have little to fear from the invention of the motor car, but in ten years perhaps, electric cabs (sic) would be in use". So spoke Sir George Sitwell at a dinner given by Scarborough cabmen in February 1897. Just six months later on August 20th 1897, fourteen Electric Bersey cabs left the depot of the London Electric Cab Company in Juxon Street, Lambeth. Charging the same fare as the horse cabs. They immediately drew forth the unanimous condemnation from the London Joint Trade Committee who protested at any further licensing of these vehicles. (1)

The world's first self propelled taxi, "the Bersey" introduced into London by the London Electric Cab Company in 1897.

Described as coupe's to carry two people, they were reminiscent of the old family coach. Painted black and yellow, their motive power was supplied from forty accumulator cells carried in a tray beneath the body. They weighed 14 cwt. and could propel the cabs for fifty miles without having to be recharged.

Designed and constructed by C.W. Bersey, they quickly earned themselves the nickname "'umming birds".

By the spring of 1898 the original cabs were withdrawn from service and replaced by fifty new vehicles supposedly of a better design. The new cabs were nowhere as silent as the earlier models, breakdowns were frequent and the drivers became reluctant to drive them. Nevertheless, they were praised by the Commissioner of Police who remarked "should motor cabs come generally into use, the effect on the traffic of the metropolis will be most marked". He was referring to the fact that as the new cabs were only half the length of a horse drawn cab there would be a drop in traffic congestion.

In May 1899 a still newer version, some seventy in number, made a tour of the West End to attract the public's attention. This resulted in a bitter attack from those who were against the new form of transport. In what can only be described as Luddism nearly all the national papers carried grossly exaggerated stories of breakdowns, accidents and injuries to fares. All the more remarkable since none of the cabs on this occasion carried passengers. (2) Within a few months the company was forced to suspend operations, nevertheless it was the first attempt anywhere in the world to operate a service to the public using self propelled vehicles.

The horse cab thus gained a temporary respite but in 1903 the first petrol engine cab, the Prunel, was licensed to ply for hire in London. It ran unchallenged for nine months when two more were licensed but by the end of 1904 they had departed from the London scene. The breach in the dam, once made, became much wider and more models made their appearance, Vauxhalls, Fords, Rationals, Heralds, Argylls and Unics were all on the road by 1906. By early 1907 they had been joined by Renault, Adler, Mascot, Adams Hewitt, Simplex, Sorex and Jeantard. Even so, their numbers were small as the figures below indicated. (3)

Year	Hansoms	Growlers	Motor cabs
1903	7,499	3,906	1
1904	7,137	3,992	2
1905	6,996	3,935	19
1906	6,648	3,844	96
1907	5,592	3,866	723

It will be seen that the motor cab was replacing the Hansom cab, the reason being that the early cab, like the Hansom, was a two seater with little accommodation for luggage. On the other hand the 'growlers' carried four people and had ample space for luggage. As a large proportion of cab work in London consists of journeys between railway stations, the early motor cabs and Hansoms were of little use until the four seater cabs with roof racks came along. Even after luggage space had been provided on motor cabs the 'growlers' were still in demand, because the railway companies would not allow motor cabs on their stations due to problems over insurance.

This was resolved in 1910 and almost immediately the old 'growler' was doomed and between 1910 and 1914 they had declined from 2,721 to 1,159 and during the same period Hansoms had further decreased to 386 and motor cabs had increased to 8,397. The Hansoms had declined at a rate of 1,000 a year and thousands were sold for firewood at £1 each. The demise of the horse drawn cab had taken place over a period of ten short years.

Despite the introduction of a petrol engine, early motor cab manufacturers persisted in imitating the horse cab. As is evident by this 1905 Vauxhall cab.

Until March 1907 the introduction of the motor cab had been of a piecemeal nature. Then, on March 15th 1907, five hundred Renault taxis, the largest fleet of motor vehicles anywhere at that time assembled, left the premises of the General Cab Company Ltd., on the corner of Brixton and Camberwell New Road in South London, to ply for hire on the streets of the capital. (4) These two seater Renault cabs were very similar in design to the cabs working in Paris. Since June 1906 the company had been running one Renault fitted with a taximeter although the taximeter was not approved until 1907. The company had been waiting to launch it's operation since June 1906 because it was not going to run cabs without meters.

The company's Chairman, Mr. Davidson Dalzeil M.P. was severely criticised for going 'foreign' for not only were the vehicles French but most of the company's capital came from France, mainly from the Compagnie Generales des Voitures. The set up was strikingly similar to the setting up of the London General Omnibus Company in 1855 with capital from France, though the omnibuses were British built, bought out with French money. The General Cab Company Ltd., was not only French but so were the vehicles. In 1908 the General Cab Company Ltd. merged with the United Cab Company to form the London General Cab Company Ltd., though they both continued to operate independently. As late as 1934 the London General had it's 'French connection' via the Banque d'Alsace et de Lorraine and the Compagnie Generale d'Exploitation, though by then both companies were in the hands of the Paris receiver.

Considerable controversy surrounds the introduction of the Renault taxicab. On January 4th 1911, J.S. Pritchley, a member of the R.A.C. Club, read his paper, "The Evolution of the Taxicab", to members of the club. (5) During the discussion that followed a Mr. H. Sturmey, a greatly respected member of the motor industry told the audience that the 'Conditions of Fitness' drawn up by Scotland Yard in 1906, requiring a 25 foot turning circle and 32 inches between the outside edges of the front springs were impracticable and the Society of Motor Manufacturers and Traders had objected to them. This regulation was intended to give the cab greater stability for the safety of the public, yet at the same time enable the vehicle to turn round in one movement. In order to achieve this it required the engine to be mounted some way back and several companies were experiencing great difficulty with this part of the regulations.

By the time the British companies, including Austin, Argyll, Adams and Humber had overcome the problem the French Renaults were on the streets. Meanwhile Mr. Sturmey had discovered that the distance between the front springs on the French cabs was 26 inches instead of the regulation 32 inches, thereby making a big difference to the design of the cab. He wrote to Scotland Yard pointing out that the Renaults which had been licensed did not come up to the official requirements. The Assistant Commissioner replied that it was true, those vehicles did differ but they were experimental and it was thought that in the public's interest they should be given a trial. The fact that the public's interest would have been better served had similar opportunities been given to British companies did not occur to the Assistant Commissioner. There was never any official explanation as to why a foreign company had been shown this preference or indeed why it had been thought desirable to consider 500 Renaults as experimental. Clearly the regulations had been relaxed to suit the French company at the expense of their British rivals. The 'Conditions of Fitness' were subsequently altered in 1907 and many British built cabs followed within the next few years.*

The first motor cabs licensed from 1903 to March 15th 1907, operated on the fare structure laid down for horse drawn cabs under the act of 1869. It was not until the act of 1907 (7th Edward 7th C 55) that the Home Secretary was able to fix the fare for motor cabs. It has always been understood that under these acts the Home Secretary has unfettered discretion to fix the fares either on the basis of time, distance or both. In the exercise of this discretion he must bear in mind three major points. The tariff must not impose an unnecessary burden on the public, it should not be such as to stifle the industry and it should be sufficient to allow a reasonable remuneration to the drivers' for their exacting work. (6)

In 1906 a Select Committee of the House of Commons made the unanimous recommendation that the privilege cab system at London railway stations should be abolished and that taximeters of the Horo - Kilometric type should be made compulsory taximeters on motor cabs but optional on horse drawn cabs. The recommendations for abolishing the privilege cab system and approved taximeters were accepted by the government of the day, but the fare tariff was not; let us examine the privilege system first. (7)

The privilege cab system in London began in 1839 when the London to Birmingham Railway Company made an agreement with a cab proprietor named Moss, to supply twelve new four wheeled cabs for the exclusive use of the company at Euston station. (8) All the other railway companies followed suit as soon as their London termini were built. Only the Southern Railway at Waterloo Station did not take up the privilege system. By 1877 the privileged cabs at Euston Station had increased to 130 with each cab paying one shilling a day for the privilege of being allowed into the station. In 1877 the charge was increased to one shilling and sixpence.

The majority of London's cabmen detested the privilege system which allowed some drivers an advantage over the unprivileged. In return for being the only cabs allowed into a station, the proprietors were required to guarantee a certain number of cabs at all times, even on Sundays. They were also required to punish drivers who were drunk, insolent, or who refused to be hired and those who were guilty of overcharging. The railway companies were ignoring the fact that all cabdrivers, whether privileged or not had to abide by

**For a detailed history of the motor cab in London see, Taxicabs, a Photographic History, by Philip Warren and Malcolm Linskey. Almark 1976 and 2nd edition Taxi Trade Promotions Limited 1981.*

the strict Public Carriage Office regulations which more than covered those insisted upon by the railway companies.

The railway companies maintained that the privilege system guaranteed them a supply of cabs when they were most needed but all through the privilege era, ordinary street cabs were called into stations to cope with the excess of passengers left behind by the privilege cabs. For this they were charged a penny entrance fee to the station and were nicknamed 'Bluchers' by the privilege drivers, after the Prussian Field Marshal who arrived at the Battle of Waterloo only to perform the work that was not done.

There were no such problems at Waterloo and Vauxhall stations on the London and South Western Railway. Any cab was admitted to these stations on payment of a penny, for which payment the company provided the drivers with a waiting room and water for the horses. The non-privilege cabmen always claimed that if all stations were 'open' they were confident that on payment of a penny there would be no shortage of cabs.

By 1906 privilege cabs in London numbered 1,695 and they were located at eighteen stations. Payments to the railway companies varied from one shilling a day at King's Cross Station, to £40 per annum at Clapham Junction, where fifteen cabs provided the London, Brighton and South Coast Railway an income of £600 per annum. The largest number of privilege cabs operated from Paddington Station, where 290 cabs provided the Great Western Railway with an annual income of £2,262.

Victoria Station, c. 1895. The horse cabs ranking for fares are "privileged cabs" a system that prevailed until 1907.

In 1895 a Departmental Committee of Inquiry recommended the abolition of the privilege system but it was allowed to continue. The number of privilege cabs then were slightly fewer than in 1906, nevertheless they provided the railway companies at thirteen mainline stations with £10,618 in 1895 from a total of 1,462 cabs. (9)

In September 1896, no doubt as a result of the government's refusal to implement the findings of the 1895 Committee of Inquiry, the cabmen took steps to resolve the situation themselves, by refusing to work for a proprietor who operated part of his fleet as privilege cabs. After several weeks the strike began to peter out and in an effort to force the issue, drivers refused to take passengers inside station forecourts, setting them down with their luggage outside the station. This action on their part, resulted in prosecutions based on the assumption that a railway station, though private property, was within the meaning of "to any place" for a cabman was bound to take a passenger. (10) A driver was convicted by a magistrate for refusing to drive through the arch of Euston station, though requested to do so by the hirer. A later hearing by the Divisional Court refused to allow the driver to state a case. (11)

Following this case the London Cabdrivers Union were no longer in a position to withstand a long struggle so soon after the strike of 1894 and the strike came to an end with the drivers resolved to continue the struggle at a later date. They were never to put that resolve to the test for the Select Committee of 1906 recommended that the privilege system be abolished. It's general findings were:-

"We may point out that Palace Yard is always well provided with cabs without any privilege system, as is Waterloo station. With regard to the alleged necessity of the privilege system to secure the safety of passenger's luggage - overlooks a fairly obvious fact, namely, that more luggage is taken to a station by non privilege cabs then is taken away by privilege cabs, with no apparent loss. In our opinion, shelter from the weather and a warm and lighted room in which drivers may rest or take a meal would always offer an inducement to drivers to frequent the stations. We recommend, therefore, the abolition of the privilege system without further delay and the passing of whatever legislation may be necessary to achieve this.".

Passing the necessary legislation proved difficult. The railway companies had a strong lobby in both Houses of parliament and a good many M.P.s were representing the railway's interests. Despite the opposition the Commons divided to vote 176 to 24 for the abolition of the privilege system. The struggle did not end there, however, for during the Bill's passage through the Lords the section relating to the abolition of the privilege system was defeated. Most of the opposition had come from the Duke of Northumberland and Lord Balfour who were of the opinion that "the public are to be inconvenienced for the sake of their own servants".

The Commons was angry at the decision taken by the House of Lords. The Home Secretary said that the whole Bill, including the taximeter regulations was in jeopardy and after some discussion the Bill was sent back to the Lords. Ramsey MacDonald and Mr. Gladstone were asked to draw up reasons as to why the Commons disagreed with the Lords. Their statement said, "because two committees, a Departmental Committee and Select Committee of the House of Commons, after hearing evidence from both sides, have recommended that the privilege system should be ended at London Railway stations, at any rate experimentally and the House of Commons after debate has declared itself emphatically to be of the same opinion". (12)

This time the Lords were persuaded to accept the Bill as it stood and it received the Royal Assent on August 28th 1907. At first all cab were required to pay a 1d on entering a railway station but the railway companies dropped this charge in 1917. Although the abolition of the privilege system was to be experimental, it was prolonged indefinitely by the Act of 9th Edward 7th C46. That act gave Home Secretaries powers to grant a privilege status to a railway station if it is in the public's interest to do so.

Section two of the 1907 act, which abolished the privilege stations came into effect on January 1st 1908. Section one dealing with fares gave the Home Secretary immediate powers to make orders fixing the fare and his first order came into force on March 15th 1907. Ignoring the recommendations of the 1906 Select Committee and the advice of the Society of Motor Manufacturers and Traders who had given evidence to the Select Committee for a fare of one shilling a mile and 3d per quarter of a mile thereafter, the Home Secretary fixed the fare for motor cabs at 8d for the first mile and 2d per quarter mile thereafter.

The question of who retained the extras charged for additional passengers over the first two and for luggage carried outside, did not immediately arise because the first motor cabs were only licensed to carry two passengers. Prior to the advent of the motor cabs and taximeters the extras had always been retained by the drivers simply because there was no way of recording them. But toward the end of 1908 when the four seater cabs came along, with space for luggage as well, the proprietors immediately claimed the extras.

In October 1911 the London Motor Cab Proprietors Association decided to risk a head on confrontation with their drivers. On October 31st, 1911, a driver named Bryant who worked for the National Cab Company at Hammersmith was told that he had been 'seen' at Paddington station and that he owed 4d in extras. Bryant refused to pay and he was told not to report for work the next day. By six o'clock that evening 600 men were on strike and the London Cabdrivers Union called a mass meeting to be held the next day.

The meeting was held at the Empress Hall, Earl's Court, where the Johnson-Wells fight was about to be staged and the ring was used as a platform. Alfred Smith, the union's president, called for the re-instatement of

Bryant and a return to the position before the L.M.C.P.A. appointed their observers to check on cabs carrying more than two passengers. The delegates were given full powers to obtain fair conditions of employment and the drivers pledged not to return to work until negotiations were successful. (13)

The two sides met for the first time on Thursday, November 3rd, by midnight there was no agreement and the meeting broke up. By then some 15,000 drivers, mechanics and washers were on strike and the L.M.C.P.A. garages were at a standstill. At the heart of the problem was the low fare set by the Home Secretary in 1907 and the refusal by Winston Churchill when Home Secretary in 1911, to grant an application for an increase of fares applied for by the L.M.C.P.A. Desperate to keep their company's solvent the proprietors had decided that the extras, which amounted to £50,000 per annum, should rightfully belong to them.

Cabmens wives showing support for their husbands in the 1912 strike at a mass meeting in Kennington Park.

Meanwhile as the strike entered it's second week, some 500 drivers at the invitation of the Rev. Dr. Darlington, vicar of St. Mark's Church, Kennington Oval, were offered the Vicarage garden hall as a resting place during the remainder of the strike with refreshments being provided. Dr. Darlington was president of the St. Mark's Taxidrivers Brotherhood and was largely responsible for setting up the soup kitchens in the crypt of the church for the benefit of wives and children of the striking drivers. Kennington Oval was the focal point for the strike with the union's offices at 30 Brixton Road and the London General Cab Company's garage, the largest of the L.M.C.P.A. garages just a few yards away on the corner of Brixton Road and Camberwell New Road. (14)

On November 23rd, after a meeting between the two parties at the Board of Trade had ended in deadlock, they both agreed to abide by the decision of a Court of Arbitration to be appointed by the Board of Trade. It's terms of reference were, "what are the fair and proper conditions of service and payment under which the cabdrivers should work, on the assumption that the existing fare remains unaltered". Pending the court's decision the drivers returned to work.

The Court of Arbitration announced it's decision on March 12th, 1912, substantially in favour of the drivers. The court's award contained four major points. "The extras should belong to the drivers, their commission rate was to be 25 per cent, the employees to supply petrol to the drivers at 8d a gallon and if the price of petrol varied by more than 12 per cent on January 1st of any year compared with the previous January, either party can go to the conciliation board who shall vary the price to be paid by the driver so that it is in the same relation to the average 8d a gallon paid at present". (15)

The award did not please the L.M.C.P.A. who thought that the arbitrators had gone beyond their terms of reference by including conditions which were never intended to be discussed. On the other hand the drivers were very pleased with the outcome and Mr. Harry Gosling, president of the Transport Workers Federation told them it was their duty to carry out the terms of the award. "The very essence of collective bargaining", he said, "was to ensure to the other side that if they (the drivers) made a bargain it would be kept". Within a year that statement was to have a hollow ring.

There can be little doubt that the proprietors had been dealt a serious blow, coming on top of Winston Churchill's refusal a few months previous to increase the fares. There is little information on the true state of the large cab companies at that time. The London General Cab Co. Ltd., had been forced to arrange a drastic reconstruction of it's affairs, involving a reduction in capital of fifty per cent or roughly £1½ million. The company had not paid a dividend since 1909 and in March 1912 the share liability was £822,946 there were debts of outstanding debenture of £536,972 and it's assets were £1,300,000. (16)

In November 1912 the price of petrol rose from 8d to 1/1d a gallon. An increase of 70 per cent, greatly exceeding the threshold set by the Court of Arbitration in March of that year. A few days later the L.M.C.P.A. announced that from January 1st 1913, the drivers would have to pay the full amount of the increase, a rise of 1/3d a day on their petrol costs representing a 20 per cent cut in wages. (17)

At a mass meeting called by the union at Lambeth Baths, Alfred Smith, the union's president said, "we wish to abide by the Court of Arbitration's award but the men cannot bear the huge increase demanded by the L.M.C.P.A., who will make no concessions. I warn the masters that the time is coming when it will not be a fight to reduce petrol prices but a fight for free petrol". (18) A call to strike was backed by 4,695 to 177 against.

Both sides met at Gwydr House, Whitehall, on December 30th 1912, but the L.M.C.P.A. refused to depart from the terms of the award given in March 1912. Following that meeting, Alfred Smith criticised the oil companies who were paying a dividend of 20 per cent on their shares while the cab companies were hard pressed to survive. Why was it, he asked that the price of petrol supplied to the London General Omnibus Company was half that charged to the cab companies, who used more petrol than the bus company?

The Times in it's editorial of January 3rd said, "the cab trade is at the mercy of those who fix the price of petrol, a sensible way out would be to raise the fare, which any other business would have done, passing on the increase to the consumer. But the cabs in London are the buses of the Parliamentarians who had control of the fares they paid".

During the first week of the strike the old London Cabdrivers Union changed it's name to the London and Provincial Licensed Vehicle Worker's Union. It's new president was a Mr. Russell, formerly secretary of the National Cab Company Ltd., and one of it's executive committee was Ben Smith, later to be knighted and to serve in the Cabinet under Winston Churchill in the second world war. The newly re-organised union immediately set about organising the drivers in the employ of the London General Omnibus Company. In 1922 the L.P.L.V.W.U. merged with the General Worker's Union and other smaller unions to form the Transport and General Worker's Union.

On January 24th there was a breach in the ranks of the L.M.C.P.A. when the London Improved Cab Company accepted the terms of 8d a gallon and their 150 cabs commenced work the next day. Considerable pressure was now brought to bear on the L.M.C.P.A. and on February 16th, after all along refusing to go to the conciliation Board, they announced that they would now attend a meeting.

As with the 'extras' strike in the previous year, the area around Kennington Oval took on the proportions of a city under siege as marches into the nearby West End and demonstrations outside the garage of the London General Cab Company nearby, were organised from the union's office in Brixton Road. Thousands of men, women and children met daily in Kennington Park which had become a focal point for the strike and where the Chartist movement held meetings during the 1830's. Here the strikers and their families discussed the latest moves and arranged assistance for those badly in need and where mock executions of blacklegs were staged. The Rev. Dr. Darlington again threw open the crypt of St. Mark's Church, placing it once more at the disposal of the strikers, who set up soup kitchens to feed the hungry.

With the strike entering it's ninth week some proprietors were experimenting with cheaper fuel, using a device invented by the British Motor Cab Company of Grosvenor Road, Pimlico. This invention enabled an engine to be started on petrol and when the engine became hot, to switch over to paraffin, then available at 10d a gallon. Following an agreement with the union, 300 of the British Motor Cab Company's vehicles commenced work on March 17th with this device fitted, with others to follow as soon as they too could be adapted.

It was not long before other companies began to capitulate and on March 18th, W.G. du Cros of Acton who operated 600 cabs and employed 1,000 drivers agreed to meet the union's demand for petrol at 8d a gallon. A few days later on March 23rd the union and the L.M.C.P.A. met at the R.A.C. Club, Pall Mall, where an agreement was signed for a full return to work with the drivers paying 8d a gallon for their petrol. The cost of the three month strike had been enormous. The union had paid out £40,000 in strike pay and the owners had lost over £1million.

The threat by Alfred Smith at the beginning of the strike that it would "soon be a fight for free petrol", was no idle boast. In October 1917 the trade had asked the Home Secretary, Sir George Cave, for an increase of fare" a flat rate charge of a shilling a mile every mile" but he had refused, offering instead a 6d surcharge on every journey. The Joint Trade Committee comprising the L.M.C.P.A., the union and the union's owner-drivers branch agreed that from October 17th all cabs would remain in their garages. Having reached this decision, the L.M.C.P.A. and the owner-drivers subsequently changed their minds and accepted the Home Secretary's offer of the 6d surcharge. The union, furious at losing free petrol, which had been promised to them in return for their support for a 50 per cent fare increase, decided to demand free petrol.

The L.M.C.P.A. and the owner-drivers stood firm, blaming the Home Secretary for their position, for he knew that the drivers would demand free petrol if the surcharge instead of a fare increase was accepted. The refusal of the union's owner-driver branch to join the strike was the reason for it's breakaway from the union after the war, joining the Owner Driver's Association. By December 20th, 1917, the strike was over, resulting in victory for the union. The decision to award the drivers free petrol was announced by Sir Arthur Stanley in the House of Commons.

Not until 1920 did the London cab trade receive it's "shilling a mile, every mile", nearly ten years after the inquiry of 1911 had turned it down. By then the British Motor Cab Company, the London Improved Cab Company, the F.I.A.T. Cab Company and many others were finished. The London General Cab Company and W.G. du Cros still had sizeable fleets but nothing like their former size. Who was to blame? Various Home Secretaries, upholding the interests of the Parliamentarians? The intransigence of the large proprietors? The rapaciousness of the drivers? Perhaps we will leave it to history to decide.

Whoever was to blame, it had resulted in the disintegration of the large efficient cab fleets of the L.M.C.P.A. Instead, the London cab trade had become a hotch-potch of small proprietors (with the exception of a few) who, with the owner drivers and the journeymen drivers over the past sixty years have spent more time arguing amongst themselves rather than come together for the common good.

There is now considerable doubt as to whether the Home Secretary had powers to fix fares for motor cabs under legislation passed in 1869, more than thirty years before the first motor cab plied for hire on the streets of London. This doubt first manifested itself during the Committee of Inquiry of 1911. (19)

A principal witness at this inquiry was a Mr. William P. Byrne C.B., Assistant Under Secretary of State at the Home Office. He said, "the Secretary of State had been advised by the Attorney General that his discretion regards to the tariff for taxicabs was not limited by the earlier acts at all, just because the provisions of those acts relating to fares, related only to horse cabs. This was announced in the House of Commons and it has universally been accepted ever since. It has never been opposed or questioned in the law courts". (20)

The Home Secretary had indeed announced it in the House of Commons but not because he thought it politic to do so but because his statement had been elicited by John O'Connor, M.P. (Kildare N.) in April 1907 who asked, "whether the minimum fare for hiring hackney carriages is fixed by law having regard to the provisions of 31 & 32 Victoria C134 and 32 & 33 Victoria section 9 and is the recent order issued by the Home Office fixing fares, within such provision and if not will the regulations to these fares be withdrawn". (21)

Mr. Gladstone replied (the statement referred to by Mr. William P. Byrne) "the only fares fixed by my recent order for taximeter cabs are the fares set out for motor cabs in schedule K as advised by the Attorney General". That the Home Secretary had grave doubts as to the legality of his order of March 15th 1907 is now evident. His original intention of doing without an act of Parliament was abandoned as he came under constant pressure. Reluctantly he was forced to introduce, on August 1st 1907, a Bill destined for a quick passage through Parliament. Before coming to that we should perhaps examine how Mr. Gladstone misled Parliament, the trade and the public with his order of March 15th. 1907. The answer comes from the evidence submitted by Superintendent Bassom of the Public Carriage Office during the Committee of Inquiry of 1911.

Replying to a question put to him by Sir Archibald Williamson, M.P., chairman of the committee, he said, "it was at that time necessary to consider whether, having regard to the provisions of section 9 of the act of 1869 (32 & 33 Victoria C115) that the Secretary of State would have the power to fix a fare commencing at 8d. which would of course be lower than that payable at the time of the passing of the act. It was considered, however, that under the provisions of section 45 of the London Hackney Carriage Act of 1831, (1st & 2nd William IV C22) as the driver could agree to carry a passenger for a sum less than the legal fare authorised and could not demand or accept more, he would, by agreeing to drive a cab for which a lower tariff was authorised, tacitly agree to carry at those fares". (22)

Section 45 of the 1831 Act gives drivers discretionary powers to accept a fare lower than the authorised fare but having done so, could not, on reaching the destination ask for more. The driver was under no obligation to accept a lower fare, yet the Home Secretary and the Attorney General, in collusion, had made a discretionary and non obligatory situation into a compulsory one. Thus, they had applied the full power of the law where in fact it had no power.

Pressure was again applied by John O'Connor, M.P. on April 23rd 1907, when he asked the Home Secretary, "whether the minimum fare fixed by law was one shilling; whether motor cabs with or without taximeters are hackney carriages and how can the Right Hon. Gentlemen, within the provisions of the law, fix a fare less than one shilling". With incredible effrontery, Mr. Gladstone replied, "any lower scale indicated by the taximeter as payable by the hirer would be a contract scale as recognised by section 45 of the 1831 act". (23)

In this sense a contract is an agreement freely entered into by the driver to charge a lower fare. The Home Secretary had made it mandatory and he did not have the power to do so. The London Cabdriver's Union was the only section of the trade who sought to oppose the Home Secretary and they announced on April 24th 1907, that steps were to be undertaken to bring the matter before the courts so that any doubts might be removed but for some reason they did not proceed with the action.

On July 3rd. 1907, John O'Connor again tackled the Home Secretary in Parliament, when he asked Mr. Gladstone, "whether the motor cabs at present in London were running illegally". Mr. Gladstone replied that it was not so; "no difficulty", he said, "had arisen under the new order with regard to motor cabs". (24) Less than a month later he introduced the 1907 Act of Parliament (7th of Edward 7th C55) to cover up his stupendous blunder of March 15th 1907.

Some form of legality had to be drawn over this sad spectacle and Mr. Gladstone introduced the Bill on August 1st. It was read a second time on August 5th and committed to Standing Committee B on August 9th., who reported back on the 14th. The Bill was read a third time, passed by 176 votes to 24 against and sent to the House of Lords where, as we have seen, a protracted debate ensued on that part of the Bill dealing with the abolition of the privilege cab system. Not one word was mentioned concerning fares or any suggestion of impropriety by the Home Secretary or the Attorney General except for one amendment put by Ramsay MacDonald "but no fare shall be less than sixpence". (25)

No one doubted the integrity of the Home Secretary and the Attorney General, with the exception of John O'Connor M.P. Even the Committee of Inquiry in 1911 failed to grasp the impact of what had been revealed to them. The drivers, well organised in the London Cab Drivers Union were determined to have their share of a small cake and a long and bitter struggle developed as we have seen between the drivers and the proprietors. The large fleets were decimated and the ranks of the owner driver grew on a low fare structure supported by a 70 hour week.

References used in Chapter Twelve

1. R.A.C. Journals, December 8th 1910, p. 389. (RAC Library)
2. Ibid.
3. Metropolitan Police Reports, 1900/49 Parly Papers. (GRL)
4. Commercial Motor, June 1907. (SMA)
5. R.A.C. Journals, January 1910. (RAC Library)
6. Departmental Committee on Taxicab Fares. 1911. (GRL)
7. Select Committee on Cabs, Parly Papers, Reports & Minutes of Evidence, 1906 Vol. 7.
8. Ibid.
9. Departmental Committee on Cabs. 1895. Vol. 6.
10. 16th & 17th Victoria C33 S7.
11. Ex Parte (Kippins) 1897, 1 QB 1 Grantham v Wright.
12. For details of the debate and proceedings in the House of Commons and Lords see Journals of the House of Commons (7th Edward 7th) Vol. 162pp. 407/461.
13. The Times, November 3rd, 1911 p. 8. (Brit. Mus. Col.)
14. Ibid. November 7th, 1911 p. 8. (Brit. Mus. Col.)
15. Ibid. March 11th, 1912 p. 6. (Brit. Mus. Col.)
16. Ibid. March 20th, 1912 p. 18. (Brit. Mus. Col.)
17. Details of drivers earnings, cost of fuel etc., can be found in the Departmental Committee on Taxicabs, Reports & Returns, Minutes of Evidence. (1911) (GRL).
18. The details of the petrol strike and the events of 1917 have been freely drawn from The Times (Brit. Mus. Col.) between November 22nd 1912 to March 20th 1913 and between October 16th 1917 and December 21st 1917.
19. Departmental Committee on Taxicabs, Reports and Returns, Minutes of Evidence, 1911.
20. Ibid. p. 12. Q.22.

21. Hansard, Parliamentary Debates, Vol. 172, with 4th series, 3rd April to 23rd April 1907.
22. Departmental Committee on Taxicabs, Reports and Returns, Minutes of Evidence, 1911.
23. The Times, April 23rd. 1907. p.6.
24. Ibid. July 4th 1907. p.6.
25. House of Commons Papers, 1907, Vol. 5.

Chapter Thirteen

"In the public's interest"

The years immediately following World War I were years of chaos for the London cab trade. Towards the end of the war spares had become almost impossible to obtain and many cabs had been kept on the road by cannibalising others. In 1919 and 1920 this problem was aggravated when several thousand cabmen could not find work after their demobilisation because of the shortage of cabs. This shortage served to push up the price of second hand cabs and Palmers of Tooting were selling Unics, Vinots and Fiats for more than they had cost when new some seven to eight years previously.

The ex-servicemen complained bitterly that while they were standing idle some 400 to 500 cabs were out of commission because of the ten inch chassis clearance rule laid down by the new Conditons of Fitness. Consequently, many proprietors had sold off these cabs for conversion to light delivery vans and other types of vehicle. (1) Official figures tell the story. By the end of the 1914 - 1918 war the number of cabs had fallen from 8,338 in 1913 to 3,821 in 1918. By 1923 the number of cabs had risen to 7,283 though still more than 1,000 fewer than in 1913. Scotland Yard was quick to issue a statement refuting the accusation that it was the ten inch chassis rule which was causing the shortage. It said:-

"The licensing authority had not insisted on the 10" clearance. Several companies had asked that this rule be waived in order that they could put cabs on the road. In March (1919) the Ford Motor Company had sought permission to place 500 cabs in London, though they were not up to standard. Again permission was given because of the cab shortage but nothing further had been heard from this company". (2)

Against this controversial background, the William Beardmore Motor Company Ltd., launched it's Mk I taxicab. This company was a large engineering concern and made it's cabs at the old Arroll-Johnson car company's works at Paisley. Later, the taxis were produced at it's Anniesland (Glasgow) factory after car production had ceased there. A subsidiary company had been set up with a capital of £¼ million to supply the cabs for cash or on hire purchase and by November 1919, agreements had been completed and contracts signed for 1,120 cabs.

It was mainly these cabs which had helped to bring the total number of cabs licensed in 1923 to 7,283. But the increase in the number of cabs was to bring the London cab trade into confrontation with the powerful and influential Lord Ashfield and as a result a long and bitter struggle was to continue into the

1930's. Apart from being chairman of several railway companies, Lord Ashfield was also chairman of the London General Omnibus company. "Some remedy" he told a meeting of shareholders in 1924, "must be found for competition that is destructive", (3) a statement that embraced the cab trade as much as it did the independent bus operators.

Lord Ashfield was the driving force behind the growth of London's public transport system. For almost forty years he dominated the growth of the buses and the underground railway system. He had a dream of one single authority for London's transport, a dream which was shared by Herbert Morrison. It was Morrison who eventually sponsored a Bill which became law in 1933, establishing the London Passenger Transport Board.

Lord Ashfield's plan to do away with competition from the independent bus operators and London's taxis was made possible by the Road Transport Act of 1924 and from the London and Home Counties Traffic Advisory Committee set up by the authority of that act. But the arrival of that act on the statute book was as the direct result of the transport strike in 1924. The bus and tramdrivers wages had recently been reduced from £2.0.0. a week to £1.5.0. The drivers were seeking a rise of 8/- but the L.G.O.C. were resisting because, they said, there was no money to pay for it. Until the reduction in wages the company had been strike free since 1905 but while wages had only increased by 69 per cent since 1905, the cost of living had increased by 79 per cent during the same period. (4)

The two principal witnesses at the Court of Inquiry investigating the strike were Ernest Bevin, then General Secretary of the Transport and General Workers Union, and Lord Ashfield. Both were seeking the elimination of competition. Lord Ashfield was empire building and the independent bus operators were in his way, while Bevin on the other hand, saw the elimination of the non-combine buses as a means to higher wages for his members. He knew that with the street's of London open only to Ashfield's L.G.O.C. the company's revenue would increase and his claim for higher wages would be substantiated.

Lord Ashfield told the inquiry, "clearly, the present methods for dealing with passenger transport in London cannot possibly secure to the public, employees, or to those who have invested in these undertakings, a satisfactory position. If you leave competition open to free play, in the end it brings disaster. You can have competition in almost every other form of industry but you cannot have competition in transport". The chairman of the inquiry asked Bevin and Lord Ashfield "if a promise on the part of the government to introduce and press forward legislation would make the position a negotiable one?" (5) Both replied that it would and the Road Traffic Act of 1924 was theirs as a result.

The definition of the term omnibus was wide enough to include motor coaches, of which no more than 400 were operating in the Metropolitan Police area. By the end of 1927 these coaches were beginning to operate in London in a manner which brought them into competition with the ordinary omnibus. Although some prosecutions were obtained the Commissioner of Police was advised that there were practical difficulties in gaining convictions against the coach operators and from 1928 onwards, coach operation in London increased rapidly.

It was the strict control of omnibuses which greatly contributed to the growth of coach operation. They were able to expand almost without restriction because of the difficulty, pending new legislation, of exercising any control over the new form of transport. There was no control of fares, anyone could buy a coach or pay a deposit to obtain one on hire purchase and then operate services to which ever destination he required.

London's buses were soon afforded the protection they needed by the Road Traffic Act of 1930. Under the act the Traffic Commissioners were told that they should have "special regard to the desirability of restricting the operation of motor coach services in the Central London area". (6) So successful was this special regard that from a total of 3,558 applications for coach licences, only 2,091 were granted.

In 1933 the London Passenger Transport Board was formed by merging buses, trams and the underground railway under one body. Small wonder that Lord Ashfield was able to say that, "the formation of the L.P.T.B., with the elimination of competition between the different groups, has rendered the development of bus operation on entirely different principles and it is desirable to consider whether traffic difficulties can be relieved by taking the fullest advantage of the unified control which has been conferred on the Board by the London Passenger Transport Act of 1933".

It was Lord Ashfield's avowed intention to relegate taxis to the position where they would not conflict with buses. This he achieved by using his position as chairman of the London and Home Counties Traffic Advisory Committee, on which the cab trade had no representation. He was not seeking to abolish taxis but to restrict their movement and to curtail their growth. Between 1925 following the formation of the Traffic Advisory Committee and 1933 with the appointment of the London Passenger Transport Board, Lord Ashfield had met with considerable success.

Successive governments had always claimed to be "acting in the public's interest", a phrase which covers a multitude of decisions designed to benefit one particular group of persons, who somehow, manage to surround themselves in a cloak of anonymity. Between 1925 and 1933 London's cab trade survived three massive onslaughts, which were designed to bolster the omnibus company where there was considerable 'public' investment.

The decision early in 1925 by the Home Secretary, Sir William Joynson-Hicks, to appoint a committee to consider the introduction of a two seater cab, came as a bombshell to the cab trade. There had been no previous mention of such a prospect, questions had not been asked in the House of Commons, neither had there been 'letters' to The Times.

The committee was appointed on March 31st, under the chairmanship of Mr. Basil Peto, M.P. and reported it's findings on June 17th 1925. It's principal object was, "to consider whether it is desirable in the public interest to licence to ply for hire as cabs, any type of four wheeled vehicle constructed or intended to carry less than four persons, and, if so, to make recommendations on the rates of fare which should be fixed". The committee was also charged to take into account "that the convenience of the public must be considered before any hardship to vested interest". (7)

Only one person supported the case for a two seater cab. He was Mr. Rene W. Owen, the managing director of White, Holmes & Co. Ltd., of Hammersmith, who was proposing to build such a cab. He maintained that the majority of passengers did not want four seats and the fact that it required a much heavier engine to propel the larger cab made it more costly to run. A cheaper cab he thought, would be a better commercial proposition because it would attract new passengers and would run fewer wasted miles. His figures, however, were based on the theory that there would be more hirings and there was no way, short of practical experience of proving or disproving his assumption.

For it's part, the cab trade, proprietors, owner drivers and journeymen drivers, were unanimous in their opposition to the two seater cab. They were adamant that the existing cabs fully met the public's requirements for there was nothing the two seater can could do which the four seater cab could not do, but the converse could not be said. It was the union's view that two seater cabs would not be able to cope with extra passengers and luggage at railway stations and it was unreasonable to expect four seater cabs to exist on that work alone. "It is the combination of being able to obtain fares on the streets and at railway stations that has made it possible to provide the public with the cab service it has today". (8)

But the cab trades best case was the anology of 1907, given by Superintendent Bassom, of the Public Carriage Office, who told the committee of inquiry, "in accordance with recommendations of the 1906 Select Committee, small folding seats were allowed inside but for the use of which drivers could not make a charge. Other makers then begun to put on cabs with full seating capacity, which proved if anything more popular than the smaller cabs, so that the management of the General Cab Co. were induced to alter their existing cab bodies at considerable cost to meet the new demand".

The committee of inquiry were of the opinion that the smaller cab, plying at a lower fare, would undoubtedly cause hardship and loss to the owners of the existing type of cabs. It was their view that the best solution would be to have lower fares all round, rather than have two rates of fare, one for four seater and one for two seater cabs. If no agreement for a reduction of fares could be reached, then on the balance of the public interest, two seater cabs should be admitted and a lower fare authorised.

Following these recommendations the cab trade associations called for a mass meeting to be held at the South London Palace, in London Road near the Elephant and Castle. At that meeting, held on Sunday, February 7th, 1926, it emerged that all sections of the trade, with the exception of the L.M.C.P.A. were firmly of the opinion that there was no need for a lower fare or a two seater cab. The L.M.C.P.A. representing the major companies said that to prevent the two seater cab, lower fares would have to be accepted.

The general view of the meeting was that there had been no call for the general public for a reduction in fares or for a two seater cab. The present situation they felt, was purely the result of a press campaign by certain newspapers representing the omnibus interest and that it was being forced on the trade by backstairs methods both inside and outside the House of Commons. The cost of altering taximeters at the time of the fare increase in 1920 had cost £20,000 and it was estimated that to alter them again would cost £25,000, "who will foot that bill" asked Mr. S.H. Elford of the Owner Driver's Association. (9)

Many London M.P.s were not happy with the situation and they pressed upon the Home Secretary the desirability of a further meeting with the cab trade representatives; to which he agreed. At this eleventh hour meeting on March 23rd, the Home Secretary rejected their proposals of 6d for the first half mile, 3d for each one third of a mile and waiting time reduced from 6/- to 4/- per hour. The following day the Home Secretary issued a statement that he was permitting the use of two seater cabs at a fare of 9d for the first mile and 3d for each third of a mile. Announcing his intention in the House of Commons, Sir William Joynson-Hicks said, "am I to say that the two seater cabs should not be put on the road and that Londoners should not have the privilege of a cheaper ride because this would be injurious to the existing cab trade". (10)

Was there another reason for his apparent intransigence? A contemporary of the time speaking of Sir William Joynson-Hicks, called him "a self opinionated busy body, vain, with a great deal of self esteem who thought of himself as a real force in the London passenger vehicle industry". His connections with the London General Omnibus Company were impeccable. His father, Henry Hicks, had been appointed Vice Chairman of the L.G.O.C. in 1891, while he himself had been the company's solicitor. In that capacity he had played a notable part in the merger with the Underground Electric Railways of London Ltd. (11) It seems strange that a man with such a background should have been given ultimate power over London's taxi trade.

The new regulations came into force on April 6th. 1926 and the Home

Office fully expected some 500 of the smaller cabs as a result of the new proposals. Almost immediately a cab appearing to answer to the requirements was put on show. It was a KRC which closely resembled a four seater cab. It's manufacturers, Messrs. White, Holmes & Co. Ltd., claimed that it's 10 hp engine and overall weight of 18 cwt. gave it a performance of between 35 and 40 mph. However, the cab trade pledged, in a manifesto published the following day, "not to buy or drive a two seater cab".

It soon became apparent that all was not well with the project. On Thursday, June 23rd. 1926, the Home Secretary said in the House of Commons in a reply to Sir F. Meyer, M.P. (Great Yarmouth) that "an approximate date when the two seater cab would be ready to ply for hire could not be stated. Three firms had taken active steps with regard to production. One was experiencing difficulty owing to the coal strike, another was not satisfied with the trial tests of the engine, while a third had submitted a specimen chassis which revealed many defects". (12)

There is considerable evidence to suggest that Sir William Joynson-Hicks was misleading the House of Commons. Within five days of his statement to the House, a KRC with a laundalette body was presented at the Public Carriage Office for approval. Far from being a chassis the KRC was a fully completed cab ready for work and was approved on June 9th. 1926. (13)

The last attempt to introduce a two seater cab to London was with this Cape bodied Morris Chassis complete with sliding doors in June 1929.

Not until February 7th. 1927, did the Home Secretary make another statement about the two seater cab, when, in reply to a question put to him, he said, "I hope the two seater cabs will be ready by the spring". Again he did not disclose the fact that apart from the KRC approved the previous June, another cab, a two seater had received full approval. This was a Beardmore two seater, chassis number 25101 which was approved on October 19th. 1926. (14) Not another two seater cab was presented at the Public Carriage Office until Beardmore presented another cab on February 18th. 1928; it was not approved. Between then and October 1928, so confident were the major cab manufacturers that a two seater cab would never appear that no fewer than eight different models of four seater cabs were presented for approval.

The final seal on the death of the two seater came on June 21st. 1929, when a Mr. Gowan presented for approval a 'Cape' body cab (so called because Mr. Gowan came from Capetown) on a Morriss G. Chassis, with two seats. It was rejected with a long list of defects. The two seater was dead, killed by the determination of the cab trade not to give way to pressure from Parliament. Not one two seater cab was ever purchased or plied for hire on the streets of London.

References used in Chapter Thirteen

1. Commercial, Motor February 1919.
2. The Times, March 28th, 1924 p. 9.
3. Ibid. February 22nd, 1924 p. 22.
4. Ibid. March 24th. 1924. p. 17.
5. Ibid.
6. Annual Report of the Traffic Commissioners 1931/2 to P.J. Pybus, Minister of Transport. (GRL)
7. Parly Papers, 1925. Two Seater Cab Committee (CMND 2466) (GRL)
8. Ibid. p. 12.
9. The Times. February 8th. 1926. p. 7.
10. Ibid. March 30th. 1926 p. 11.
11. History of London Transport, Barker & Robbins. (GRL)
12. The Times, June 4th, 1926 p. 8.
13. P.C.O. (Motor Cab Approval Type Book) P.C.O. Records.
14. Ibid. p. 63.

Chapter Fourteen

"A breach of faith"

On April 27th. 1927, almost two years after the Home Secretary's threat to lower fares if the two seater cab was not accepted, he announced a reduction in cab fares of 25 per cent, 6d for the first mile and 3d for each succeeding quarter of a mile. This was considerably lower in fact, than those proposed by Sir William Joynson-Hicks for the two seater cabs. The Home Secretary was not prepared to give any concessions on the Conditions of Fitness, which may have resulted in a cheaper cab, believing that "it is essential to have really strong cabs in London and there must be no whittling down of the margins of safety".

The new fare came into force on May 1st 1927, and the following day the Joint Trade Committee accused the Home Secretary of a breach of faith. At a meeting between trade representatives and the Home Secretary on April 5th at the Home Office, an agreement had been reached whereby the trade would accept a reduced fare if the Home Secretary cancelled the two seater cab order, gave permission for advertisements to be displayed inside cabs and that the lower fare would be for an experimental period. Following the reduction in fares the Home Secretary did not cancel the two seater cab order neither would he allow advertisements inside cabs. (1)

The Home Secretary denied there had been a breach of faith saying, "I never pledged that two seater cabs would be forbidden to be licenced, without grave injustice to the manufacturers who for the past year have been working on the designs for two seater cabs". He was accused in the House of Commons by Ben Smith M.P. of speaking "at least beside the truth", saying, "the letter that was sent to the press contained statements that were other than the truth and I ask the Right Hon. Gentleman, in the light of the statement made by him in my presence to the cab trade delegates that he would withdraw the two seater cab". (2) At this point, because of the uproar in the House, the Speaker intervened saying that the matter had gone beyond the question stage and would have to be taken up at a later date.

Within a month of the lower fares coming into force, the J.T.C. asked the Home Secretary to reconsider. Most of it's members felt that if it went on too long, many would be made bankrupt. Although there had been a slight increase in the number of people using cabs, there was still an overall drop in takings of 22 per cent. The effective return after driver's commission had been paid was 4d a mile which was not enough to ensure commercial viability.

Fares were now only 12 per cent higher than they were in 1917 while the cost of living was up by 55 per cent since then. On the other hand all other types of transport fares had increased by nearly 100 per cent over the pre- war figure. Costs too had risen, apart from a current drop in the price of petrol, which at this period was fluctuating. The price of cabs had increased by 50 per cent, road tax had increased to £15 per annum and the taximeter rental had recently increased from £5 to £12. It must also be borne in mind that it was very costly to maintain cabs to the very high standard demanded by the Public Carriage Office. Apart from that, rent, rates, wages for mechanics and washers etc., were all higher than pre-war.

DECREASE OF FARES. *May, 1927.*

Old Fare s. d.	New Fare s. d.	Old Fare s. d.	New Fare s. d.	Old Fare s. d.	New Fare s. d.	Old Fare s. d.	New Fare s. d.	Old Fare s. d.	New Fare s. d.
1 0	0 9	7 3	5 6	13 6	10 2	19 9	14 10	26 0	19 6
1 3	1 0	7 6	5 8	13 9	10 4	20 0	15 0	26 3	19 9
1 6	1 2	7 9	5 10	14 0	10 6	20 3	15 3	26 6	19 11
1 9	1 4	8 0	6 0	14 3	10 9	20 6	15 5	26 9	20 1
2 0	1 6	8 3	6 3	14 6	10 11	20 9	15 7	27 0	20 3
2 3	1 9	8 6	6 5	14 9	11 1	21 0	15 9	27 3	20 6
2 6	1 11	8 9	6 7	15 0	11 3	21 3	16 0	27 6	20 8
2 9	2 1	9 0	6 9	15 3	11 6	21 6	16 2	27 9	20 10
3 0	2 3	9 3	7 0	15 6	11 8	21 9	16 4	28 0	21 0
3 3	2 6	9 6	7 2	15 9	11 10	22 0	16 6	28 3	21 3
3 6	2 8	9 9	7 4	16 0	12 0	22 3	16 9	28 6	21 5
3 9	2 10	10 0	7 6	16 3	12 3	22 6	16 11	28 9	21 7
4 0	3 0	10 3	7 9	16 6	12 5	22 9	17 1	29 0	21 9
4 3	3 3	10 6	7 11	16 9	12 7	23 0	17 3	29 3	22 0
4 6	3 5	10 9	8 1	17 0	12 9	23 3	17 6	29 6	22 2
4 9	3 7	11 0	8 3	17 3	13 0	23 6	17 8	29 9	22 4
5 0	3 9	11 3	8 6	17 6	13 2	23 9	17 10	30 0	22 6
5 3	4 0	11 6	8 8	17 9	13 4	24 0	18 0	30 3	22 9
5 6	4 2	11 9	8 10	18 0	13 6	24 3	18 3	30 6	22 11
5 9	4 4	12 0	9 0	18 3	13 9	24 6	18 5	30 9	23 1
6 0	4 6	12 3	9 3	18 6	13 11	24 9	18 7	31 0	23 3
6 3	4 9	12 6	9 5	18 9	14 1	25 0	18 9	31 3	23 6
6 6	4 11	12 9	9 7	19 0	14 3	25 3	19 0	31 6	23 8
6 9	5 1	13 0	9 9	19 3	14 6	25 6	19 2	31 9	23 10
7 0	5 3	13 3	10 0	19 6	14 8	25 9	19 4	32 0	24 0

Levy's Ltd KING'S CROSS

32-34 York Road, King's Cross, London, N.1

Telephone - NORTH 4112/3.

The foremost Taxi-Cab Garage and Service Depot in London.

A fare conversion chart demonstrating the reduction in fares in May 1927. Issued by Levy's, a famous North London taxi garage to their drivers at the time.

Following the refusal of the Home Secretary to review the position, the right wing Unionist Movement led by Sir Oswald Mosley, saw fit to align itself with the cab trade. As a result of this, the movement did gain a considerable following from among the non Jewish drivers. Pressure applied by the Unionist Movement had the desired effect and the Home Secretary announced that as a result of Sir Oswald Mosley's visit to the Home Office, he was setting up a small technical committee to examine whether it was desirable to make any changes in the design of taxicabs which would make them cheaper. (3)

The existing regulations did not allow brakes on all four wheels, yet every police vehicle had four wheel brakes. Even the petrol tank on taxis were non standard fitting, being placed under the driver's seat and not at the rear as with other vehicles. Fitted in this manner the passengers would be less exposed to risk if the tank burst following an accident and the petrol caught fire. The committee was appointed on July 5th. 1927, under the chairmanship of Captain Douglas Hacking, O.B.E. M.P. Parliamentary Secretary of State at the Home Office.

The Times commenting on the appointment of the committee said "if something is not done, eventually the law of supply and demand must have it's way and bring about considerable reductions in the number of taxis in the streets". Apparently many of the papers' readers agreed. On June 1st. 1927, a Mr. William Shand had written:-

> "Sir,
>
> The recent reduction in taxicab fares does not appear to have led to the increase use of taxicabs which was expected and the industry, particularly the owner driver, seems to be badly hit. I suggest that the public would be well satisfied if the authorised charge reverted to what was previously shown on the meter".

Another letter dated July 27th. read:-

> "Sir,
>
> From all that emerges out of the multiplicity of controversy on the subject of taxicab fares, it would appear that something like the old rate of fare will need to be introduced.
>
> Signed, G. Seaton,
>
> Headley, Hants.

These letters and others in similar vein seemed to bear out the cab trades claim that the call for a lowering of the fares did not come from the public. The controversy raged throughout the remainder of the year without being resolved. The Home Secretary had reaffirmed himself as the guardian of the public's interest and he was not prepared to reopen the question of fares. "I would desire to remind taxidrivers", he said, "that they are a privileged licensed class and it is in their own interests to make the new fare work satisfactorily. In my view, civility and an obliging spirit on their behalf will do much to bring about the desired increase in the number of passengers". (4) Faced with a reduction in wages of 25 per cent it must have been difficult to keep alive the obliging spirit.

In January 1928, came the long awaited report into the Conditions of Fitness regulations. It recommended that advertising should be allowed inside cabs that the chassis 10" ground clearance be reduced to 7" and that the 25 foot turning circle should be increased to 40 feet. The Home Secretary said that he was willing to accept advertisements inside cabs but he was not in favour of reducing the 10" chassis ground clearance. He had been advised he said, by both Scotland Yard and the London Traffic Advisory Committee that the turning circle should not be increased to 40 feet "for it would result in diminished mobility and add to traffic congestion". (5)

Later, when pressed by a group of M.P.s led by Sir William Bull, the Home Secretary reversed his decision regarding the 10" clearance rule, allowing a 7" clearance, and permitting brakes to be fitted to all four wheels. The reduction in the chassis height was especially welcomed by the trade and it was the direct result of the Austin Motor Company's future involvement with the London cab trade.

One of the major distributors at the time was Messrs. Mann and Overton Ltd., who had the franchise for Unic taxis, which the company imported from France. The Unics were expensive because of the high import duty and following the reduction of fares, sales of these vehicles plummeted. Following the reduction in chassis height, W.T. Overton immediately recognised the potential of Austin's Heavy 12/4 chassis as being suitable for London and he approached Sir Herbert Austin with a view to purchase them.

Sir Herbert Austin was at first opposed to the idea because he felt that any association with taxicabs would be considered 'infra dig', but W.T. Overton was persistent and eventually persuaded Sir Herbert that it made good business sense for Austin to be part of the London taxi scene. A contract for 500 chassis was signed in 1929 and the first Austin Heavy 12/4, known affectionately in the trade as 'the high lot' entered service on June 7th. 1930. It had a Dyer & Hobson body and the brakes were actuated on all four wheels. More important was the price, a modest £380 or £50 deposit and £11 per month. The cost of a cab had nearly halved and it was this plus the expected revenue from advertising which the trade hoped would keep it going through the difficult years ahead. (6)

The combination of Austin chassis and Mann & Overton expertise was to prove the dominating factor in the supply of taxis into London. Five years later in 1935, from a total of 1,515 new cabs entering service, 1,178 were Austins. The Austin cab continued to dominate until the outbreak of war in 1939. After the war the Austin cab once again dominated the sales of all new cabs as proprietors and owner drivers opted more and more for the new models as they came along, to the final exclusion of all other makes.

The expected revenue from advertising did not materialise. Responsibility for obtaining the advertisements lay with the Cab Proprietors Council (CPC), a representative body of all owners. In January 1930 they announced that they were abandoning any further attempts to arrange for advertisements in cabs, and as the existing contracts expired the advertisements would be withdrawn. The CPC made every endeavour to promote the success of advertising and had distributed £2,000 to it's members but severe opposition had come from vested interests, mainly newspapers and the L.G.O.C., who resented the intrusion of a new medium. The claim made by Sir William Joynson-Hicks that the revenue from advertising would partly offset the reduction in fares could not now be justified.

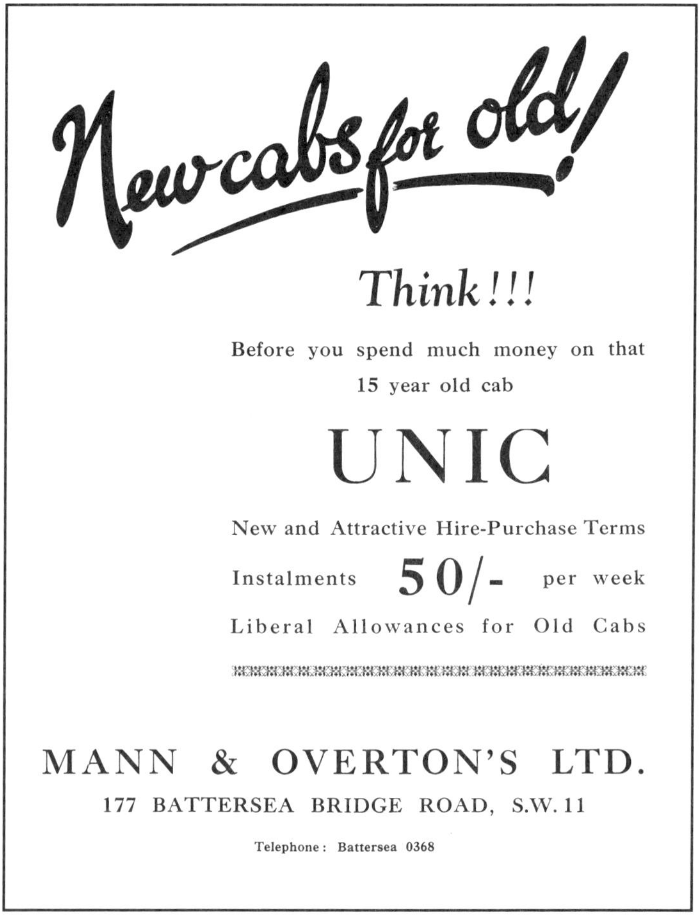

A 1929 sales advertisement by Mann & Overton's Ltd, extolling the virtues of hire purchase for Unic cabs just prior to their involvement with Austins.

The combination of reduced fares and high costs had driven many owner drivers to seek the indulgence of the hire-purchase companies. It was clear that the reduced fare had not resulted in an increase of passengers and for many medium sized firms the drop in fares led down the road to bankruptcy. The fate which befell one such company, Frary & Johnston Ltd., of Stockwell in South-West London, was similar to that which befell many others.

During the bankruptcy proceedings in 1932 it was stated that "..the reduction in taxicab fares affected their business considerably and the following rise in petrol duty had caused a heavy decline. Police restrictions with regard to their vehicles forced them to keep a good class of stock and their declining capital meant that they could not purchase outright. The recent increase in the price of petrol had been the last straw". (7)

The larger companies could weather the storm but only at a price. The largest cab company at this time was the London General Cab Company Ltd. It operated 570 taxis and employed 1,000 men. At the beginning of 1929 it's paid up capital was £67,000 and it's gross profit for that year was £25,188. By 1932 it had made a loss of £5,940. The Coupe Motor Company Ltd., with a capital of £33,232 had a gross profit in 1929 of £10,195, by 1932 their balance sheet showed a profit of only £2,454. (8)

The price of fuel is of prime importance to the passenger carrying industry, far outweighing the cost of vehicles, which being of sturdy construction and lasting over a large number of years have a low depreciation value for the original capital investment. In April 1928 the price of petrol soared from 1/-½ d a gallon to 1/4¾d a gallon and reached 1/7d a gallon in March 1929. From that peak the price fluctuated until September 1932 when it stood at 1/4½d having fallen as low as 1/2½d in July of that year. At the end of September 1932 the price rose to 1/7½d a gallon, the price referred to in the bankruptcy proceedings of Frary & Johnston Ltd. (9)

On February 11th. 1933, a new Home Secretary, Sir John Gilmour, announced an increase of fare from 6d for the first mile to 9d. The proprietary side of the trade accepted the increase but the drivers did not, for they were convinced that the rise would cost them dear. It was common practice at that time for the driver, when asked by a passenger "how much", to reply "one sixpence". Often, the passenger, especially if he or she were not regular riders, would mistake the answer as "one and sixpence" and proceed to give the driver two shillings.

The increase of fare was to be recorded by a 'sticker' until such time as the meters could be altered. It was the use of this 'sticker' which precipitated the strike that commenced on August 2nd. 1933, at the garage of W. G. Du Cros Ltd. The T. & G.W.U. pointed out that when the fares were reduced in 1927 the task of changing some 8,000 meters was not accomplished until 1928 and the drivers were not prepared this time to wait eighteen months while the meters were changed. (10)

By August 4th. the strike had spread to the London General Cab Co. Ltd., where all the drivers came out on strike. There were indications that the strike would spread and by the following day the Coupe Cab Co. Ltd. and Punter's Garage Ltd. had stopped work. The strike was then made official by the union and by late evening the number of drivers on strike had increased to 5,000 and 75 per cent of London's cabs were out of service.

Earlier in the day the L.M.C.P.A. had made an offer that pending the alteration of the meters, drivers of those cabs with 6d. meters would be permitted to retain 2d of the 3d increase. The strike was eventually settled on August 14th. 1933, when the L.M.C.P.A. issued a statement saying, "the settlement means that as each cab is fitted with a revised meter the driver goes back to 30 per cent commission. Meanwhile the driver retains the whole 3d". (11) Significantly, all the meters were altered by the end of November, just four months after the increase.

References used in Chapter Fourteen

1. The Times, May 3rd 1927, p. 13. (Brit. Mus. Col.)
2. Ibid. May 6th, 1927, p. 11. (Brit. Mus. Col.)
3. Ibid. June 17th. 1927. p. 14. (Brit. Mus. Col.)
4. Ibid. June 25th, 1927, p. 13. (Brit Mus. Col.)
5. Ibid. February 28th. 1928. p.11. (Brit. Mus. Col.)
6. Taxicabs, A Photographic History. Philip Warren & Malcolm Linskey, Almark 1975, and second edition Taxi Trade Promotions 1981.
7. Steering Wheel, January 25th. 1930. p. 185, from the authors private collection but which are also in the Brit. Mus. Library.
8. Taximen and Taxi owners in London, W. Fox. Published by the Labour Research Department, 1935. from a copy in the author's private collection.
9. Ibid.
10. Ibid August 10th 1933, p. 142.
11. Ibid. August 19th. pp. 242, 243, 244, 245.

Chapter Fifteen

"Cruising cabs"

In The Times of Monday, June 26th, 1926, there appeared the following letter.

> "Sir,
> I suggest as an experiment to prevent cruising cabs, that by regulation, cabs should only be hired from ranks in certain streets, i.e. Piccadilly, Bond Street, etc., between specific hours of daylight.
> Signed, George Maxwell".

A few weeks later, Colonel Ashley, M.P., Minister of Transport said that something must be done to reduce the number of vehicles causing congestion". It had been, he said, "the unanimous vote of London Traffic Advisory Committee". (1) This committee was chaired by Lord Ashfield, the man dedicated to make London's buses pay their way. In September 1926 the Advisory Committee proposed that certain streets within a three mile radius of Charing Cross should be closed to cabs plying for hire, with the exception of those on a rank. This meant that cabs within this area would not be able to pick up a fare, even if hailed, in the very streets where most of their work was obtained.

At a mass meeting of the cab trade, held in the South London Palace on September 12th. Mr. W.H. Tucker, secretary of the Joint Trade Committee told those present, "many ranks in Central London have been taken away, in any case, congestion in London is mainly due to buses. London's streets were never designed for such ponderous vehicles too large and cumbersome to expect anything else but congestion". The cab trade was now embattled on two fronts for they were, at the same time, opposing the attempt by the Home Office to introduce the two seater cab.

Almost a year had passed when, on the recommendations of the London Traffic Advisory Committee, the Minister of Transport issued regulations in August 1927, forbidding unhired taxis to loiter except for picking up or setting down passengers and drivers were not permitted to allow the cab to stop elsewhere other than on a cab rank. Though not as drastic as the original proposals, drivers could not risk driving at a speed which was too fast should a fare hail him.

The new regulations would have given the buses complete domination in Central London. The authorities knew that there were sufficient ranks in London for only 4,000 taxis, yet some 8,000 were licensed. They had little alternative but to cruise looking for work. Not only were they being denied the right to pick up fares in Central London between 8.00 am. and 7.00 pm., even worse, Charing Cross Road, Piccadilly, Coventry Street, Shaftesbury Avenue, Regent Street, Oxford Street, Tottenham Court Road, the Strand and Kingsway were virtually closed to cabs that were plying for hire between 8.00 am and midnight. (2)

On May 26th. 1931, the Minister of Transport proposed new regulations for cruising cabs, to be effective from January 1st. 1932. Again it had been the London Traffic Advisory Committee who had initiated the proposals. They extended the area under control to include Chelsea, Kensington, south as far as Vauxhall Bridge and north to High Holborn including Southampton Row. (3) For the first time taxis were to be banned from making "U" turns in Oxford Street, Regent Street and Bond Street. This brought protests from the cab proprietors that the 25 foot turning circle which was insisted upon by Scotland Yard, added £100 to the cost of the cab, yet they were being denied the right to turn round in the very streets which the cabs were designed to do.

At this time there were four members of the Traffic Advisory Committee, particularly concerned with London. They were Sir H. Walker (railways), Mr. F. Picks (London General Omnibus Company), Mr. W.F. Mallender (the Association of Omnibus Proprietors) and Mr. J.H. Turner (London Cartage and Haulage Association), in addition it's chairman was Lord Ashfield. Yet, though there were some 8,000 taxis and nearly 11,000 taxidrivers in the London cab trade, they had no representation on this powerful body who were framing regulations to the detriment of the cab trade in favour of the bus interests.

The Taxidriver's League, a newly formed organisation closely allied to the Unionist movement, called a mass meeting in Hyde Park in an organised protest at the new regulations. The meeting was addressed by Mr. L.W. Nicholls who complained that no member of the cab trade was represented on Traffic Advisory Committee. "It is dominated" he said "by our competitors, the London General Omnibus Company. We object at this attempt to make the capital's cab service the scapegoat in the traffic congestion problem".

If anyone was to blame for cruising cabs, it was Scotland Yard. Cab rank places had dropped from the 4,000 available in 1927 to 3,515 in 1931, despite the fact that a deputation from the cab trade had visited Scotland Yard to request more spaces, they had been told that it was not possible. It would appear that Scotland Yard's decision not to increase cab rank space had been influenced by recommendations made by Lord Ashfield that "in our view no additional space should be allocated for cab ranks in Central London". (4)

"Oxford Street is not Ashfield Avenue", was a slogan adopted by the cabdrivers. Because of the reduction in fares and the general depression throughout the country, the cab trade required every facility to conduct it's business. In the areas where demand for cabs was greatest, ranking accommodation was totally inadequate, yet cab ranks were abolished and replaced by bus stops, which increased in numbers. For example, the cab rank and shelter in Duncannon Street, off Trafalgar Square, was removed so it was said, because of the obstruction it caused, but in it's place bus stops were erected which stand there to this day, greatly adding to the congestion. (5)

Meanwhile, a deputation from the cab trade who had met the Traffic Advisory committee argued that the congestion in Central London was not the fault of the cabs, which had barely increased in numbers for ten years but was entirely due to the increase in size and number of omnibuses and coaches. They complained that the regulations seemed designed entirely in the interests of the omnibus companies with a view to eliminating cabs altogether. So acute was the problem that many drivers were afraid to enter the "danger zone" for fear of prosecution.

Lord Ashfield, Chairman of the London General Omnibus Company was a scourge on the London cab trade throughout the !920's and 30's.

Lord Ashfield, in his annual message to shareholders in February 1931, showed to what extent bus and coach traffic had increased. The associated companies had, in 1930, carried between them 117 million more passengers than in 1929, an increase of six per cent, "due in large part", said Lord Ashfield, "to the consolidation of subsidiary companies with the London General Omnibus Company". During this period London had also expanded with more than a 1/4million people moving into London, requiring travel facilities.

Green Line Coaches Ltd., a subsidiary of the L.G.O.C. commenced operation in 1930, carrying 4,000,000 passengers in the first year and at the beginning of 1931 were carrying 200,000 a week, some 10 million a year if Lord Ashfield's figures were correct. The cab trade's view that the size of the omnibus was a major cause of obstruction was supported by the fact that the L.G.O.C. had introduced the model T bus in 1930 and by February 1932, nearly 2,000 were working in London. (6)

A resolution passed by the Joint Trade Committee in July 1931, called upon the Minister of Transport "to rescind the regulations regarding Oxford Street insofar as they relate to the taxi trade, to withdraw the Unhired Cab Regulations (1927) and to abandon the proposed extension of those regulations". The proposed extension of the 1927 regulations had been authorised by Sir Herbert Morrison, Minister of Transport, to become operative on January 1st. 1932. Before that date, in September 1931, he left that position as the result of a Cabinet reshuffle and his place as Minister of Transport was taken over by Mr. P.J. Pybus, M.P. The cab trade waited to see if he would heed the request made to the former minister to withdraw the regulations.

Mr. Pybus announced his decision in July 1932, and although the cab trade had not won all the concessions they were seeking, they were nevertheless pleased at the outcome. The ban on "U" turns in Oxford Street, Regent Street and Bond Street was lifted and here the cab trade owed much to the various shopkeepers associations, who viewed the proposed restrictions on cabs with considerable apprehension. Several banned right hand turns were restored but the waiting restrictions in Oxford Street were allowed to stand.

In the event these new regulations were never ratified but where the 1927 regulations applied there was considerable evidence to suggest that the Metropolitan Police were being over zealous in their interpretation of the regulations. Prosecutions for loitering, caused by drivers waiting to 'put on a rank' or for 'being on foul' i.e. exceeding the number of cabs allowed on a rank, (both of which were as the result of there being insufficient ranks) were running at 200 a month with fines up to a maximum of 5/-. It was not uncommon to see lines of taxis outside Central London magistrates courts, while their drivers were inside answering a summons.

The trade magazine, Steering Wheel, in it's editorial of January 6th. 1934, said, "the police authorities in London have been and are engaged in a wholesale round up of taxidrivers who commit offences against the loitering regulations. During the first seven months of 1933 some 867 drivers were prosecuted". It was not unknown for an over zealous police officer to book a driver of an empty cab simply for giving precedence to the driver of a cab carrying passengers.

The matter was brought to a head in 1935 when Dr. O'Donovan M.P. (Mile End) asked the Home Secretary in the House of Commons, the number of taxidrivers which were summoned by the police in 1932, 1933 and 1934. Sir John Gilmour replied, "within the Metropolitan Police District summonses against cabdrivers for offences arising in the course of their employment, was 920 in 1932, 1,747 in 1933 and 2,319 in 1934. The number of cabs licensed for the same years respectively were 8,121, 8,025 and 8,181". (8)

By 1937 there were signs of a softening of attitude by those in authority. As early as January of that year Mr. H. Alken-Trip, Assistant Commissioner of Police said, "everyone knew that more cab ranks were necessary in the West End in order to prevent the cruising cab. The commissioner had managed to increase the number of ranks in the past year but it was obvious that more were needed".

The cab trade also derived a great deal of pleasure from a report by the Traffic Commissioners in March 1937, which revealed a difference of opinion between them and the London Passenger Transport Board, over a suggestion that only a shuttle service of buses should be permitted in busy streets. The commissioners expressed the view that the traffic problems of Central London could be eased by the Transport Board prescribing a periphery around Central London on which there should be situated terminal bus stations; a shuttle service would then operate within that periphery. This plan, according to Commissioner G.E. Robinson "would remove the congestion in Central London caused by processions of nearly empty buses in the West End". (8)

In the entire report there was not one word about cabs. In the years following the Second World War the controversy over cruising cabs died down. Only occasionally would the London County Council and latterly the Greater London Council mention cabs in connection with transport. There was a gradual change when the G.L.C. became responsible for London Transport, officials began to adopt a more hostile attitude towards the cab trade when they originally wanted to exclude taxis from bus lanes.

As one crisis abated so another loomed. In 1937 Scotland Yard instituted the 'yellow badge' licensing system for the suburban areas of London. This is a restricted form of licence which enabled the holder to work within two and half miles radius of certain ranks which are generally sited adjacent to railway stations such as those at Plaistow, Wimbledon and Ealing. It was then relatively easy to obtain one of these licences because the knowledge examinations necessary to acquire one are considerably easier than the examinations for a full green badge licence.

It was intended to attract local men during the period of heavy unemployment and also to draw off some of the drivers from the Central London area, thereby creating more work for those remaining. Today (1994) there are approximately 2,000 yellow badge drivers from a total of some 17,000 licensed drivers. A yellow badge driver cannot ply for hire outside the area for which he is licensed, though some obtain licences for adjoining areas.

This new licensing system angered the private hire car trade who previously had looked upon suburban London as their own preserve, entirely without justification it can be said, for a London cabdriver is licensed to ply for hire anywhere within the Metropolitan Police District. By February 1938 a new kind of private hire car operator known as 'streamliners' had emerged. So called because they used new, small saloon cars fitted with taximeters and who were steadily encroaching on Central London operating as pseudo taxis charging a lower fare.

Their incursions caused considerable alarm within the licensed trade with the result that the Joint Trade Committee had a meeting with the Home Secretary, Sir Samuel Hoare. Their complaint was that while the licensed trade was tightly bound by regulations, unlicensed vehicles were free from any form of control. The drivers were not subject to medical tests, knowledge test or for any criminal record check, neither were their vehicles subject to any kind of testing as to their public safety. The only restriction they faced was that, in theory, they were not permitted to ply for hire on the streets.

The eminent Barrister, Sir Walter Monckton, K.C. had been briefed by the J.T.C. and he had asked the Home Secretary for private hire cars to be subject to similar legislation which governed the operation of taxis. (9) Meanwhile, a new aspect of the 'streamliners' had become evident. A certain number of licensed drivers had joined them, not only to drive the cars but to run their own 'streamline' groups. Those who drove the new cars were better off than when driving a taxi. They were paid £2 a week plus 1/8d in the pound commission. They worked ten hours a day and in addition received a paid holiday, unheard of in the cab trade, then or now.

On June 22nd. 1938, Sir Samuel Hoare announced that he was setting up a committee of inquiry and it's terms of reference were to include the taxi and private hire trade in England and Wales and it's chairman was to be Sir Clement Hindley. The committee's task was to review, first as regards London and second with regard to England and Wales, the legal provisions applying to taxis and motor vehicles not so licensed. They were to consider what services were or should be provided by each of the two classes of vehicles and to see whether any changes in the law was desirable.

Once again the British Union of Fascists were to intervene in the affairs of the London cab trade. There was no mistaking the enthusiasm which marked a meeting held in the Memorial Hall in Farringdon Street on July 4th. 1938, addressed by Sir Oswald Moseley. His speech lasted two hours and some 2,000 cabdrivers gave him tremendous applause when he spoke on "the British Union and the problems of the taxi industry". He attacked alien financiers and combines and pledged his support in tracing those behind what he called "the private hire car racket". Under his system he said, "the taxi industry and every other industry would be ruled by it's own organisation unless it adopted unfair means and attempted to hold the country to ransom". (10)

The Hindley interim report was published in February 1939. It's principle recommendations were a scheme for the control of private hire vehicles to ensure that they did not infringe the cabs privilege of plying for hire and that the distinction between cabs and hire cars should be more precisely defined. A satisfactory way of achieving this, the report stated, would be to define by statute the term plying for hire. This term should be so phrased as to include vehicles which are advertised as being for hire while standing on private property where they were open to the view of the public. This would include open fronted garages, car parks, courtyards or hotels and blocks of flats etc. Hindley did not think it necessary to control private hire car fares. (11)

The outbreak of the second world war in 1939 brought considerable relief from the 'streamliners' as hundreds were put out of business because of petrol rationing. Their allocation was insufficient to sustain the dead mileage of returning to their base, whereas taxis could seek out the nearest rank. Another casualty of the war was the Hindley Report, sunk without trace and never to be revived.

In October 1970 the long awaited Maxwell Stamp Committee Report was published (12), subsequently described as "a lie dressed up as the truth". One of the major findings of the report stated that: "The (licensing) authority should be an independent body corporate, governed by a Board appointed by the Greater London Council. (13) However, the government decided against taking up the report's recommendations.

In February 1976 the GLC's Department of Planning and Transportation, drew up a confidential report, not intended for publication. (14). At that time discussions were taking place between the Home Office and the GLC as to how the control of London taxis should be transferred from the Home Office to the GLC, one of the recommendations put forward by the Maxwell Stamp Committee's report. A major stumbling block was the Metropolitan Police Commissioner's objection to the GLC's precept to carry out the responsibilities of licensing. Whether the GLC's Department of Transportation and Planning's report was intended to support the GLC's case is a matter for speculation. More probably the report represented the council's permanent official's view of what could be done to prop up the capital's declining bus transport. What better way to do it than by creaming off some of the 100 million passengers carried annually by London's taxis. (15)

The report blamed the taxi trade for the shortage of bus drivers and the delays caused to buses by taxis picking up, setting down and performing 'U' turns. Complaining at the competition between the two modes of transport the report stated: "Observations suggest that people often stand in a bus queue in the hope of a bus arriving but are quite prepared to take a taxi should one pass by". It compared the frequency of services: "buses are seldom timetabled in the West End of London," it said: "but taxi services, although untimetabled, are more predictable in their operation".

Whereas intending bus passengers can only obtain the services of a bus at a bus stop or terminal, intending taxi passengers can hail them in the street, hire them at a rank, telephone a cab rank or one of London's radio circuits. A person waiting for a bus can expect a minimum of five minutes for a bus as opposed to three minutes for a taxi. In practice though waiting for a bus can exceed 15 minutes and in peak times when demand is heavy, taxis can be unobtainable.

The report was critical of the low taxi fares which meant that with four people sharing a cab it only cost twice as much as travelling by bus. "If we take the Underground service into account then three people can travel by taxi up to a distance of six miles for the same fare as the Underground. If four people travel by taxi it is often cheaper than the Underground. People use taxis because they save a considerable amount of time and where time is money are better value than buses. Taxis are better for comfort and pricing, for ease of travel with heavy luggage and because of the highly regarded door-to-door travel".

The main causes for concern were the possible competition for drivers between taxis and buses, at the expense of the bus. The delays caused to buses by taxis in the Central London area and competition for passengers, which reduces public transport usage and revenue. The report concluded by saying: " Legislation to control taxi operation in certain areas could take the form of a complete ban on taxis in certain areas, or streets, entry to a street restricted to carrying passengers only and control in the form of authorised stopping places only. (15)

Some fifty years separated this report from the original Cruising Cab regulations put forward in 1927 by the London Traffic Advisory Committee. History does not repeat itself, it is simply that different groups of people, when facing a similar situation, will inevitably come to the same conclusion in these cases using the cab trade as a whipping boy.

References used in Chapter Fifteen

1. The Times, July 25th. 1926. (Brit. Mus. Col.)
2. Ibid. August 18th. 1927. p. 7. (Brit. Mus. Col.)

3. Ibid. May 27th. 1931. p. 9. (Brit. Mus. Col.)
4. Steering Wheel, July 25th. 1931. p. 242.
5. The Times, July 21st. 1931. p. 8.
6. Ibid. February 26th. 1932. p. 20.
7. Steering Wheel, March 30th. 1935. p. 51.
8. Traffic Commissioners Report of March 1937, reviewed in Steering Wheel, December 1937, p. 229.
9. Steering Wheel, March 26th. 1938. p. 148.
10. Ibid. July 16th. 1938. p. 109.
11. Interim Report of the Inter-Departmental Committee on Cabs and Private Hire Vehicles. (Cmnd 5938) February 1939.
12. Home Office Departmental Committee on the London Taxi Trade, October 1970, Cmnd. 8443.
13. Ibid. Chapt. 13 para. 5 p.124.
14. GLC Department of Transport and Planning PT/TN/FI February 1976, as 5/8 p.8. In the possession of the author.
15. Home Office Departmental Committee on the London Taxi October 1970, Cmnd. 8443. Chapt. 4 para 4.45 p.47.

Chapter Sixteen

THE MODERN INTERLOPER

It is generally believed that Michael Gotla's abortive attempt to break the hackney carriage laws begun in 1961. This was not so for as far back as 1959, Isaac Wolfson's General Guarantee Company backed this venture by acquiring for £15,000 a 51 per cent controlling interest in Welbeck Motors, to whom it proceeded to loan £1 million. (1)

The Home Office, cast in the role of Pontious Pilate, washed its hands of the matter, sharing the government's view that minicabs were an extension of the private hire car trade and as such were to be welcomed. It regarded the existing law as adequate to protect the licensed taxi trade but as events unfolded it became obvious that there were those who were determined to see that the law was abused. The government continually stated that as plying for hire had no statutory definition, it was difficult to obtain convictions. Yet, they and previous governments had had ample time since the Hindley Report of 1939 and the Runciman Report of 1953, to define plying for hire by law.

The minicab company owned by Isaac Wolfson and managed by Michael Gotla, had to acquire some degree of respectability and to that end the services of two Members of Parliament, Rupert Spier MP and Gresham Cooke MP, were obtained. It was their task to soften up the public, preparing the way for the minicab venture. It began when Rupert Spier, MP for Hexham, said in a statement in the House of Commons on November 7th, 1960, seven months before the first red Renault Dauphines took to the streets:-

"London's cabs are unable to meet the needs of the public and I suggest the introduction of mini taxis and motorised rickshaws which would require Home Office approval". (2)

In reply to Rupert Spiers statement, Mr. Denis Vosper, Minister of State at the Home Office said: "There are three arguments against their use, they would not be strong enough to stand the wear and tear as the average yearly mileage of a London taxi is 40,000; they had been tried in 1928 but there was no demand for them and the limited demand would not justify their manufacture". Having failed to gain the government's open approval, the projectors switched their campaign to a more receptive channel - the press. The Times of March 2nd, 1961 said:-

"Men of wealth have been heard to cry out against the taximeter - men who think nothing of signing away many thousands in a seconds wiggle of a pen, but find it very painful to sit helplessly in the back of a taxi watching their money dripping away in threepenny stages".

The writer in The Times seemed blissfully unaware of the fact that some sixty years previously the paper had been in the van of the campaign for the introduction of the taximeter.

The red Renault Dauphine minicabs were launched by Welbeck Motors on June 19th, 1961, amid a storm of ballyhoo whipped up by the press. "The gay little minicabs", the Daily Mail described them. "If the project is a failure", said The Times, hedging it's bet, "then it will have been a glorious failure". From a Conservative election pamphlet came the words of encouragement: "Let us Conservatives applaud the acumen and initiative of men who are bringing us a cheaper cab service". (3) On the same day the government broke the silence it had steadfastly maintained since the previous November.

"The government does not propose to allow the privilege of plying for hire, which is confined by legislation to licensed taxicabs, to be enjoyed by vehicles which are not subject to proper controls administered by a public authority and who are driven by people who also are not subject to proper control".

That statement has a hollow ring when viewed from the standpoint that in November 1994, there are at least 35,000 minicabs working in London without public control, who ply for hire openly from the kerbside, outside sleazy minicab offices, who flagrantly break the law, laws confirmed by several High Court stated cases.

During the first week of Welbeck Motors minicab operations, the licensed trade was advised by the Transport & General Workers Union, "to leave them alone".

CABMAN!

Your Living is in Danger!
Mini Cabs are increasing Daily
The Crisis Committee needs your support
at a
MASS MEETING
to be held at
CENTRAL HALL
WESTMINSTER
on
Monday, 28th August
7p.m. Doors open 6.40 p.m.

Entrance by Copy Licence only

Come and hear what has been done, what is going on now and what YOU can do to help

2/- Car Park available at Storeys Gate and Lawrence Yard, Marsham Street

Printed by Viking Poster Services Ltd. Cyde Works, Clyde Road Wallington.

A leaflet issued by the Crisis Committee calling for a mass meeting only five weeks after the launch of Welbeck Motors in August 1961.

By August 28th however tempers were rising and some 4,000 drivers packed into Central Hall, Westminster. There were angry scenes as the drivers were told by union officials: "To beat this menace the only way you can beat it, with the active assistance of the authorities". (4)

The active assistance of the authorities was not forthcoming and towards the end of July 1961, London's taxi drivers began to hit back. The apparent ineffectiveness of the T & G W U had led to the formation of an unofficial body, the London Cab Trade Crisis Committee. Its first meetings were held in a room above the 'Victoria' pub near Mornington Crescent, Camden Town. It later moved to the 'Pembury Tavern' in Dalston and from there to its own offices in Fitzroy Street, near Tottenham Court Road.

Almost immediately the Crisis Committee plunged into action by calling a boycott at West London Air Terminal in Cromwell Road, where the management had actively supported the use of minicabs. Despite attempts by the police from Earl's Court Road Police Station, to break the picket line, the boycott was successful. The situation was resolved after executive members of the Crisis Committee met the management of the air terminal and only one or two minor incidents occurred here throughout the remainder of the crisis.

Until October 1961 the licensed taxi trade had met with some success in bringing actions against Welbeck Motors. This it was forced to do in the absence of any attempt by the police to uphold the law. But soon events were to turn against the licensed cabmen and on October 1st, following a case at Great Marlborough Street Magistrates Court, concerning a case where two young women had hailed a minicab in Fulham Road. Mr. Leo Gradwell, the magistrate, dismissed the charge and awarded costs to Welbeck Motors. This particular kind of offence was said by Mr. Denis Vosper at the Home Office to be illegal; Leo Gradwell disagreed with him. (5)

On the same day in the same court, when 22 minicab drivers were summonsed, again before Leo Gradwell, he dismissed the charges against them, telling the defendants that he had a great deal of sympathy for them. (6) Contrast this with the attitude taken by the courts against licensed cabmen who were defending their jobs in face of an onslaught by big business and those in authority; the very people who should have been defending the cabmen, for statutory control, implies statutory protection.

Between August 23rd and November 27th, 1961, 37 taxidrivers were prosecuted by the police arising from incidents involving minicabs. Of these fifteen were found guilty, three summonses were dismissed, five cases had been adjourned, eleven were waiting to be heard and three men had been sent for trial. (7)

The most significant of these cases were those which concerned M. Nally; D. Johns and M. Krushner. Micky Krushner was originally sentenced to two months imprisonment by Leo Gradwell, the minicab sympathiser, at

Great Marlborough Street on November 20th, 1961. An appeal was immediately lodged by the Crisis Committee on his behalf and was heard at the London County Sessions on January 4th, 1961. During cross-examination the minicab driver admitted swerving in front of Micky Krushner at least six times, his passenger said he didn't swerve at all. There were other inconsistencies but it was to no avail; Micky Krushner was sent down.

The case of Nally and Johns united the cab trade as nothing else had done since the days of the two seater cab controversy. Both were committed for trial at the London County Sessions on November 23rd, 1961, where they received a three month prison sentence and were disqualified from driving for three years. This was following an incident in Brompton Road when they tried to prevent a minicab, driven by the son of a police sergeant at Harrow Road Police Station, from picking up a passenger who had hailed it in the street.

One of Welbeck Motors red Renault Daulphines with a taxicab close behind which is probably deliberately boxing it in, c. 1961.

A few days later on November 27th, the Crisis Committee called a mass meeting at Speaker's Corner, Marble Arch. It was attended by over 4,000 cabdrivers and a resolution was passed calling for a 48 hour strike, to be followed by a march through the West End of London, as a protest at the harsh sentence passed on Nally and Johns and other cabdrivers. Both the strike and the march were a huge success and within 24 hours of the strike ending, both Nally and Johns were released from Brixton Prison on bail. The action of the Crisis Committee had been fully vindicated.

On January 23rd, 1962, Lord Chief Justice Parker and two other judges squashed the prison sentence and the three year ban on driving, substituting instead a fine of £100. Lord Parker said: "There was very grave doubt whether a taxi driver sentenced to imprisonment or disqualification would ever be granted a licence again. Only in extreme cases would it be right to inflict a deterrent sentence that would deprive the men of earning their living as taxidrivers". (8) Had the sentences on Nally and Johns not been squashed, they could easily have earned a living as minicab drivers on their release from prison.

Meanwhile, amid all the excitement of Nally and Johns, the strike and the march, the resignation of Michael Gotla from the board of Welbeck Motors had gone unnoticed. The following statement appeared in The Times: "The General Guarantee Corporation has today sold its 51 per cent interest in Welbeck Motors to Mr. R.S. Walker. Mr. Gotla has also sold his 25 per cent interest to Mr. Walker and has resigned as managing director. Mr. Gotla said: "I have been grossly misrepresented, as a result, the hate of the whole taxi trade has been levelled at me. If the cab drivers think my resignation is a victory then they are mad". (9)

It was heavily rumoured at the time that Mr. Isaac Wolfson as he then was, had been told that the controversy surrounding his minicab venture was likely to cost him his coveted knighthood. Whatever the reasons were he did receive his knighthood not long afterwards.

The cab trade was jubilant, first Nally and Johns had been vindicated and now Gotla had gone, for despite Gotla's statement the licensed taxi trade looked upon him as the arch villain. The whole venture had been his idea, nurtured during the years he had run a legitimate hire car company.

The final demise of Welbeck Motors was not to occur until 1965, when, on July 17th the company faced a petition for its compulsory winding up. It had been brought by the City of Westminster for rates amounting to £2,652 and the Inland Revenue who were owed £8,750 and a total liability of £50,000. An Order was made for the winding up of the company. (10)

In November 1961, the first steps had been taken to fulfil one of the main functions of the Crisis Committee, as stated by the committee's secretary, Philip Rose, at a mass meeting the previous August. This was to bring a test case to the High Court. The opportunity arose following the loss of a case at Becontree Petty Sessions which had been brought by the Crisis Committee. Leave was given to appeal which was fixed for May 30th 1962. When the early editions of the evening papers hit the streets with the news that the Crisis Committee had won, there were scenes of jubilation as cabdrivers openly congratulated one another.

The long awaited Divisional Court case of E. Rose v. Jones and Welbeck Motors and the police case of Newman v. Vincent and Welbeck Motors were heard consecutively on May 31st and June 1st. The three judges,

Lord Chief Justice Parker; Mr. Justice Winn and Mr. Justice Brabin decided that a prima facie case of unlawfully plying for hire had been made out against Welbeck Motors Ltd and their two drivers. In both cases the summonses had been issued after the minicabs had been seen stationary in the street. (11)

It subsequently turned out to be a hollow victory. Had the Crisis Committee lost the case, then the government would have been forced to bring in new legislation, for it had maintained all along that the existing legislation was adequate. As it was minicabs were increasing every day and it was not possible to take them all to court. Despite the trade's vindication in the High Court, proving that the law was and is still strong, the Metropolitan Police have, in the past 31 years, abjectedly washed its hands of upholding the law. Perhaps the real culprits though are the successive conservative and labour governments, who, though fully aware that the law required changing, refused to take any action. It can only be speculation as to why.

During the run up to the High Court case, Sir Hugh Lucas-Tooth MP and Robert Mellish MP, sought leave to introduce a Bill in the House of Commons on May 16th, 1961, which sought to amend the law relating to hackney carriages in London, by imposing restrictions on the use of two way radio for hiring vehicles. It also sought to define plying for hire and to make it illegal to use the words cab or taxi except where they applied to licensed vehicles. (12)

With Michael Gotla and his financial backers departed from the scene of battle, Rupert Spier MP, was left naked in the chamber. All he could do now was to make fun of the situation saying: "It is high time the winds of change blew through the Public Carriage Office, it was festooned with cobwebs, strewn with horse manure and had an all pervading smell of horses. The London cab trade wanted a monopoly and a scarcity of cabs". (13)

If the winds of change are required anywhere, then the storm could do with blowing through the House of Commons first. Rupert Spier knew full well that the Public Carriage Office only implemented the law they didn't make it. He also knew that there is no limitation on cabs or drivers in London, only an economic limiting factor. Taxis increase when it is financially viable to do so, in the same way that other forms of private enterprise increase. The taxi trade has a disadvantage that other businesses do not have, its income is strictly limited by Parliament.

The Bill was moved by 164 votes to 86 but as predicted it was not proceeded with. Six years were to pass before another Bill was presented, which became the 1968 London Cab Act. Primarily dealing with advertisements on private hire cars, the Act was ineffective from day one. On April 17th 1973, during the second reading of a Bill which was to become the 1973 London Cab Act, Lord Campion in the House of Lords, replying to Lord Avebury who had moved the Bill, said: "There is no doubt at all that when we passed the 1968 London Cab Act we thought it was reasonably foolproof. Subsequent events have shown that it was not the case". (14)

This Act gave the Home Secretary powers to make orders plugging any loopholes and during the same debate Viscount Colville of Culrose, Minister of State at the Home Office said: "I think there is no doubt that the only way of achieving the necessary flexibility in order to plug up the holes that are made in the law by the unscrupulous, is to have this completely flexible procedure. As to the timing of the orders that will follow the first order, I want it to be very quick". (15)

Alas, no orders have been forthcoming and both the 1968 and 1973 Acts are dead letters. Within two years of the passing of the 1973 Act it was being overturned in the courts as magistrates and judges pronounced in favour of the minicab companies. Thousands of minicabs work the streets illegally, in full view of the public, who are free to walk into a minicab office and hire a minicab parked outside as if it were a taxi parked on a rank. Hindley, Runciman, Maxwell Stamp, the years roll by and nothing is done while the law is held in utter contempt.

References used in Chaper 16

1. The Times June 7th 1961
2. Ibid. November 8th 1960
3. From a Conservative Party local election pamphlet in the possession of the author
4. The Times June 19th 1961
5. Ibid. October 2nd 1961
6. Ibid.
7. From the records of the Crisis Committee in the possession of the author.
8. The Daily Express January 24th 1962.
9. The Times November 25th 1961.
10. Ibid. July 28th 1965
11. Stones Justice Manual Vol. 2 1975 page 4281 (Rose v Welbeck Motors Ltd (1962) 2 All E.R. 801; 126 J.P. 413; Newman v Vincent (1962) 2 All E.R. 806; 126 j.p. 417.
12. Parliamentary Debates (Hansard) House of Commons May 6th 1962.
13. Ibid.
14. Ibid. House of Lords April 17th 1973.
15. Ibid.

CONCLUSION

Looking back over the years to Oliver Cromwell's Ordinance of 1654, which established the principle of a licensing system and control for hackney carriages plying for hire in London, two dominant features stand out; central government's obsession with controlling one particular trade and, particularly since 1831, with not allowing the licensed trade's income to move in relation to outside market forces. Secondly, in latter years, but especially since 1961 following the Welbeck Motors minicab venture, with allowing unlicensed vehicles to perform exactly the same kind of work as the licensed trade yet show no intention of controlling their fares, vehicles, owners and drivers.

This benevolence to the unlicensed trade, permitted by a Conservative government in 1961 but nurtured by successive governments since then, was permitted because of the inability of the public transport system, to provide a service flexible enough to deal with the spontaneous travelling requirements of millions of Londoners, outside the central area. By curtailing the fares which are charged for London's taxis, governments have ensured that the licensed trade can only work cost effectively inside the intensive hiring area of central London.

Unintentionally or not, governments, particularly in 1973 with VAT and in 1989, by insisting on the compulsory adoption of the wheelchair access facility, have added very high additional costs on London's licensed taxi trade. At the same time they have not permitted fares to rise high enough to compensate for the imposition of these additional costs.

Prior to April 1973, the London licensed taxi trade was seeking zero rating when VAT was introduced, but the Chancellor of the Exchequer, Anthony Barber, flatly refused to do so. In a rare moment of support for the cab trade from the other main political parties, the Labour Party, who had unsuccessfully moved an amendment to the 1972 Financial Bill, seeking zero rating (which was defeated) and the Liberal Party, both issued statements supporting the taxi trade's case for zero rating.

The governments own Select Committee for Urban Transport (section 52) stated: "Taxicabs provide a personalised form of public transport ...... we recommend that consideration should be given to relieving taxis from VAT by zero rating in the same way as all other forms of public transport".

The government continued to rely on the feeble excuse given by the Secretary to the Treasury at a meeting with trade representatives in March 1973 that: "Taxi fares are not likely to form a high proportion of the expenditure of low income families and it therefore seems appropriate to include them in the scope of this broadly based tax". The trade's answer to the minister at this meeting was: "We would remind the government that the fares of luxury jet aircraft are not likely to form a high proportion of the expenditure of low income families either, yet they are zero rated". (1)

TAXI

THE NEWSPAPER OF THE TAXI TRADE

Volume 3 No. 18 5p 1 February 1973

VAT: Zero Rating Likely

Government prices freeze may sway Home Office to zero rate the Cab Trade. . .

ZERO RATING on Value Added Tax now looks more likely than ever following two recent moves in Parliament.

The Licensed Taxi Drivers Association's magazine, 'Taxi' was optimistically predicting zero rating for the cab trade as late as Feb, 1973.

The imposition of VAT added approximately £150. to the price of a new taxi. VAT on the driver's rental charge, added approximately £3.20 per week, which was alleviated by a 3p surcharge on each fare, roughly equating to the VAT charge. This 3p surcharge was subsequently incorporated into the metered fare. Over recent years the VAT on the price of a new taxi has varied between £3000 and £3500 depending on the model purchased, while the VAT on the driver's rental charge varies between £28 and £35 per week, depending on the age of the vehicle rented.

On 1 January 1989, Minister of Transport, Michael Portillo MP, altered the Conditions of Fitness which govern the construction of London type taxis. The new Conditions made it compulsory that after 1 January 1989, all new London taxis must have a wheelchair access facility. This added £1,500 to the price of a new taxi. It is envisaged that by the year 2000 all London taxis will have this wheelchair access facility. Not only has a Conservative government heaped the unjust VAT on London's taxi proprietors and drivers, it has made the taxi trade pay for the cost of providing a social service, i.e. the transport of disabled people in their wheelchairs. Though the government did allow a 11 per cent increase of fares in 1989, to compensate for the additional cost, it was only four per cent above the increase applied for. Inflation soon eroded that increase and the taxi trade has never caught up.

When it is considered that anyone with a driving licence (and often without one or the correct insurance) can purchase a secondhand car under £1,000 and become a minicab driver, is it any wonder that their fares are cheaper than licensed taxi fares. To put a second-hand four year old London taxi on the road today would cost about £13,000 and a new taxi would cost approximately £21,500. Not only is there an 'unlevel playing field', the London taxi trade is operating on a mountain slope. This is the chief reason why the London licensed taxi trade can only work cost effectively inside the intensive hiring area of central London.

It is no coincidence that the bulk of the establishment live and work inside this area; it is they who call the tune and while they have no objection to millions of Londoners travelling in unlicensed and very often uninsured cars, of doubtful safety, driven by people of dubious backgrounds, they do not rely on that type of vehicle for themselves.

It is worth recalling the editorial statement in The Times of January 1913, commenting on the strike of that year: "The cab was at the mercy of those who fix the price of petrol, a sensible way out would have been to raise the fares, which any other business would have done. But the cabs of London are the buses of the Parliamentarians who have control of the fares they paid".

Three statements of fundamental importance made by government bodies and which reflect official attitudes must be taken into account. First, the trade has always been viewed from the standpoint that: "The convenience of the public must be considered before any hardship to vested interest". (2) Second, "We have conceived it our duty not to ignore the trade's interest". (3) Thirdly, of great importance to the future position of London's licensed taxis, in view of the Green Paper issued in October 1993, is the statement made in the Hindley report of 1939: "The law governing public service vehicles was based on the principle that unregulated competition in the field of public transport is against the public interest". (4)

In later years various governments have ignored this precept and have permitted, indeed, have encouraged a two tier system of licensed and unlicensed vehicles. They have rigorously controlled the fares of licensed taxis to the point where they can only operate reasonably profitable in a restricted area.

Why then has the licensed taxi trade not opted out of the licensing system and work as unlicensed vehicles? It is not an easy question to answer but it is due to several reasons. The licensed owners and drivers have a considerable stake in the trade. It takes between two and three years to complete the 'Knowledge of London', including the suburbs and the police driving test. They have a considerable personal investment in the trade which could not lightly be given up.

But probably the most valid reason for remaining in the licensing system is the strong desire we all have to live and work within the law. "It is almost certainly true that most of us respond better to demands made upon us than to offers of an easy life, so long as we feel that the demands are made on everyone, just as on the whole we prefer to be law abiding but resent others being allowed to breach the law with impunity". (5)

It has been obvious to succeeding governments since 1938 (the war years excepted) that there has been something fundamentally wrong with London's licensed taxi trade. First there was the Hindley report of 1939 but the outbreak of war in September of that year saw the report consigned to the dustbin. In 1953 there followed the Runciman Report and though as we shall shortly see, two of its recommendations were acted upon, almost the entire report suffered a similar fate that befell the Hindley Report. In 1969 we had the Maxwell Stamp Report and it too was not acted upon.

On 1 April 1984, the control of London's licensed taxis passed from the Home Secretary to the Secretary of State for Transport who delegates his authority to the Assistant Commissioner of Police, Territorial Operations. The day to day control is carried out by the Public Carriage Office. By tradition the Home Office deals with crime and allied subjects. It was only natural then that its attitude to the capital's taxi trade was one of 'magistrate to a 'delinquent'. It had no jurisdiction over transport and its administration of the cab trade was anomalous.

On the whole the taxi trade welcomed the change, at last the trade was under a government department that understood transport and its needs. Sadly the change has achieved nothing of note. The Transport Act of 1985 gave authority for shared taxis but the public, except on rare occasions do not support it. Had the Department of Transport done its homework they would have discovered that the public want to hire a taxi because of its exclusivity, they do not want it to act as a bus.

Michael Portillo, Minister of Transport, with Carl Turpin, Chairman of Reliant Motor Group, celebrating the opening of the Reliant Metrocab assembly plant in Tamworth in 1990. The Metrocab, originally developed by Metro Cammell Weymann in 1986,was the first purpose built wheelchair accessible taxicab.

The Department of Transport hailed the wheelchair access facility in London's taxis as a huge success, it would have been had the cost been borne by the government and not the trade. Despite the fact that half of London's taxis have this facility, very few actually have the opportunity to carry wheelchair bound passengers, except those radio circuits who operate the Taxicard travel scheme, funded by the London Boroughs. People in wheelchairs simply do not come onto the streets to hail a taxi and even by the year 2000 when all London's taxis have this facility, it is still doubtful if disabled people will be so inclined as to hail a taxi in the street.

In July 1988, David Mitchell, Minister of Transport wrote to various trade bodies and licensing authorities in England and Wales (Scotland has separate legislation) and other interested groups. Enclosed was a questionnaire asking the view of those concerned, as to how the future of the trade should evolve. He wrote: "In its White Paper 'Building Businesses not Barriers', the government considered difficulties which inhibit the growth of existing businesses and the birth of new ones".

Referring to taxis it said: "The government will review, in the light of experience of the 1985 Transport Act, whether further relaxations in the taxi and hire car regimes are desirable". The 1985 Transport Act hardly affected the London taxi trade, it was mainly seeking to deregulate taxis in England and Wales, outside London, which, except in some areas it conspicuously failed to do. It also gave councils discretionary powers to subsidise the cost of the wheelchair access facility, in those licensing areas where the London type taxi is used. The great majority of councils decided not to use this discretionary authority. This discretion was not allowed in London because Parliament is the ultimate licensing authority and the Treasury would have had to bear the cost!

The Department of Transport was already preparing for this review, they were anxious that the views of those actively involved in the taxi and hire car trades, and the views of consumers, transport authorities and those enforcing regulations should be heard. On 11th May 1989, Michael Portillo, the new Minister for Public Transport said, referring to the White Paper: "Last year the Department of Transport completed an internal review of taxi and private hire legislation for England and Wales .... In the case of London, it has become clear that the high standard of service and propriety offered by taxis are highly valued by the public .... I therefore do not propose to legislate to change the present arrangements, neither do I intend to alter the present distinction between the taxi and the hire car trades".

Although another opportunity had been missed, the London taxi trade was somewhat relieved, for one of the proposals, put forward by the London Boroughs was, that they should be the licensing authority for minicabs, which would have been a disaster. In 1992 the Minister of Transport, Steve Norris, set up a Working Party which included representatives of the licensed taxi trade and minicab companies. The object was to study the situation in London and to report back to the Minister with their suggestions for proceeding further.

After nearly a year of discussion no agreement could be reached and the working party was disbanded. Then, on 2nd June 1993, in an announcement to the London Taxi Board and the trade press, the Minister said: "It may not be sensible to look at the regime in London in isolation from the rest of the country.

The government has therefore concluded that it is right to undertake a fundamental review of the laws on taxis and minicabs throughout England and Wales in their entirety, for which I will be responsible. I propose to issue a Green Paper setting out the various relevant issues and indicating possible areas of reform". (6)

Steven Norris, Minisiter for Passenger Transport launching the long awaited Parliamentary Green paper in 1993.

The Green Paper was launched on 27th October 1993 and at the press conference where the Green Paper was issued, the Minister said: "This consultation document is not a statement of Government intentions although we have made our views known on some issues. We believe, for example, that wheelchair accessibility is important and should remain a feature in any taxi licensing regime. We also think there is a strong argument for having as near to a single framework as possible for the whole of England and Wales. Above all, we believe the law should be understandable, relevant and enforceable". (7)

Many of the problems affecting the licensed taxi trade in London could be solved if there was a change of control. Currently, the day to day business of licensing proprietors, drivers and vehicles, mechanical inspections, conducting the Knowledge of London examinations, taximeter testing and handling lost property etc. are carried out by the Public Carriage Office at 15 Penton Street, London N1.

As it is presently constituted under the Metropolitan Police, via the Department of Transport, the Public Carriage Office is too restricted to meet the needs of the London Taxi trade. It can only carry out the obligations laid upon it in 1851 by Sir Richard Mayne, the Metropolitan Police Commissioner, all of which is looked upon purely from the public's point of view. Control of the London taxi trade by the Metropolitan Police is restricted and autonomous. The constraints which this form of control places on the licensed trade, while at the same time allowing unlicensed cars and their drivers to operate freely, makes a mockery of having a licensing system at all.

A Public Carriage Office should have the authority, directly mandated from the Secretary of State for Transport, to effect changes similar to the powers vested in the Hackney Coach Commissioners by the Treasury Lords. These changes should come about after consultation with the London Taxi Board, on which all the major groupings within the London taxi trade are represented, and not by imposition. Above all, the taxi trade should be able to set the level of its own fares, for the licensed taxi trade is private enterprise, albeit under statutory control.

If the financial return was higher, either by increased fares or a government subsidy for the wheelchair access facility, there would be greater incentive for more cabs to be fitted with modern, computerised data transmission two way radio and Automatic Vehicle Location systems. While it is true that London's radio taxi circuits are very modern, trend setters in the taxi world, it has taken nearly 40 years to reach this high level, simply because the financial capital was not there to effect it quicker. If, as the government say, we can only have clean, pure drinking water if we pay higher charges, then, by definition the public can only have a better, more efficient cab service if the public are prepared to pay for it.

The London taxi trades inability to invest in it's own future reflects largely on the low fare structure that it operates on. This fact attracted the attention of The Times, whose edition of 13 August 1951 said: "It has never been reasonable to accuse the London taxi trade of taking part in a prices wage spiral. They kept their prices steady, astonishingly enough, for all the seventeen years from 1933 to 1950 ... Then there was an increase in 1950, but since then six spiralling years have gone by without an increment".

Had The Times known, it could have told its readers that between 1654 and 1950, London's hackney carriages basic fare never rose above one shilling a mile. Those six spiralling years and the next seven lay like a dead weight on the trade. By 1952 petrol prices were rising and London taxis were then powered exclusively by petrol engines. One proprietor, Mr. J.M. Birch, who had experience of diesel engines in another part of his business, sought to reduce the fuel costs by using the Standard Motor Company's 2 litre diesel engine unit, once used as a tractor engine, It was badly under powered and it was not until Austins made their own 2.2 litre diesel engine in 1954 that satisfactory results were obtained.

By 1953 the London taxi trade was in crisis. In 1951, the Chancellor of the Exchequer had doubled the purchase tax on new vehicles and by 1953 the number of taxis had declined to 5,273. The rising fuel costs only served to increase the pressure. In 1953 the Runciman Committee was appointed to examine the London taxi trade. One person to give evidence was Mr. W.T. Overton, Managing Director of Mann & Overton Ltd. founded in 1897. In 1905 they acquired the franchise to distribute the Unic taxi, in London, commencing with the French Unic. In 1953 they had been the distributor of the Austin taxicab for 23 years and are now one of the two distributors of the modern Fairway Driver, manufactured by Carbodies Ltd of Coventry. Both companies trade as London Taxis International Ltd., part of the Manganese Bronze group of companies.

W.T. Overton then, was in the best position to lay before the Runciman Committee the forlorn state of the trade, brought about by the imposition of double purchase tax. When the report was published, it recommended that: "vehicles built to a specification which complies with the Conditions of Fitness laid down by the Metropolitan Police Commissioner, for the purpose of the London Cab Order 1934, should be exempted from purchase tax". Runciman went a stage further and suggested that: "The London type cab should be freed altogether from the operation of the Hire Purchase and Credit Sales Agreement Order 1952". (8) From the Hindley Report of 1939 to the Green Paper of 1993, these were the only items of real benefit to the London licensed taxi trade.

The government accepted both these points and the number of cabs began to increase, but it was the carrot to keep the financially weak trade pegging along. All the savings in costs from the conversion to diesel engines and the freeing of the purchase tax controls, were frittered away subsidising a low fare structure. Apart from the 6d surcharge during the Suez crisis of 1956, fares were not increased until February 1964. This meant that in the 31 years from 1933 to 1964 there had only been two fare increases and the minimum charge had risen from one shilling for two thirds of a mile in 1933, to two shillings for three fifths of a mile in 1964. Between 1914 and 1933 taxi fares in London were always below the cost of living index. They reached parity in 1933 and from then until 1976 they were never equitable.

The licensed taxi trade in London is faced with serious shortcomings in the present licensing system. It operates on a low fare structure, solely for the benefit of the public, yet because of the trades limitations the public are denied the service it should receive. Because the system cannot suppress the unlicensed minicabs or take effective action when minicabs break the law and because police on the beat have virtually washed their hands of the law breakers, it works against the public interest.

What then should replace the existing system? The nucleus for a new system of licensing and control already exists in the shape of the Public Carriage Office, for it is inconceivable that such a body should be disbanded, should there be new legislation. It has the experience, the goodwill of the trade and it is the finest body of its kind in the world, if looked at from the viewpoint of licensing taxis and drivers and for ensuring that both are of a high standard.

The Public Carriage Office should become the controlling body for the licensed taxi trade in England and Wales. As far as it is necessary to be responsible to Parliament that responsibility should remain, as it is now, with the Department of Transport.

The country should be divided in regions, consistent with the number of taxis in each region. Each region would have a Public Carriage Commissioner, answerable to the Public Carriage Office in London. It is essential that each region should have a degree of autonomy, enabling them to deal efficiently with local needs. District Councils, who currently licence taxis and private hire cars, would be spared the cost they are always complaining of. The licensing authorities are empowered to charge their taxi drivers, proprietors and operators, the cost of administration and licensing in their districts. These costs have rocketed in the past few years and it is widely believed that many councils inflate their costs in order to raise revenue.

A major advantage enjoyed by the London taxi trade is the continuity of control provided by the Public Carriage Office. There are very few changes in policy unless it stems from central government. In the licensing areas outside London, except perhaps the larger towns and cities where there is some continuity of licensing. In many of the smaller towns and in rural or semi rural areas, licensing policy can change every time there is an election, either because the political colour of the council changes, or because new councillors are elected without there being any political change.

A major feature of areas outside London should be some form of rationalisation. For example, some councils insist on wheelchair accessible taxis, others do not; some councils will provide adequate rank spaces, others will not; some councils have either deregulated or have a policy of issuing a tranche of licences annually; others have no more taxis licensed now than they did before the 1985 Transport Act. Some councils will permit signs on private hire cars, others will not; some councils say taxis must be a certain colour or a mix of colours, such as Bournemouth or Brighton, other councils will permit five door saloon cars, others will not; some councils have a strict policy of the number of years a vehicle can be licensed for, other councils have no restrictions and some councils permit zoning and others do not.

Throughout England and Wales there are some 360 licensing authorities and no two fares are the same. Brighton and Hove are so close to one another that you pass between them, without knowing that you have left one town and entered the other, yet there is a 15 per cent difference in fares. A similar situation exists between Hastings and Rother District Council. Further afield, Stockport, Manchester, Tameside and Macclesfield are all fairly close to one another, yet there are very different fare levels with Stockport's fare being nearly 50 per cent less than that of Manchester.

In London, what are referred to as minicabs should have three years to change and adapt as part of the licensed taxi trade. By then they must be using the London type taxi and proprietors and drivers must conform to the same licensing conditions which apply to the existing taxi drivers. The greater majority of minicabs operate in the inner and outer suburbs and new legislation should ensure that they continue to work those areas they now work as minicabs, outside a four mile circle from Charing Cross. They must wear the same yellow badge already worn by the licensed suburban drivers and the police plate affixed to the rear of the taxi must also be yellow.

If, as it has been suggested, there are 30,000 minicabs in London, then, following the same police vetting which applies to London's licensed taxi drivers, a spectacular drop in their numbers would follow and the final number could be between 15,000 and 20,000, possibly less. It is no use the police saying it would not be possible to appoint sufficient ranks for all these additional taxis, for 30 odd years they have been ranking outside minicab offices, many of them situated in main roads, which the police have seen fit to ignore.

There is one difficulty which could occur, that is the question of whether the two manufacturers of London's current taxis could supply sufficient vehicles. Perhaps it would be necessary to extend the time to change vehicles or perhaps to licence different vehicles which would have to be wheelchair accessible. The existing manufacturers would have every incentive to produce more of the current taxis, which would create better employment prospects in the Midlands.

A newly constituted Public Carriage Office should have the powers to effect these changes and any other changes thought to be necessary, after full discussions with the trade. Two important changes must be considered. Currently, applicants for 'the knowledge' do not have to pay for the cost of the examinations, which can take two years or more. The cost of these examinations are borne by those already licenced, from the annual licence fees for drivers and proprietors. This is an unfair burden for them to carry and any new legislation should include the authority to make a charge on new entrants.

There is also a good case for hiving off the 'knowledge of London' examinations to the existing knowledge schools, who have been established for a number of years. The Royal British Legion Taxi Driver's Training School, established in 1928 and Knowledge Point School, established in 1987, are two examples. Both of these schools have exceptionally high standards, as indeed do several other schools. The Public Carriage Office would still have to licence the applicants, once they are satisfied that they have reached the required standard.

A feature of any new legislation should be the abolition of the charges made by British Rail, in areas outside London, for the right of taxis to pick up BR passengers arriving at their stations. In some towns these charges are up to £600 per cab per annum. All licensed taxis should also have free access to airports. At Heathrow, the British Airports Authority charge between £16,000 and £20,000 a week to use the airport. This cost is not passed on to the customer.

The Public Carriage Office should have powers similar to those of the Traffic Commissioners. Their control must be firm but fair and they must have powers to approve and implement different methods of operation. Above all they should be empowered to adapt taxi operation to the needs of the travelling public, provided it is remembered that the taxi trade is essentially private enterprise and must be allowed the same freedom to operate, within certain guidelines, as all other forms of private enterprise.

Despite a chequered history, London's cab trade celebrated 300 years of continuous licensing at the Guildhall in May 1994, hosted by the Fellowship of Hackney Carriage Drivers and in the presence of The Rt. Hon. The Lord Mayor, Paul Newall and H.R.H. Prince Michael of Kent.
The trade now awaits the challenge of new legislation for the new century.

References used in the Conclusion

1. Cab Trade News Vol.4 April 1973, in the possession of the author.
2. Parliamentary Papers, 1925, Two Seater Cab Committee (CMND)
3. Interim Report of the Hindley Inter-departmental Committee on Cabs and Private Hire Vehicles para. 55 CMND 5938 9GRL)
4. Ibid. para 50
5. Sir Robert Lowe-Hall, KCMG, 23 September 1961, in the Economist, entitled Britain's Economic Problems. (GRL)
6. Department of Transport Press Notice No. 218, 1 June 1993.
7. Ibid. No. 419, 27 October 1993
8. Runciman Committee's Report on London's Taxicabs CMND 8804
9. The Case for Tariff Reform in the London Cab Trade. Sidney Pearce B.Sc.(Econ.)
10. The Stockport Express Advertiser, 22 September 1993.

Appendix A

A record of all the major Acts of Parliament between 1654 and 1973 wholly or partly concerned with legislation affecting hackney carriages, Sedan Chairs, short stage coaches and in some instances, stage coaches. These acts only applied to London.

Acts of the Inter-regnum 24th June 1654.
14th Charles II C2 1662.
5th & 6th William & Mary C22 1694.
9th Anne C23 1711.
10th Anne 1712.
11th Anne 1713.
12th Anne 1714.
1st George 1st 1714.
3rd George 1st 1716.
12th George 1st 1726.
16th George II 1743.
18th George II 1745.
30th George II C22 1757.
33rd George II 1760.
1st George III C15 1760.
4th George III C36 1764.
7th George III C44 1767.
8th George III C21 1768.
10th George III C44 1770.
11th George III C24 1771.
11th George III C28 1771.
11th George III C29 1771.
12th George III C49 1772.
24th George III C27 1784.
26th George III C72 1786.
32nd George III C47 1792.
38th George III C93 1798.
39th George III C47 1800.
42nd George III C78 1802.
44th George II C87 1804.
48th George III C87 1808.
54th George III C14 1814.
55th George III C159 1815.
57th George III C125 1817.
1st & 2nd William IV C22 1831.

2nd & 3rd William IV C120 1832.
3rd & 4th William IV C48 1833.
6th & 7th Victoria C79 1843.
13th & 14th Victoria C7 1850.
16th & 17th Victoria C33 1853.
16th & 17th Victoria C127 1853.
32nd & 33rd Victoria C115 1869.
59th & 60th Victoria C27 1896.
7th Edward 7th C55 1907.
London Cab Act 1968.
London Cab Act 1973.

The London Cab Order 1934 which is still in force was made by the authority of the Home Secretary under powers derived from the act 1869. The Act of Common Council of 1683 was not Parliamentary legislation but it controlled hackney carriages in the City of London between 1683 and 1694.

Appendix B

Other enactments not wholly concerned with hackney carriages (Road Traffic Acts are not included) containing sections which specifically refer to hackney carriages, or to which hackney carriages are included in the general form.

Metropolitan Paving Act, C29 s 65 1817.
The Highway Act, 5th & 6th William IV C50 ss 72/78 1835.
The Metropolitan Police Act, 2nd & 3rd Victoria C47 ss 52/54 1839.
The Cruelty to Animals Act, 12th & 13th Victoria C92 1849.
The Metropolitan Streets Act, 30th & 31st Victoria C134 (selected parts) 1867.
The Infectious Diseases (Prevention) Act, 53rd & 54th Victoria C34 s11 1890.
The Disease of Animals Act, 57th & 58th Victoria C57 ss 4/22/44/51 1894.
The Locomotives on Highways Act, 59th & 60th Victoria C36 1896.
The Motor Car Act, 3rd Edward 7th C36 1903.
The Post Office Act, 8th Edward 7th C48 s68 1908.
The City of London (Streets Act) 9th Edward 7th C117 ss2/4 1909.
Licensed Hackeny Carriages and Sedan Chairs outside London

Prior to the Town Police Clauses Act, 1847, C 14, the larger towns in England and Wales each had their own Act of Parliament, as per example:-
Bristol.

32nd George III C57 1792.
Also see House of Commons Journals Vol. 44 p. 545.
Newcastle-on-Tyne
3rd George III C55 1763.
Also see House of Commons Journals Vol. 29 p. 464.
York.
3rd George III C48 1763.
Also see House of Commons Journals Vol. 28 p. 69.

Following the Town Police Clauses Act of 1847, Parliament enacted the Town Police Clauses Act 1889 C14 (see section six). These two acts were the only acts of Parliament until the 1976 Local Government (Miscellaneous) Provisions Act, C57 Part II as 45 to 80. This act may only be adopted by District Councils if the act of 1847 is in force throughout it's area, or if in force in part of it's area, then in that part only.

Appendix C

"London 13th June 1828.

The Duke of Wellington presents his compliments to the Commissioners of Hackney Coaches, and begs leave to refer them to the enclosed plan from Mr. Gye M.P. which he had forwarded to the Duke.

Plan submitted to His Grace the First Lord of the Treasury for an additional number of Hackney carriages, for use in the Metropolis and it's vicinity.

It is an admitted fact, that the laws now in force for the good order of Hackney Coaches, are of very little, if any service, as the public will not trouble themselves to lodge complaints and attend the police to establish them; and hence arises the dirty state of these vehicles, their want of repair, and almost total inattention to either the safety or the convenience of the public.

It is, therefore, respectfully submitted, that the only remedy for these evils is competition. The projectors of the present plan would not, however, have ventured any suggestions on the subject at this moment, were they not assured that the rapid increase of the buildings and the population around the Metropolis, not only afford ample room for a large additional number of hackney carriages, but render such an accommodation absolutely necessary.

It is the determination of the projectors, if they are permitted by His Majesty's Government to carry their ideas into execution, to promote by their example a total change in the hackney Coach system, and which nothing but competition can effect and they have no doubt of the very great public advantage being the consequence.

The Cabriolets have been to a certain degree useful, but they are deficient in many points of view. They are very unsafe, having but two wheels, and the driver riding in the carriage is extremely objectionable, particularly to females, and much greater accommodation ought and can be given at the price permitted to be charged by the Cabriolets.

It is the principle object of the present plan, to most materially improve the one horse Hackney Carriage, and to unite all the safety and convenience of the Hackney Coach with the lightness and speed of the Cabriolets; in short, to furnish the Metropolis with small coaches upon four wheels, to be drawn by one strong horse and to carry four passengers at the present Cabriolet prices; this can be effected without difficulty, affording the parties fair remuneration for their capital and attention. The parties would undertake to immediately provide for public use, carriages of three distinct kinds, viz.

One hundred small coaches, to be drawn by one horse, to carry four persons at the present Cabriolet fares; the driver to be seated on a dickey. The carriages will invariably be sent out in the most perfect repair as to their safety, with patent wheels and the insides kept uniformly clean and fit for well dressed females to ride in. The fares and regulations to be precisely similar to those which now govern the Cabriolets.

One hundred small chariots, to carry three person, on the same principles as the coaches. One hundred Barouchets, to take three persons principally for use in the summer season, to have an additional lining of calico and the carriage being open would greatly tend to the convenience and amusement of the public, and will no doubt prove a great public accommodation.

The drivers are to be dressed in liveries en suite; and means will be adopted to insure the most perfect civility from them, and to prevent any overcharge or imposition being practised.

Carriages on something like the principle herein proposed, are at use in Bath, Bristol and Cheltenham etc., and are universally patronised as most useful and agreeable conveyances for the public accommodation.

Signed: Frederick Gye, M.P. for
Chippenham,
141 Fleet Street,
10th June 1828.

Appendix D

Copy of a letter from the Commissioners of Hackney Coaches to His Grace the Duke of Wellington, dated 16th June 1828, reporting on Mr. Gye's plan for establishing three hundred four wheeled Hackney Carriages to be drawn by one horse.

Hackney Coach Office,
16th June 1828.

My Lord Duke,

We have the honour to acknowledge the receipt of your Grace's note of the 13th. instant, referring to us a plan for Frederick Gye M.P. (herewith returned to your Grace) for establishing three hundred four wheeled hackney carriages to be drawn by one horse.

We beg to assure your Grace that our best attention has been given to the state of the Hackney Carriages in this Metropolis, and to the proper accommodation which the public ought to derive from, and after the most mature consideration, we have every reason to think that no better description of carriages than those now in use can be introduced with advantage to the public. We are at the same time of the opinion, that if any carriages could be brought out by which the public could be accommodated at a cheaper rate than what they pay now, it might be advisable to give them a fair trial. This might certainly be done by allowing four wheeled hackney coaches and chariots to be drawn by one horse instead of two; and should your Grace think it proper to approve of this being done, it will be necessary that an Act of Parliament should be had for the purpose, the present acts expressly providing that all four wheeled hackney carriages should be drawn by two horses.

We at the same time, beg to submit to your Grace, that it would be most unfair to the present Hackney Coach owners to allow Mr. Gye to have the monopoly he applies for, not only because we have reason to think that the money necessary for establishing the description of carriages in question (which would not be less that £65,000) would be raised by a Joint Stock Company, but, as it would be manifest injustice to the old established Hackney Coach owners, who would be ruined if they were not allowed to exchange their present description of carriage for those specified in Mr. Gye's application to your Grace.

We beg leave to take this opportunity of adding, with reference to what Mr. Gye asserts respecting the insufficiency of the present Hackney Coach laws, that if we were furnished with those additional powers which we have repeatedly applied for, we should then be able to enforce the supply of a better and cleaner description of carriages than some of those now in use.

Signed: Edward Jesse)
Thomas Marrable) Commissioners
Edward Gwatkin)

Appendix E

Copies of two MEMORIALS, with the answers of the Lords of the Treasury, relative to the application of George Shillibeer, Coach Builder and Livery Stable Keeper, for licences to work Ten Cabriolets, to be constructed upon an improved principle.

To the Right Honourable the Lords Commissioners of His Majesty's Treasury.

The humble Memorial of George Shillibeer, Coach Builder and Livery Stable Keeper, residing and carrying on business at 12 Bury Street Bloomsbury Square.

Showeth,

THAT your Memorialist has for sometime past been desirous of obtaining a licence to work Cabriolets; and your memorialist now most humbly solicits Your Lordships to give directions in such a way as may appear to meet to the Honourable Commissioners of Hackney Coaches, to grant him a licence for ten Cabriolets, which your memorialist undertakes to build and construct on a plan that shall render it unnecessary for the driver to be placed by the side (as is now the case) of the person or persons occupying the Cabriolet, it being the intention to form a separate seat for the person who drives.

That your Memorialist being a coach builder, as well as proprietor of a respectable livery stables, would be able to supply vehicles superior to the generality of Cabriolets at present about the streets, and which your memorialist undertakes should be drawn by good horses and driven by civil men, who should be clean in their persons which is too obvious is not the case with the drivers of very many who now hold plates, and for the due performance of his duty, should your Lordships be pleased to grant the prayer of this memorial, the responsibility of your Memorialist, he trusts, will be a security to the public.

And your Memorialist, as in duty bound, will every pray,

George Shillibeer,

3rd November 1827.

Appendix F

To the preceding memorial the Treasury returned the following answer.

Treasury Chambers,

20th November 1827.

To Mr. George Shillibeer,

12 Bury Street,

Bloomsbury Square.

Sir,

Having laid before the Lords Commissioners of the Treasury your Memorial praying for licences to work Ten Cabriolets upon an improved principle, I am commanded by My Lords to acquaint you that they cannot comply with your request.

I am sir,

Your obedient servant,

W. Hill.

Some two months later following his return from Paris, George Shillibeer petitioned the Treasury Lords again.

To the Right Honourable the Lords Commissioners of His Majesty's Treasury.

Sheweth,

That your Memorialist addressed a memorial to your Lordships dated 3rd. November last, praying for an order to the Commissioners of Hackney Coaches to grant him the necessary licences to work Ten Cabriolets, upon an improved principle; which memorial was taken into your Lordships consideration, and a negative reply was received by your Memorialist from Your Lordships, dated 20th. November 1827, at which period your memorialist was in Paris.

That your Memorialist, throwing himself upon your lordships kind consideration, ventures again to memorialise Your Lordships, beseeching you to reconsider his case, by which he most humbly hopes Your Lordships will yet be pleased to grant his request.

Your Memorialist being engaged in the coachmaking business, and that of livery stable keeper, feels himself peculiarly well qualified to conduct a Cabriolet Establishment with credit to himself and satisfaction to the public, and having for sometime past been desirous of obtaining plates to work Cabriolets, has made repeated applications at the hackney Coach Office relative thereto, but always received the answer, "that no more licences would be granted".

Your Memorialist stated, at different periods within the last three years, when at the Hackney Coach Office, the improvements that appeared to him might be made in the construction of public Cabriolets, by placing the drivers seat apart from the fare; and asked to build one, subject to any alteration in the plan the Commissioners might think fit to point out, wherebye the comfort and the convenience of the public might be consulted; but was informed that the Commissioners had determined not to issue any more licences. It was therefore, with considerable surprise Your Memorialist learnt on repeating his application at the hackney Coach Office that the Commissioners had received Your Lordships order to issue twenty more licences to two persons who had presented a plan to Your Lordships for building the Cabriolets upon an improved principle, WHICH PLAN YOUR MEMORIALIST SUGGESTED UPWARDS OF TWO YEARS AGO, but, from not being aware that Your Lordships would increase the number, declined making application for that sanction which Your Lordships have so lately granted to two other persons, who have not that facility that your Memorialist possesses, he being engaged in a business contributing largely to the means of affording this description of public convenience, he being both coachmaker and livery stable keeper.

Your Memorialist, therefore, most respectfully beseeches Your Lordships to grant the prayer of his Memorial, CONCEIVING THAT THE IMPROVEMENTS ACTED UPON BY OTHERS ORIGINATED WITH HIM, and trusts Your Lordships will not allow his ignorance of the mode of application to operate at his disadvantage, and as he is prepared to prove to Your Lordships that the improvement was suggested by him at the Hackney Coach Office more than two years ago, he most earnestly entreats Your Lordships to give an order to the Commissioners to grant him ten licences, and extend the number to thirty on the new principle, your Memorialist feeling a hope that Your Lordships will not consider it a matter of much import to increase the gross number to 130 instead of 120, as a public convenience must be benefited in a proportionate degree by doing so.

George Shillibeer,
23rd January 1828.

The following answer was returned to the preceding memorial.

Treasury Chambers,
11th February 1828.

To Mr. George Shillibeer,
12 Bury Street,
Bloomsbury.

Sir,

Having laid before the Lords Commissioners of His Majesty's Treasury your second Memorial repeating your former application for licences to work ten hackney cabriolets, I am commanded to acquaint you, that My Lords see no reason to depart from their former determination on this case.

I am sir,
Your obedient servant,
George R. Dawson.

Appendix G

An account of some of the financial disbursements made by the Treasury from money received from hackney Coach licence fees between 1694 and 1743. Source, the Calendars of Treasury Books and Papers.

1. £400 for the use of the Royal Hospital Chelsea.
2. 752.18.6. to Charles Fox, Lord Coningsby and Captain Philip Griffin for the troops in Ireland.
3. To George Knowling and Edmund Starr and company, owners of the ship 'Rose' for two months hire of her in the West Indies. £206.
4. £1,126.5.9. to pay the officers of Steenbocks and Recterens Regiment now leaving England.
5. £300 for Eppingers Dragoons.
6. £118 for Captain Sanderson on behalf of his son, who, at the time of his

death at the siege of Namur was a captain in the Royal Regiment of Foot.

7. £100 to Captain William Hyde on account of his pay from April 1st 1694 - January 17th 1697, as a Captain in one of the four companies now at New York.
8. £375 for Lt. Col. Duncannon of Lord Larnes late Regiment in considera tion of the loss of his clothing at Dixmude.
9. £342 paid to the cost of the forces in Newfoundland, viz, the construction of Fort William.
10. £300 to be paid towards the maintenance of the four companies of soldiers in New York.
11. £500 paid to the Navy Treasurer for the seamen's wages.
12. £2,535 paid to the Earl of Ranelagh for unspecified military purpose.
13. £400 paid to the arrears of the West Indies Regiment.
14. £782 paid to the out pensioners of the Royal Hospital, Chelsea.
15. £150 paid to Mrs. Winifred Hillbourne for a piece of ground on which was erected Fort Clifford In Northumberland.
16. £242 to be paid to Colonel Spottiswood for the transportation of himself and his family to the Colony of Virginia, as the new Governor.
17. £20 to be paid to Elizabeth Gulliford, administratrix of Captain William Webster, for the use of the said Captain's children.

Bibliography

MANUSCRIPTS

Guildhall Record Office

Misc. MSS (various) 190.3 212/213
MSS 212.4 212.6
Remembrancia volumes and indexes
Reportorys of the Court of Aldermen
Small MSS (various) Nos. 1/3/10

Public Record Office

Accounts (various) E.101 Henry II to George III
Hackney Carriage Accounts (AO) 119
Hackney Coach Papers (T) 289
T22 1704 - 1921 62 volumes

British Museum

Add. MSS. 18047
Harl. MSS. 4115

King Edward VII School, Witley, Surrey

Records of Bridewell Prison

Primary Printed Sources

Acts and Ordinances of the Inter-regnum

Acts of the Privy Council
Acts Public & General
All England Law Reports
Annals of the Royal Statistical Society 1834 - 1934 (GRL)
Annual Reports of the Metropolitan Police Commissioner
Annual Reports of the Traffic Commissioners 1931/2
Bibliotheca Lindesiana (GRL)
British Imperial Calendars
Calendar of State Papers Domestic
Calendar of Treasury Books
Ibid. Papers
Chronological Index of Patents
Cobbett's Parliamentary Debates
Concise Dictionary of English Etymology
Hansard (Commons)
Hansard (Lords)
Historical Manuscripts Commission Reports
House of Commons Journals
House of Commons Papers
House of Lords Journals
House of Lords Papers
Journals of the Royal Society of Arts
Middlesex County Records
National Dictionary of Biography
Parliamentary Papers (Reports and Returns)
Proclamations (small) (GRL)
Public Record office (Treasury Papers) registers, plates etc, No. 1.
Ibid (Misc.) Expired Commissions (Hackney Coaches)
Records of Lord Bath (Longleat Library)
Records of the Commissioners Library (New Scotland Yard)
Records of the Public Carriage Office (Motor Cab Approval Type Book)
Royal Calendars
Statutes of the Realm
Statutory Instruments (Home Office)

Guildhall Reference Library

Abstract of Bye-laws 21.47
Articles to be observed by W. Huggins 21.61
Bill advertising coaches leaving Snow Hill 8.162
The Case of the 400 Hackney Coachmen 11.71
The Case of the 700 Hackney Coachmen 11.77
The Case of the poor hackney coachmen 11.75
The Case of the unlicenced chairmen 11.76

The Case to raise £2,000,000 11.67
Hackney Coachmen and taxation 28.79
Pamphlets - Guildhall Reference Library
Account of a coaching inn 9010
Account of coaches in and out of London 1700 3095
Citizens Guide 7155/6
Le Guide de Londres 494
The Hackney Coachmen (1797 pamphlet 76.95
Letter on hackney coach fares 1319 pamphlet 13.19
Licence number, names and addresses of 400 licenced coachmen pamphlet 276
London's cabs and cabmen's grievances 7385
Prime Minister's papers 1801 - 1902 10631
Regulations for Hackney Coaches 5670
Roads and Travel before Railways 61
Rules and Bye-laws for hackney coaches (1654) 8716
Newspapers, periodicals and magazines
Commerical Motor
Cornhill Magazine
Economist
Flying Post
Gentleman's Magazine
Geographical Magazine
London Gazette
London Illustrated News
London Mercury
Loyal London Mercury
Mercurius Politicus
Monthly Recorder
Public Adviser
Punch
Social Science Review
Steering Wheel Magazine
Temple Bar Magazine
The Times
Books
Barker & Robbins. History of London Transport. Vol. I. Allen & Unwin, 1963.
Brown, T. Amusements serious and comical. London. 1702.
Burgess, F.W. Coach Building. Routlege. 1919.
Clunn, H.P. The face of London. Spring Books. London.
Cohen, H.J. The law of cabs in London. London. 1889.
Copeland, J. Roads and their traffic, 1750 - 1850. David and Charles,

Newton Abbot, 1968.
Corbett, E. Old coachman's chatter with remarks on driving. Bentley. 1890.
Cressett, J. Reasons for suppressing stage coaches. (BM)
De Laune, T. Angliae Metropolis, or the present state of London. 1690 (GRL)
De Saussure, L. A foreigners view of England. trans. J. Murray. 1902.
Dickens, C. Sketches by Boz. Collings, London & Glasgow.
Dowell, S. The history of taxation in England from the earliest times. Longman.
Harper, G.C. Stage coach and mail days of yore. Chapman. 1903.
Humerous, H. History, origin and progress of the Watermen's Company.
Jackman, .T. Developement of transportation in modern England. (BM)
Knights London (GRL)
Loftie, J. History of London (Supplement). Stanford, 1884.
Loftie, L. Packhorse, wagon and post, London. (GRL)
Lowe, C. Four national exhibitions in London. Fisher & Unwin. 1892.
Lucas, C.P. The beginning of English overseas enterprise, Clarendon Press, 1917.
Macaulay's History of London, Westminster Edition.
Macausland, H. The English carriage. Batchworth Press, London, 1931.
Maudesly Athol. Horse and Highways. London, 1888.
Mitchel & Ley, History of London Life.
Moore, H.C. Omnibus and cab. London. 1901.
Montgomery, J. 1900, the end of an era.
Moylan, J.F. Scotland Yard. Putnam, London, 1929.
Murray, J. Conversations with the Duke of Wellington, 1831 - 1851. 1889.
Priestly, Harold. The years of change.
Reid, J. The evolution of the horse drawn vehicle.
Richardson, A.E. The old inns of England. Batsford. 1925.
Richardson, A.E. Georgian England, 1700 - 1820. Batsford. 1948.
Huess, R. Londres et Angleterre en 1700. (GRL)
Searle, H. Turnpikes and tollbars. Hutchinson. 1930.
Shevichaven, H.D.J. The story of the London parks. (GRL)
Scot. Byegone pleasures of London.
Sekon. Locomotion in Victorian London. OUP 1938.
Sissons & French. Age of Austerity. Penguin.
Stow, John. Survey of London. Everyman edition.
Strong, I.A.G. The rolling road. Hutchinson, 1956.
Taylor, J. Carriers cosmographie. London. 1634. (GRL)
Thornbury. Old and new London. Cassell.
Thrupp, T. History of coaches. Kerby, London, 1877.
Waterman & Poet. Tracts and works of J. Taylor. (GRL)
Wheatley, Henry, ed. Samuel Pepy's Diary. Bell, 1919/21.

Guides and Directories in the Guildhall Reference Library

Berridge, R. Rates of stage coaches, hackney coaches and chairs. 1728.
Brown, J. Laws concerning travel. London, 1718. (GRL)
Edwards, J. Tabulae distantiarum.1800 - 1801.
Fielding, J. Guide to coach and chair rates.1786.
Guiseppi, M.S. Guide to the contents of the Public Record Office. 1963.
Hampshire Directory, 1852/5/9 - 1867.
Lowndes, T. A guide to stage coaches, 1779 - 1797.
Moggs Omnibus and coach guide. London 1844.
Philips, R.A. A dissertation concerning the present state of the roads. 1737.
Pigot's general directory, 1844.
Post Office directory (small) 1844/5/6.
Quaife, J. The hackney coach directory. London. 1817. (GRL)
Shopkeepers and assistants guide to stage coaches, 1768 - 1828.
Simons, M. A direction for the English traveller. 1645. (GRL)

Index

C

M

R

S